Topophilia
Topophobia

This book is about the love and hate relations that humans establish with their habitat, which have been coined by discerning modern thinkers as *topophilia* and *topophobia*. Whilst such affiliations with the *topos*, our manmade as well as natural habitat, have been traced back to antiquity, a wide range of twentieth-century cases are studied here and reflected upon by dwelling on this framework. The book provides a timely reminder that the qualitative aspects of the *topos*, sensual as well as intellectual, should not be disregarded in the face of rapid technological development and the mass of building that has occurred since the turn of the millennium.

Topophilia and Topophobia offers speculative and historical reflections on the human habitat of the century that has just past, authored by some of the world's leading scholars and architects, including Joseph Rykwert, Yi-Fu Tuan, Vittorio Gregotti and Jean-Louis Cohen. Human habitats, ranging broadly from the cities of the twentieth century, highbrow modern architecture both in Western countries and in Asia, to non-architect/planner designed vernacular settlements and landscapes are reviewed under the themes of topophilia and topophobia across the disciplines of architecture, landscape studies, philosophy, human geography and urban planning.

Xing Ruan is Professor of Architecture at the University of New South Wales and is the author of *Allegorical Architecture* (2006) and *New China Architecture* (2006). He has published on a wide range of topics concerning legible relations between humans and the built world in some of the world's leading scholarly journals, as well as professional magazines in China and Australia.

Paul Hogben is a lecturer in architecture at the University of New South Wales. His research focuses on promotional politics and the discourse of architecture over the twentieth century. This research has been published in *Architectural Theory Review* and *Fabrications*, the journal of the Society of Architectural Historians, Australia and New Zealand.

Topophilia and Topophobia

Reflections on twentieth-century human habitat

Edited by Xing Ruan and Paul Hogben

Routledge
Taylor & Francis Group

LONDON AND NEW YORK

First published 2007
by Routledge
2 Park Square, Milton Park, Abingdon, Oxon OX14 4RN

Simultaneously published in the USA and Canada
by Routledge
270 Madison Ave, New York, NY 10016

Routledge is an imprint of the Taylor & Francis Group, an informa business

Typeset in Univers by
Keystroke, 28 High Street, Tettenhall, Wolverhampton
Printed and bound in Great Britain by
TJ International Ltd, Padstow, Cornwall

British Library Cataloguing in Publication Data
A catalogue record for this book is available from the British Library

Library of Congress Cataloging in Publication Data
   Topophilia and topophobia: reflections on twentieth-century human habitat/edited
   by Xing Ruan and Paul Hogben.
      p. cm.
   Includes bibliographical references and index.
   1. Architecture – Human factors. 2. Architecture – Psychological
   aspects. 3. Architecture, Modern – 20th century. I. Ruan, Xing, 1965–
   II. Hogben, Paul, 1969–.
   NA2542.4.T67 2007
   720.1'03–dc22   2007018093

ISBN10: 0–415–40323–5 (hbk)
ISBN10: 0–415–40324–3 (pbk)
ISBN13: 978–0–415–40323–8 (hbk)
ISBN13: 978–0–415–40324–5 (pbk)

Contents

Contents

Illustration credits

The editors and publishers gratefully acknowledge the following for permission to reproduce material in this book. Every effort has been made to contact copyright holders for their permission. The publishers would be grateful to hear from any copyright holder who is not acknowledged here and will undertake to rectify any errors or omissions in future editions of the book.

Alessandro Como   9.10

Anthony Browell   8.1

Architecture Review   5.8

Asim Aly-Khan   12.1–12.4, 12.6, 12.7

Bernard Rudofsky   9.2, 9.11

Centro Studi Giuseppe Terragni, Como   7.1

China Architecture and Building Press   6.3, 6.5, 6.6

CityRail and STA, Sydney   12.8

Daniel O'Hare   11.2–11.6

Eduardo Persico   7.3–7.6

Fondation Le Corbusier, Paris   4.1

Fonds Alberto Sartoris, Archives de la Construction moderne, École polytechnique
    fédérale de Lausanne   7.2

Harriet Edquist and Richard Black   8.4

Jean-Louis Cohen   4.4, 4.5, 4.8–4.10, 4.12–4.14

John Harbeson   6.2

John Murray Publishers   10.1, 10.2

Louis Kahn   6.7

Marco Albini   7.7–7.13

Michael Nicholson   8.2, 8.3

National Gallery of Victoria, Melbourne   8.6

Peter Kohane   5.6, 5.13– 5.15

Philadelphia Museum of Art   5.1–5.3

P.M. Letaruouilly   5.10

State Library of Queensland   11.1

Sue Ann Kahn   5.11

Tati estate, c/o Jérome Deschamps   4.2

The Boyd family   8.5

The Getty Research Institute, Los Angeles   9.1, 9.3–9.9

University of Pennsylvania and Pennsylvania Historical and Museum Commission
    5.4, 5.5, 5.7, 5.9, 5.12

University of Pennsylvania Yearbook   6.1

Xing Ruan   6.10, 6.11

Notes on contributors

Jean-Louis Cohen trained as an architect and historian in Paris, and has taught in Europe and North America. Since 1994 he has been a professor at New York University's Institute of Fine Arts. His research has focused on twentieth-century architecture and urban planning in France, Russia, Germany and North Africa, resulting in numerous exhibitions and publications on both sides of the Atlantic. Among his many books are *Le Corbusier and the Mystique of the USSR* (1992), *Scenes of the World to Come* (1995), *Casablanca, Colonial Myths and Architectural Ventures* (2002) and *Above Paris* (2006).

Alessandra Como is an architect. She studied in Naples, Italy, where she also received a PhD in Architectural Design. She has taught at the Washington State University, at the Architectural Association, in various schools in Italy, and at the University of Manchester. At present, she teaches studio courses and history and theory at the Università di Salerno, Italy. She is currently working on a study of narratives and geometric structures of the English landscape garden: text in publication.

Vittorio Gregotti is the founder of Gregotti Associati International, and a Professor of Architectural Composition at the IUAV in Venice. He has been a Visiting Professor at the Universities of Tokyo, Buenos Aires, São Paulo, Lausanne, Harvard, Princeton, Cambridge, and MIT. He was the editor of *Casabella* from 1982 to 1995. Gregotti was responsible for the introductory section of the XIII Triennale (Milan 1964), which won the international Grand Prix. Through his teaching, practice, and writing, Gregotti's voice has influenced almost every recent architectural debate. Some of his recent architectural works include a new university building at Bicocca in Milan (2004), Pujiang Promotion Center in Shanghai (2003), and New Porta Susa railway station in Turin (2002). He is the author of, among others, *New Directions in Italian Architecture* (1968) and *Inside Architecture* (1996).

Paul Hogben is a lecturer in architecture at the University of New South Wales. His research focuses on promotional politics and the discourse of architecture over the twentieth century. This research has been published in *Architectural Theory Review* and *Fabrications*, the journal of the Society of Architectural Historians, Australia and New Zealand.

Ross Jenner is Associate Head of the School of Architecture and Planning, University of Auckland, New Zealand. He has exhibited and published in the USA, Italy, Australia and New Zealand, and was Commissioner for the New Zealand Section of the XIX *Triennale di Milano*. His PhD from the University of Pennsylvania was on the topic of lightness in modern Italian architecture. Recent publications include: articles in *Interstices: Journal of Architecture and Related Art, Lotus International*, and entries in the *Encyclopedia of Twentieth Century Architecture, Routledge Encyclopedia of Contemporary Italian Culture* and *Tangled Destinies: National Museum of Australia*.

Peter Kohane is a Senior Lecturer in the Faculty of the Built Environment at the University of New South Wales. He has previously taught at RMIT and the University of Pennsylvania. His research has led to many publications on nineteenth- and twentieth-century architecture in Australia, Britain and America. He is currently completing an Australian Research Council-funded project, which explores the relationship of the principle of decorum to the practice of architecture. His publications include: *James Barnet* (co-authored with C. Johnson and P. Bingham Hall) (2000); "Eclipse of a Commonplace Idea: Decorum in Architectural Theory" (with M. Hill), *Architectural Research Quarterly* 5, 1, 2001; "Order and Variety in the Work of C. R. Cockerell," *Fabrications* 10, 1999; and "Louis I. Kahn and the Library: Genesis and Expression of Form," in *Via 10: Ethics in Architecture* (1990).

Neil Leach is an architect and theorist. He teaches at the Architectural Association, London, and has been Visiting Professor at Columbia University, New York, Professor of Architectural Theory at the University of Bath, and Reader in Architecture and Critical Theory at the University of Nottingham. Among his many publications are *The Anaesthetics of Architecture* (1999), *Millennium Culture* (1999), *China* (2004) and *Camouflage* (2006).

Harry Margalit is Associate Professor and Head of the Architecture Program at the University of New South Wales. He has degrees in architecture and fine arts, and has published extensively on Australian modernist and contemporary architecture in both the academic and professional press. Recent publications include "The State of Contemporary Architecture in Australia," *Architectural Theory Review* 11, 1, 2006, and "The Brick Pit Aerial Walkway, Sydney," in *Topos: The International Review of Landscape Architecture and Urban Design* 57, 2006. He is also a partner in the Sydney architectural firm of Quinton-Margalit Architects.

Peter Murphy is Dean of the Faculty of the Built Environment and Professor of Planning and Urban Development at the University of New South Wales. His primary interests are the economics of urban land use, the management of growth and change in large urbanized regions, and urban and regional economic development. He is co-author of *Immigration and Australian Cities* (with Ian Burnley) (1997), *Surface City: Sydney at the Millennium* (with Sophie Watson) (1997) and *Sea Change: Movement from Metropolitan to Arcadian Australia* (with Ian Burnley) (2004).

Daniel O'Hare is Associate Professor of Urban Planning at Bond University on Queensland's Gold Coast. Previously he coordinated the postgraduate Urban Design Program at Queensland University of Technology. He holds a PhD and MA in Urban Design from Oxford Brookes University, and a Bachelor of Town Planning from the University of New South Wales. His main research interest is in the transformation of coastal tourism areas into urban regions.

Xing Ruan is Professor of Architecture and Chair of Architecture Discipline Group at the University of New South Wales in Sydney. He is the author of *New China Architecture* (2006) and *Allegorical Architecture* (2006). Xing Ruan has published on architecture and anthropology, architectural education, China's modern and contemporary architecture, as well as Australian contemporary architecture in both scholarly and professional journals. He is co-editor, with Ronald Knapp, of the book series *Spatial Habitus: Making and Meaning in Asia's Architecture*, which is published by the University of Hawai'i Press. Born in China, he received his architecture education at the Southeast University in Nanjing.

Joseph Rykwert is Paul Philippe Cret Professor Emeritus of Architecture at the University of Pennsylvania. Author of some of the most important books on architecture, his influential titles include *The Idea of a Town* (1963), *On Adam's House in Paradise* (1972), *The Necessity of Artifice* (1982), *The Dancing Column* (1996) and *The Seduction of Place* (2000). Among his numerous honours, Rykwert is a Chevalier dans l'ordre des Arts et des Lettres (1984) and has been elected to the Italian Accademia di San Luca.

Sarah Treadwell is an architect and a senior lecturer at the School of Architecture, University of Auckland, New Zealand. She teaches in the architectural design studio and lectures on issues of architectural representation. Her research areas include analyses of nineteenth-century images of architecture in the South Pacific and New Zealand. She also writes on contemporary fine art practices that reference architecture. Her publications include "Earthquake Weather," in *Drifting: Architecture and Migrancy*, S. Cairns (ed.) (2004); "The Motel: An Image of Elsewhere," *Space and Culture* 8, 2, 2005 and "Animation, the Cat and Escaping Drawing," *Interstices: A Journal of Architecture and Related Arts* 06, 2005.

Yi-Fu Tuan is Professor Emeritus of Geography at the University of Wisconsin-Madison. Widely regarded as the founder of humanistic geography, Tuan has made a profound impact on the disciplines of geography, landscape architecture, English literature and religious studies. Among his more than 200 publications, his influential books include *Topophilia* (1974), *Space and Place* (1977), *Landscapes of Fear* (1986), *Escapism* (1998) and *Dear Colleague* (2002). Tuan received the Lauréat d'Honneur from the International Geographical Union in 2000. He is a fellow of the British Academy and the American Academy of Arts and Science.

Acknowledgments

Many individuals and institutions assisted the 2005 Beijing symposium and the subsequent book project. The editors wish to gratefully acknowledge the following: Huang Juzheng, editor of *The Architect*, China Architecture and Building Press, was the co-convenor (with Xing Ruan and Joseph Rykwert) of the Beijing symposium. Together with Shi Miao, Huang Juzheng coordinated the mammoth task of securing the symposium sponsorship and organizing its logistics. Dean Professor Peter Murphy and Associate Dean Professor Martin Loosemore of the Faculty of the Built Environment at the University of New South Wales supported this publication with a book grant. The main institutional support came from the University of New South Wales, the China Architecture and Building Press and the Southeast University in Nanjing. Finally, the editors would like to thank Caroline Mallinder, from Routledge, for her immediate enthusiasm when the idea of this book was first proposed. Caroline and Georgina Johnson have been patient in the long process of the book's making.

X.R. & P.H.

Architectural Enclosure

A Prologue to Topophilia and Topophobia

Xing Ruan and Paul Hogben

To reflect on human habitat in the twentieth century, we shall begin with a comparison between a Gothic cathedral and a modern skyscraper that Yi-Fu Tuan has made in several of his publications, including *Topophilia* (1974),[1] which is one of the triggers for the current book. Tuan reminds us that a Gothic cathedral, when it was inhabited in its time, often could not be viewed in the distance as an architectural object that we moderns now are able to see in a European city: there was no wide enough open space before a cathedral in a crowded medieval city. A Gothic cathedral, therefore, was conceived and built as a confined internal world that catered to three or four senses, rather than vision alone. It is, to be precise, an architectural enclosure. The heavenly ambience in a Gothic cathedral is a simultaneous combination of music (heavenly sound as it was supposed to be!), skylight filtered through rose windows, the tactility of aged materials that invite human touch, the fragrance of burning candles, and even the subtle odour disseminated from moist stone. The bodily experience of an architecturally confined world evokes emotions as well as thoughts through many senses. A modern skyscraper, a significant hallmark of the twentieth century, often built in steel and glass, caters mainly to our vision. The verticality of a modern skyscraper is not an internalized world; it is by contrast an outward viewfinder with stacked offices or apartments. Even the summit of a skyscraper is about the view: either a restaurant, or simply a viewing platform, on the top floor of a high-rise tower, occasionally offering visitors an opportunity to expand their horizon. The glass and shiny metallic surfaces are too sleek to register senses other than vision, let alone stimulate them emotionally as in a Gothic cathedral.

Such a comparison perhaps can be tested in many other parts of the human habitat in the twentieth century, ranging from cities, institutions, leisure centers to homes, and the conclusions of more comparisons, dare we say, would be similar: the modern built world is largely a clinical and yet visual world. This generalization is further demonstrated in the new city centers in China, which are being

1

constructed at dashing speed and at vast scale in order to catch up, or even surpass what the West had achieved in the twentieth century.[2] Tuan observes that these city centers are increasingly becoming gigantic sculpture gardens. The architects and their clients are in a "gymnastic competition" with each other with isolated, and yet mammoth high-rise objects in Beijing and Shanghai. What formal novelties might still be envisaged other than turning a skyscraper into a Möbius strip, like that of the China Central Television tower (CCTV) in Beijing? The glass and steel skyscrapers of the twentieth century have been reincarnated as the gravity-defying and dazzling super-structures of today, a proverbial "beauty contest" of high-rise towers, from Beijing to Moscow, and from London to Dubai.[3]

This book grew out of a symposium with the same title – Topophilia and Topophobia: Reflections on Human Habitat in the Twentieth Century, which was held in Beijing. While witnessing a frenzy of building activity in the city, one was awestruck at the immensity and the daring of the new structures under construction at the time of the symposium, which ranged from the 2008 Olympic stadium to the CCTV tower. The visual spectacle of these buildings seems to capture a moment of joyful explosion, like that of fireworks, but frozen into static structures. For us humans, a state of ecstasy surely does not last for too long and there is often a chemical-emotional swing in the opposite direction. These buildings give the impression that an interior life is inferior to their metallic sculptured exteriors. One wonders whether they will, as architecture once did, serve as stable homes to harbor changing emo-tions, the frailties of human life, and indeed, the growing awareness that comes with time of individual mortality. If not, what emotional bonds to architecture and place can be developed and nurtured in this technology-driven, gravity-defying age?

In this book we propose to explore these questions by examining the feelings of love and aversion towards places humans have inhabited over the twentieth century. This exploration is tied to two interconnected themes – topophilia and topophobia – which provide a framework for including, hence discerning, the emotional, psychological, life-enhancing and debilitating meanings and experiences of modern architectural and urban environments.

Long ago, Gaston Bachelard reminded us of the importance of enclosed space – that of a house, which has the power to integrate our thoughts, memories and dreams: "The house thrusts aside contingencies, its councils of continuity are unceasing. Without it, man would be a dispersed being."[4] Although Bachelard had already coined the human and home relation using the word *topophilia*,[5] it was Tuan who redefined it as "the affective bond between people and place or setting."[6] For Tuan, this form of affection had both general and particular modes of expression, diffuse as a concept yet "vivid and concrete as personal experience."[7] In his book, *Topophilia: A Study of Environmental Perception, Attitudes, and Values*, Tuan describes a wide range of human experiences and environmental perceptions of the world, from the vital openness of young children to the sensual contraction of old age, from the ancient Greeks to the Indians and Anglo-Americans of New Mexico to the automobile slipstreams of Los Angeles. It is a kaleidoscope of human relations, both bodily and conceptually, to places. The book concludes by explaining that the study of environmental perceptions, attitudes and values is "enormously complex" and that "it is seldom possible to relate environmental characteristics to perceptual biases as cause to effect: culture mediates."[8] The shifting intensities and forms of topophilia, the affection and fondness developed towards places, present a broad framework for studying these culturally formed relationships.

Tuan followed the publication of *Topophilia* with further studies of the affective relationships between humans and their environments, which encompass both the familiar and comforting affirmative bonds we develop towards places, and also the negative, psychologically darker forms this relationship can take – the latter being the subject of his 1979 book, *Landscapes of Fear*.[9] Here Tuan argues that fear and anxiety are integral parts of the human experience of the world, and a significant range of these feelings is understandable in terms of the "landscapes," both physical and mental, that people create, occupy and are sometimes forced to live in. Many of these landscapes can be found in the city, ancient and modern: the sensual assault of Imperial Rome with the "breathless jostle" and "infernal din" of street traffic and commotion; the narrow and gloomy alleys of the medieval town which at night were plunged into impenetrable darkness; the dread of fire and loss of life that was a perennial concern for Chinese and Europeans living in houses made of bamboo or wood; and the many middle-class fears of the nineteenth and twentieth centuries caused by overcrowding, poverty and unemployment in such places as the teeming tenement districts of Philadelphia and New York. Tuan explains how such fears were often the motivation for action against urban chaos, resulting in the establishment of new building policies and ambitious planning schemes. It is an illuminating study of urban and architectural history, reminding us of the personal and social attitudes that have animated everyday urban life and the emotional intensities and vibrancy that such "landscapes of fear" have held in human consciousness and imagination.

In fact, the topophobic relation was foreshadowed in an earlier book entitled *Space and Place: The Perspective of Experience*, which was first published in 1977.[10] In this book, Tuan at the outset generalizes the rich and diverse relations with the human habitat, which were given loving depictions in *Topophilia*, as a compelling paradox: "Place is security, space is freedom: we are attached to the one and long for the other."[11] Such a paradox also suggests that our *philia* and *phobia* (or love and hate) relations with the *topos* can be interchangeable: the open plains to Americans may be a symbol of opportunity and freedom, and they suggest mobility, but to Russian peasants boundless space connoted desolation and despair: the emptiness and indifference of the space inhibited their capacity to act![12] Topophilia or topophobia, neither of which therefore is evoked by vision alone: it is a combination of our senses that stirs emotions and that enables us to engage with the world with both body and mind.

Joseph Rykwert, though never using the words topophilia and topophobia in his earlier work, has wrestled with the irrational aspects of our relations with the built world. Such irrational, and yet perceptive, engagements with human habitat are symbolically meaningful, albeit they often occur subconsciously and take form in collective rituals and ceremonies. In *The Idea of a Town: The Anthropology of Urban Form in Rome, Italy and the Ancient World*, Rykwert told architects and planners that there was a mutual, as well as symbolic, understanding between citizens and town patterns in the ancient world.[13] The book was conceived and first published in the late 1950s as a special issue of the Dutch review *Forum*, which was edited by architect Aldo van Eyck. The interactive and meaningful relations between the inhabitants and the built world are most vividly embodied in the physical fabric of a city, which, as van Eyck suggested in the first edition of the book, is Rykwert's reminder of what architects seemed to have forgotten:

> that the city was not just a rational solution to the problems of production, marketing, circulation and hygiene – or an automatic response to the pressure of certain physical and market forces – but that it also had to enshrine the hopes and fears of its citizens.[14]

Such architectural enshrinement is first and foremost an enclosed space for protection: a home for Bachelard, a confined place for Tuan, and voids in-between things for Rykwert. Only with sufficient enclosure and sensual tactility might emotions be registered and stimulated, which, as the ancients had proved, is the precursor of an emotional and hence meaningful interaction between inhabitants and their built world. The voids in-between things, for Rykwert, are necessarily primordial and eternal. They are both the containers and the stimuli for human activities. In his following book, *On Adam's House in Paradise: The Idea of the Primitive Hut in Architectural History*,[15] Rykwert traces an architectural history of postulating the first house, or the primitive hut, for Adam in Paradise. It may seem to be merely an irony that the recurrent reconstruction of the primitive hut, from ancient rites to the inventions of modern architects, serves the inescapable desire for renewal, but Rykwert subtly points out that the enclosure of Adam's house is notional:

> Its floor was the earth, its supports were living beings, its trellised roof was like a tiny sky of leaves and flowers: to the couple sheltering within it, it was both an image of their joined bodies and a pledge of the world's consent to their union. It was more; it provided them – at a critical moment – with a mediation between the intimate sensations of their own bodies and the sense of the great unexplored world around.[16]

Indeed, this primordial demarcation between a confined, internal world and the wild, and yet free external space is the very architectural means to house, as well as animate, our topophilia and topophobia.

But the unchanged nature of a container as human habitat, though more notional than physical, is necessary, for our changing emotions need something permanent to hang on to. Rykwert, incidentally, concluded that "Paradise is a promise as well as a memory."[17] Memory in the twentieth century was never a buzzword; it was, and still is, the novelty of technological advancement and progress that has largely preoccupied modern life. Over the twentieth century we can see the implications of both topophilia and topophobia being increasingly disregarded while we have been overtaken by the speed and the mass of building. The sheer size and quantity of the built world seem to go up with animal rather than human energy. The various avant-gardes have celebrated the seductions of newness since the turn of last century and we are continuingly amazed by the technological advancements that allow us to manipulate the *topos* through building human habitat. All of this has undoubtedly been heightened by leaps in building technology that have taken place in recent decades, and the vast building program currently being undertaken in East Asia. Whether we will be able to translate this awareness into the paradox of our love and aversion towards place and *topos*, only sustained reflection can decide.

A re-examination of human habitat that dwells on a static architectural enclosure, both notionally and physically, now seems "ridiculously *passé*" again.[18] Technological advancement has enabled future-oriented architects to predict that before long buildings and cities will change shape and size in relation to the seasons (shrinking to save energy in winter), and perhaps change according to one's mood.[19] This is ludicrous for Tuan who argues that buildings must necessarily stay the same in order to calm our fear of change and unpredictability:

> Suppose this madness can be applied to nature so that the hill in my neighborhood will obligingly loom like a mountain when my mood calls for something large? Renaissance architects couldn't have guessed that one day their Vitruvian ideal of man as measure could lead to the extremity of making man so much the measure, so much in command, that the external world, having totally merged with human fantasy, simply melts away.[20]

Digital technology, which started in the latter part of the twentieth century, and is now in full swing, seems to promise a virtual world in which any perceptive, embodied connection to the physical world, and to one another, may be redundant. The prophets of the "city of bits" foretold of bodies becoming reconfigurable cybernetic actuators and receptors, hands as telemanipulators, eyes with televisual vision and hearing with telephonic ears.[21] As "cyborg citizens" we exist in both virtual and physical worlds with an increasing incorporation of virtual life ("smart places" and devices) into the physical fabric of cities, shifting, once again, our senses of location, proximity, presence, mobility and community. But Rykwert remains unconvinced that our body, a big piece of warm hardware, may one day be sent through wires, let alone wireless cyberspace: "I suspect that even when ways will be found to turn us into information bits, we will still be the creatures of our senses."[22] While Rykwert argues that our bodily awareness must be supported and stimulated by the analogue world,[23] Tuan would point us to the weighty sensation of sinking into soft sand, the comfort of a favourite armchair, or the sting of touching a hot iron.

Responsive and immersive environments and the idea of virtual bodies configured and reconfigured within informational networks suggest that the notion of human mobility, physically and symbolically, is challenged. In respect to the promise of virtual reality, we are witnessing a shift from the idea that humans require mobility in order to experience change, emotional differences and otherness, towards an increasing degree of immobility in human life. The digital capacities of surrounding environments and software will alter and be updated, but what of the perceptual capacities and energies that result from human movement from one sensual place to another? Is this also to be simulated for our convenience? A provocative metaphor here would be that of "complacent oysters," bodies that have over-adapted to a fixed position and which consequently have lost the capacity to move.[24] The peril of the promise of a digital world, in lieu of an analogue one, is that humans may trade emotional and sensual mobility for illusion.

Readers by now must have realized that this prologue calls for attention to be paid to the learning and thoughts of Rykwert and Tuan since the middle of the twentieth century. True, but it is more. At the risk of making it too blunt, the emphasis of the necessity of an architectural enclosure is the prologue to the discussions of topophilia and topophobia included in this book, which, fortunately unlike our explicit plea for reflection here, deal with the nuances and artifice of this architectural confinement, physically and symbolically, with twentieth-century cases. For architects, planners and environmental designers, as well as those outside these professions, a conscious awareness of the demarcation between the internal built world and the space beyond must not stay in oblivion: it is worth a recurrent reminder.

The awareness of an architecturally confined interior world should, however, not be mistaken as a "fortress besieged." The post-modern concern with "defensive architecture" is based on a paranoid fear, hence the need for architecturally ensured security. Yes, sufficient enclosure protects us from fear, but it also symbolically places us in the center of our world: hearth is our topophilia; we then need to venture out. Modern gated communities and fortified institutions deny a pedestrian access to them. Even the dissolution between the interior and exterior in corporate and institutional buildings – the use of large areas of glass, has not resulted in a transparency in its symbolism. In stark contrast, such openness is often guarded by "state-of-the-art electronic surveillance" if not "gun-toting private police." This seemingly invisible fortification, as Mike Davis observes in Los Angeles, can be immediately deciphered by the underclass "Other."[25] They are, in other words, transparent panopticons! The absence of a conscious demarcation between interior and exterior, and consequently doors and windows, begs for a reflection on the primordial meanings of architecture, as well as their modern social implications in the twentieth century. But ultimately the reflection calls for action: a more humane modern world, though it will always be tinted by our ambivalence of affinity and aversion, will have to be solidified as buildings and cities, but also understood with loving maintenance by those who live within them.

In this book, the human habitat, ranging broadly from the cities of the twentieth century, to highbrow modern architecture both in the West and Asia, to non-architect/planner designed vernacular settlements and landscapes are thematically reviewed under the frame of topophilia and topophobia, with philosophical musings as well as explorative case studies. An introduction such as this one is to some extent redundant, for the first two chapters by Joseph Rykwert and Yi-Fu Tuan serve as fitting introductions to not only the pre-modern meanings of our love and hate relations with the built world, but also the chapters that follow, which offer detailed studies of this paradoxical tie with the *topos* via cases of buildings and cities in the twentieth century.

The reflection begins with a chapter by Rykwert, who reiterates the necessity of the discourse of emotion and place, hence the invention of the words *topophilia* and *topophobia*. The purpose of a reflection beyond the twentieth century is to remind us that linguistic expressions of a love and hate relationship with a place existed in the ancient world, but the expressions as well as our understanding of these relationships have become dusty throughout modern history. Rykwert is optimistic about the renewal of these relationships, and the chapter calls for an activist mentality, and indeed aims to empower individuals to more consciously acknowledge our essential *philia* and *phobia* in making a place on earth.

Along with that of Rykwert's, Tuan's chapter begins with a reflection on the pre-modern era, and although it may seem to suggest that topophobia is the psychological base for human–*topos* relationships, the key argument of the chapter is to point out a recent change to the role of architecture, which was to be enduring in order to defy time, but now the metallic brightness of buildings seems to withstand corruption and aspire to immortality at the same time, however, as being readily prone to fashion and technological innovation. In other words, the life span of these buildings is shorter. Given that it was Tuan who reinvented *topophilia* in the English-speaking world, it is only telling that Tuan is now using the changed role of architecture to beg the fundamental question of human relations with the *topos*. If technology has the ability to make us forget our mortality by giving us abundance, the question then may be whether or not architecture still has a role to create a sense of connection to our biological impulses, if it is no longer possible to relate to cosmic or religious foundations as it once was.

Neil Leach goes on to raise two important questions in Chapter 3: How are we to understand the formation of human identity in relation to the environment? And what role does place play in that process? This chapter suggests that the paradox of topophilia and topophobia forms both place and human identity. Leach theorizes that identities are established either on the horror of undifferentiated self, or the horror of the alienated self. Is identity essentially a phobia? Does this chapter, from a different angle, echo Tuan's "troubling thought" that phobia is our psychological base of *topos* relations? The arguments, needless to say, are necessary and important, but it is tantalizing to conclude that it is horror, or fear, not affection, that helps form identity.

In Chapter 4, Jean-Louis Cohen offers a tangible reflection on the modern heterotopias leading to the twentieth-century metropolis. Heterotopias and archipelagos, to paraphrase Cohen, are important hallmarks of modernity, which started as spatial segregations in order to achieve hygiene as well as social order, hence there came prisons, hospitals, factories and other institutions. Cohen, however, points to a not-quite-either-or paradox in our time: many of the "enclaves" in a modern metropolis have indeed been designed to generate happiness – a topophilia, so to speak. These pleasure archipelagos range from early department stores and grand hotels to more recent shopping malls, skyscrapers, Disneyparks and even ocean liners. The identity of each archipelago notwithstanding (to continue the discussion from Leach), Cohen calls for a positive view of modern heterotopias – that is, to use his quote of Guy Debord, that "we will play on topophobia to create a topophilia."

Topophilia and topophobia, for Peter Kohane in Chapter 5, can be seen through a relation between humans and buildings, that is, the "agreement" that can exist between a person and a room. The conversation between two people may be analogous to the conversation between a person and his/her room, while at a civic level it may become the decorum of building within the city, which again can be interpreted as a form of agreement. Kohane suggests that the work of Louis Khan formally encapsulates bodily agreement, which in other words, is based on a conviction that a building must be an internalized container in order for a civilized conversation to be held between the occupier and the room occupied.

The problem of modern architecture as a centering device is addressed by Xing Ruan in Chapter 6 on the divergent practices of Yang Tingbao and Louis Kahn, both of whom graduated from Paul Philippe Cret's design studio at the University of Pennsylvania in the early 1920s. These two architects adapted the Beaux-Arts concern with "character" and the use of *parti* and *poché* in their own work, Yang in his civic projects in China and Kahn within his various institutional buildings. Ruan recognizes this divergence, but also draws parallels in the embodiment of "character" in the buildings, theories and in the personal and professional traits of the architects. On a physical level, character is connected to the provision of enclosure through such things as "interest centers" with Yang and concentric space in the case of Kahn. On a conceptual level, character is recognized in the manner that their buildings provide a sense of being in the center for their occupants through the emotional strength gained by the warm attachment to that which is familiar or uplifting. These, Ruan argues, are admirable qualities of the two architectural trajectories: with Yang, it is the unpretentious fit to everyday life or urban context, and with Kahn, the soaring spiritual elevation his buildings were designed to provide.

In Chapter 7, Ross Jenner examines a specific architectural endeavor to overcome the gravity that holds buildings firmly in the ground. Through a study of several Italian modern architects and their works, Jenner sheds new light on levitation and the use of glass in twentieth-century buildings. A key character of the selected works, for Albini in particular, is that a place can be made out of space. Although there is no doubt that the appeal of levitation and suspension says something about modernity that has been materialized via architecture, Jenner offers a romanticized reading, which is the potentiality of a place in air, hence a possibility to be desired in modern architecture.

Harry Margalit, in Chapter 8, offers a reading of the iconic contemporary Australian house – that of Glenn Murcutt's bush pavilions, which are characterized by the dissolution between their interior and exterior. The consequence, incidentally, is the absence of an architectural enclosure, hence a transparency that, to paraphrase the author, has been employed to ward off anguish of an Australia that is still defined by a neo-colonial complex. Elsewhere, transparency in domestic architecture may warrant a psychoanalysis (for example, California's modernist houses), but in Australia however, transparency is ideological. The "darkness" that lies behind domestic life may be avoided, but it has provided an opportunity for the pursuit of works of clarity and sophistication. Phobia yet again has been transformed into philia, though Margalit nonetheless calls for a richer conception of domestic life. Since architecture does not transcend ideology, architects will need to take part in the future imaginings of a culture.

In Chapter 9, Alessandra Como tells of the little-known architectural works of Bernard Rudofsky, who is reputed for popularizing vernacular architecture through exhibitions and books, the most widely recognized being *Architecture without Architects*, published in 1964. But it is through his architecture that Rudofsky claimed the relationship between the building and the ground/*topos*. A building, for Rudofsky, is like a medicine, which should work, or be instrumental. This, as Como reveals, lies in Rudofsky's interest in "unchanged" things in life, as well as his study of architecture as solids and voids. It is the capacity of these solids and voids that register and interact with human activities that makes architecture experiential.

In Chapter 10, Sarah Treadwell presents a sensual narrative of the emotive relationship with landscape. Although this tale is specific, we are not alone in terms of these highly charged emotive experiences with a place. The earth sometimes can be a wonderland, but it also is atmospherically architecture. This resonates with earlier discussions of the definition of place, which is confined and contained to hold an ambience, which inevitably is charged with emotion. The geometry of such confinement, though subconscious to a modern person, is symbolically meaningful. The horizontality of landscape, in this tale, is pleasurable, while the verticality of a place can be transcendental. Pre-modern experience it may be, but such primordial inhabitation of a place may form much of our subconsciousness, and yet too often it is not animated in the modern built world. Does the liquid world (the animated matter) of this landscape offer hope for modern habitat?

In Chapter 11, Daniel O'Hare examines the discourse on modern tourist resorts, claiming that topophilia and topophobia can be found in the promotional material of these resorts, popular novels and films, as well as within the decision-making and political lobbying of developers and environmental activists. The construction of these resorts as places of desire is often based on a topophobic contrast to inspire topophilic attachment. O'Hare argues that resistance to the over-development and commercialization of coastal places depends on the strength of topophilic narratives, above legislative controls, and that these narratives hold significant sway over the public imagination, thus reaffirming Tuan's thesis for the study of urban geography through culturally mediated forms of perception. This chapter also provokes questions about whether the character of one place can be transported and fabricated within another.

Does the emotive relationship with the *topos* come with a "price tag"? A reflection of the predominantly twentieth-century human habitat would not be complete without an economic examination of the love and hate relationship with it. Peter Murphy does just that in Chapter 12 via an appraisal of the contemporary metropolis, in this case, Sydney. This chapter dwells on an ambivalent idea: Yes, the economy of a city and our own economic state may well influence our affections towards it, but as Rykwert argues, the rise and fall of the economy, as that of our emotions, are abrupt and irrational. How much are the love for and emotional attachment to Sydney's harbour and the Opera House based on the economic well-being of the metropolis, which in itself is unstable and susceptible to sudden change?

In an uncompromising manner, Vittorio Gregotti concludes the book with a call for a reconciliation of topophilia and topophobia. This particular angle of reflecting on the twentieth-century human habitat, when topophilia and topophobia have parted company, tells us that the modern era is characterized by boundless expansion: urban sprawl is perhaps one example of such disregard of topophilia. Gregotti reiterates his belief that the primordial architectural act is not taking shelter but marking out boundaries to create a human world.[26] This echoes the theme of the prologue: dwelling on the marked enclosure, we begin to dialogue with the world beyond. Such condition is for Gregotti a precursor of an internationalism with culturally rooted differences. Gothic architecture and its regional characteristics in England, France and Spain are but one example in this regard. Gregotti's urge for a "return of meaning to a readable differentiation" is opposed to the "new picturesque" in our time. His observations of new Chinese cities and the problems facing European cities are once again proof that the modern desire for newness in architecture, in his own words, results in "awe without marvel": "a string of colossal objects erected in aesthetic and economic competition with each other" are a "forced diversity," hence "meaningless newness." In the absence of an architectural enclosure at its most primordial level, we once again have become what Gaston Bachelard called "dispersed beings."

Notes

1 Yi-Fu Tuan, *Topophilia: A Study of Environmental Perception, Attitudes, and Values*, New York: Columbia University Press, 1974, p. 11.

2 Xing Ruan, *New China Architecture*, Singapore: Periplus/Tuttle, 2006.

3 For illustrations of these, see Georges Binder (ed.), *Tall Buildings of Europe, the Middle East and Africa*, Mulgrave, Victoria: Images Publishing, 2006.

4 Gaston Bachelard, *The Poetics of Space*, trans. by Maria Jolas, Foreword by Etienne Gilson, Boston: Beacon Press, 1969, pp. 6–7, originally published as *La Poétique de l'espace*, Paris: Presses Universitaires de France, 1958.

5 Ibid., p. xxxi.

6 Tuan, *Topophilia*, p. 4.

7 Ibid.

8 Ibid., p. 246.

9 Yi-Fu Tuan, *Landscapes of Fear*, New York: Pantheon Books, 1979.

10 Yi-Fu Tuan, *Space and Place: The Perspective of Experience*, Minneapolis and London: University of Minnesota Press, 1977.

11 Ibid., p. 3.

12 Ibid., p. 56.

13 Joseph Rykwert, *The Idea of a Town: The Anthropology of Urban Form in Rome, Italy and the Ancient World*, London: Faber and Faber, 1976.

14 Rykwert, *The Idea of a Town*, Preface to the Paper Edition, Cambridge, MA: MIT Press, 1988, p. 1.

15 Joseph Rykwert, *On Adam's House in Paradise: The Idea of the Primitive Hut in Architectural History*, 2nd edn, Cambridge, MA: MIT Press, 1981.

16 Ibid., p. 190.

17 Ibid., p. 192.

18 Rykwert felt that his idea of town planning as an art was thought "ridiculously *passé*" when city planning was dominated by "rational principles" in the 1960s. See *The Idea of a Town*, Preface to the Paper Edition, 1988, p. 1.

19 For examples, see Michael Jantzen's Windshaped Pavilions, www.walrus.com/~ddprod/ michaeljantzen, accessed 26 June 2007, and David Fisher's "Dynamic Architecture," www. dynamicarchitecture.net, accessed 26 June 2007.

20 Tuan in email conversation with Xing Ruan, 8 December 2006.

21 See William J. Mitchell, *City of Bits: Space, Place and the Infobahn*, Cambridge, MA: MIT Press, 1995, pp. 31–41.

22 Joseph Rykwert, *The Seduction of Place: The City in the Twenty-first Century*, London: Weidenfeld & Nicolson, 2000, p. 159.

23 Ibid., p. 156.

24 Lewis Mumford makes a clear distinction

> between the mainly free-moving protozoa that formed the animal kingdom and the relatively sessile organisms that belong to the vegetable kingdom. The first, like the oyster, sometimes become overadapted to a fixed position and lose the power of movement; while many plants free themselves in some degree by underground rootings and above all, by the detachment and migration of the seed.
>
> (Mumford, *The City in History: Its Origins, Its Transformations, and Its Prospects*, London: Secker & Warburg, 1961, p. 5)

25 Mike Davis, *City of Quartz: Excavating the Future in Los Angeles*, London and New York: Verso, 1990, p. 226.

26 Kenneth Frampton, "Foreword," in Vittorio Gregotti, *Inside Architecture*, trans. by Peter Wong and Francesca Zaccheo, Cambridge, MA: MIT Press, 1996, p. xvii.

1

Topo-philia and -phobia

Joseph Rykwert

We have linked the two Greek words for love and hate, *philía*, *phobia* to another Greek word, *topos*, to sum up the theme of this book. The Greeks did use the word *topos* τoπoς, generally for any place – in a book, in a body, in a landscape, in any discourse. Aristotle called his book on arguing (when its construction is independent of any subject), *Topica*. In medicine, it signifies the diseased points of the body as well as its secret places, while in our more generic usage, "topos" has to do with any region or locality, however big. The Romans translated it by *locus*, a word some have derived from the archaic *stolcus* – which in turn suggests an origin in *stare*, "to stand." Yet the Greeks do not seem to have known either an emotion they could call *topophilia* – nor *topophobia*, for that matter. Their *topos* was not anything one could love or hate. The twentieth-century usage has assimilated that word to another word for place: χωρα (sometimes χωρoς).

  Chora seems older, used by both Homer and Hesiod – while *topos* appears first in tragedy. Chora starts its life as a place enclosed, a dancing floor – as well as a dancing troupe – from which we got our "choir", "chorus" and the enclosure, some entomologists suggest, are the linked hands of dancers. The word is also related to notions of hollow and cavern, allied in turn – if rather remotely – to *chaos*; but also to χoρτoς, "garden", "orchard", "farmyard" (from which the Latin *hortus*). Aeschylus in the *Eumenides* contrasts Athena's birthplace, *choros*, with Libya, the *topos* to which it belongs.[1] All these usages suggest the reason why the Greeks, who did indeed know a love of place, called it *philochoria* or even, inverting the two words, *chorophilia*.

  Sophocles begins his tragedy about *Oedipus at Colonos*[2] – the place where, incidentally Sophocles himself was born, a few miles north of Athens – at the point when the exhausted, blinded, exiled King sits down on a stone to rest. And asks Antigone his daughter, who has been his guide:

        "To what
    region, tell me, to the city of what people have we come?"
    looking round, Antigone answers:

The place before us
is clearly holy – *πρόςω′ χ ρος δ′ öδ′ ⊇ρός* –
shaded by vines, olive trees and bay . . .

She recognizes Athens as the town in the distance – but cannot identify the *choros*; and asks her father if she should ask what the *topos* – the words seem almost interchangeable – might be. A stranger appears and tells Oedipus to move away, as he is on holy *choros*, land consecrated to the avenging Eriniyes, "daughters of Darkness and Earth, Ladies whose Eyes are terrible." The stranger tells Oedipus further that all the *choros*, all the country around, is protected by Poseidon and Prometheus, but the very *topos* where he rests "has been called the earth's brass doorsill and buttress of great Athens." In that place Oedipus is to die and leave his corpse to the Athenians as a relic that will guarantee the safety of Athens in perpetuity.

I am not concerned here with Antigone's great deeds in Thebes after her father's death, and where she is killed because she preferred divine justice to human authority. Yet I wonder if the *choros/topos* distinction, not quite clear in Sophocles (though it becomes more marked as the Greek language develops) cannot be refined through a more reflective use of language in the generation following him, by Plato.

The *Timaeus* was probably written twenty years or so after the death of Sophocles. In the course of considering some of the great themes of philosophy – chance or necessity, accident or design, the one and the many, the intelligible and the sensed – Plato posited the existence of three kinds of being: the invariant and eternal forms, *ειδιει*, ungenerated and indestructible, which need no "somewhere," *no topos* to abide; forms of the second species, which – though similarly named – are sensible, subject to opinion and in constant movement and transformation, *ιδέαι* (but also *μορφή*), and the third, the space *χωρος*, which receives those sensible forms, but is itself eternal and, like the other two, "there" before the heavens were made. Uncreated forms may only be known by the intellect, while the second kind can be appreciated by the senses. Space is not subject to change and not knowable by the senses, but is discerned by a sort of bastard (Cornford) or hybrid (Rivaud) or spurious (Jowett) reasoning; we know space as in a dream.[3]

These are the three species which the creator god, the demiurge, organizes through the rationalizing process of world-making. Plato explains that physical being has both location in and possession of place: anything that is must be someplace. The contrast is between "some – specific – location," and its containing volume. For Plato, *chora* is therefore not merely "a place" but the everlasting location and matrix of all created things. His valuation of the word and the notion, in the context of an argument crucial to his thinking, has colored the word even since.

Of course I have abbreviated Plato's exalted text summarily – but in any case the place of which I wish to speak is not the uncreated species which Plato canonized, but the more humble abode which we all too often take for granted. At this lower everyday level, Hellenistic Greeks made the distinction explicitly by reference to representation: *topographia* is the precise depiction of a place, while *chorographia* is concerned with a general impression of a locality – and geography with all the world.

That difference has an obvious application in the *Geographikis Yphigiseos*, the very first guidebook to the whole earth; Claudius Ptolomaeus, its author, explains that his book includes a *Chorographia*, as part of Geography, but that the two procedures require different skills. "Geography" only needs a kind of mathematical knowledge, and anyone – so Ptolemy thinks – can perform its operations, which, after all, only consists of drawing lines between determined points. "Chorography," on the other hand, could not be done by someone who was not a painter, *ei mi graphikos anir*.[4]

For Ptolomaeus, geography is therefore merely quantitative, and can only deal with the *poson* of a place – its dimensions and levels – while "chorography" may not require any special mathematical knowledge, but depends on a sensibility which will allow "the describer" to appreciate and set forth the quality of a place, its *poion*.[5] We sometimes forget another quality, which every inhabited place owed to the faculty it had of generating its own time. Through a calendar, which might be regulated either by the sun or by the moon, every settlement in the ancient world could have its own system of dating which was counted from some crucial event in its history (usually its foundation). More powerful political bodies would impose their calendar on subject towns and countries to signify their domination. The Greeks counted time from the first Olympic games, while the Romans fixed the foundation of the city on the feast of Parilia (April 21) of the year 753 BC. For obvious reasons, that dating, *ab urbe condita* is the one that is now most generally remembered.

The two words have inevitably changed meaning in modern parlance: we now call "chorography" any description of a region, while "topography" is the mapping of a specific district, and "geography" the mapping of the world in general – in English and French, at any rate. The great seventeenth-century physician-essayist, Sir Thomas Browne, claimed to be familiar with the "nature of several climes, the Chorography of their provinces, (the) Topography of their cities," while in his *Dictionary*, Dr Johnson says that chorography is "less in its object than geography, and greater than topography."[6] That modern version unfortunately confuses the ancient distinction which had seemed so essential to Ptolomaeus.

That is why the Greeks may also have found it easier to love a place as *chora*, since *topos*, being only quantitative, cannot carry a real emotional charge. Our own time may tend to avoid such a slippery, imprecise term which depends entirely on quality – and indeed *chorophilia* is now classed as an archaic (or even obsolete) word. Yet qualities are what endear their home to exiles. Exiles form a human group whose members need to imagine and configure most intimately and urgently the space from which they have been excluded and to which they may – or may not – long to return. In either case, it will hold them in its thrall – not by any of its exactly measurable characteristics, but by its tastes and smells and its vagaries of climate. James Joyce's *Ulysses* is one of the grandest monuments to the non-returning exile's *chorophiliac* nostalgia. But such *amor patriae* may have any number of different stimuli. It may have to do with imponderables, but also to familial attachment, or the shelter the earth may have given to the bones of the ancestors who cultivated it. Exiles may even have tilled that soil themselves, so that only its particular feel may impart the familiarity needed for emotional stability and security. Only the buildings and landscape that gave the exiles shelter in their childhood and adolescence will make them feel that absence as deprivation. That sense of deprivation was given a clinical label in the sixteenth century: nostalgia, the illness of return. It was said to have been first diagnosed among the Swiss guards of the Pope, who in the flat and sunny expanses of the Roman Campagna pined for the glaciers, mountains and meadows of their Grisons/Graubünden homeland.

In the ancient world, the loss of home was also associated with loss of freedom: as that of the Israelites when some 30,000 were taken into captivity by Shalmaneser III and Sargon II in 727 BC. They presumably constituted the land's priestly-warrior-craft-merchant classes. Judea in its turn finally fell to Nebuchadnezzar in 586 BC.[7] After the Jerusalem temple was destroyed, a series of deportations took place: it was the beginning of that Babylonish captivity which has become the commonplace of all exile dereliction. "By the rivers of Babylon we wept and sighed when we remembered Zion" has become the archetypical exile's lament[8] – and it is quite irrelevant that Mount Zion now seems an insignificant elevation to the south of old Jerusalem, dominated by a rather ungainly church built at the expense of the German Emperor William II. Many descendants of the exiles returned in the reign of the Persian conqueror Cyrus after 540[9] – the exile having lasted a nominal seventy years. Jerusalem fell finally to Titus who turned exile into the permanent condition of the Jews in 70 AD.

The Greeks, for their part, hymned a group of heroes whom they called *Nostoi*, commanders who had taken part in the siege of Troy and whose long and often tortuous voyage home was the subject of several Epics. Homer's recital of King Odysseus' return to his realm, Ithaca, was merely the most famous of them – and became the canonic account of an exile's homecoming.

Exile may have been – in the case of the *Nostoi* – a condition imposed by history, by war or conquest, or by the failure of some commercial expedition – but it could also be a punishment. The Greeks called it φυγη, *phygi*, the same word they used for escape, especially from the battlefield. Exile was imposed for murder, as it was for blasphemy – such as the uprooting of Athena's olive-trees, or the knocking the *phalloi* off some of the herms which guarded Athenian street-corners (as in the case of the beautiful and brilliant but incorrigibly opportunist Alcibiades). It was also applied (as Plato details in the Laws) to such offences as striking a parent, and that sentence could be sharpened by refusing the exile bread and water – the necessities of life.[10] Even touching such an exile was considered defiling. Many Greek cities made exile more grievous by the confiscation of home and of goods; though anyone, even someone condemned to death, could escape punishment, however awful, by going into voluntary exile. Socrates refused that alternative at his trial, as he would refuse the chance of escape offered by his rich friend Crito.[11]

The Romans gave us the word *exsilium*, which the old grammarians explained as derived from *ex* – "out" and *solum* – "ground, base, earth." No Roman exile is more famous than that of Ovid who suffered its milder form, *relegatio*, to

Tomi in what is now Constanța, in Romania. In his Epistles from Pontus and his *Tristitia*, he left the archetype of a literary exile's lament. In modern languages, we have, more recently, developed another series of concepts connected to the Italian custom of *bando*, the vocal proclamation or the affixing of written announcements of exile. A person so named became *bandito* – as Romeo was after the murder of Tybalt, his exile setting in motion the tragic machinery of his love of Juliet.

Literature has made exile a most eloquent witness to *amor patriae*, but a negative one, since it testifies to the seductive power which our home exercises on us once we have lost it. Arguably, in the twentieth or the twenty-first centuries, *amor patriae* no longer plays any role in our attachment to our dwelling. It is not always easy to feel such love for an apartment in a high-rise block or a house in a gated suburb, however stylish. Both are explicitly designed not to have those qualities which invite that affection we called *chorophilia*, since such places tend in fact to be so neutrally equipped that they can be adapted quickly for new owners. This is, of course, essential to the real-estate condition of several countries, notably the United States, where 25 percent of the population were said to change their domicile every couple of years.

The gated suburb has recently had rapid growth: at the time of writing, the Emirate of Dubai has established just off its coast (and has widely advertised) a most spectacular one, shaped in plan like the silhouette of a date-palm. Reclaimed from the sea, it will be the largest artificial island ever, and boasts an internal monorail, several luxury hotels, great shopping spaces and its own mosque – all nearing completion in 2006/7. It will be interesting to see if any of the celebrity buyers – who are said to include senator and ex-president Clinton, the Beckhams and Brad Pitt – will ever develop any form of nostalgia for it. But maybe not inviting nostalgia is one of its main attractions. The neutrality of the permanent fabric and a relatively quick turnover in ownership have induced many inhabitants of our towns or cities to carry their homes with them: their chattels are contained so neatly that wherever they choose to set up their next camp, they can appropriate a house or apartment simply by unpacking. The prevalence of cheap, disposable kitchen – and table-ware – even furniture – may soon dispense the modern nomad from packing anything but bare necessities. The alternative, a mobile home or trailer, is not so much a convenient adaptation of nomadism to modern technology but the institutionalizing of a permanent homelessness.

The old-style nomad may be mobile by definition, but is never homeless. A pastoral one, for instance, usually has two homes: a winter one in plains or valleys, and a summer one higher up in the hills. Slash-and-burn farmers – such as some Amerindian nations – may have left their land when the earth they had been exploiting was exhausted, yet they moved "in context," as it were, within a nexus of kinships and social patterns for which the physical fabric of their village was a metaphor. They moved with household goods as well as their gods. The social pattern as well as the forms of the fabric provided those farmers with a home. Such a move could not be individual: exclusion from a village would mean exile – not only from a given place, but from society, religion, the whole culture. That may be the vital implication of *chora* in Ptolemy's use of the word – that sense of not just being anchored in a specific place, but also having a life within it which is articulated by the celebration of seasonal changes.

The Industrial Revolution brought about a revaluation of time by alienating the new proletariat from the seasons before it ever affected their specific relation to place. The Physiocrats had already protested at the number of productive workdays wasted through the multiplication of religious festivals and insisted that industry was much more important than seasonal observances. It is only in the late twentieth century, and as a result of intensive trade union activity, that the number of working days in the year began to approach that of pre-industrial western and central Europe.

Yet the secularizing of the calendar has also involved a kind of *Gleichschaltung*, a flattening of time – from which the de-qualifying of space has followed, which in turn implies the reduction of any *chora* into one more *topos*. That impoverishment is one of the many ills that the Industrial Revolution brought with it in its early stages, ills that have left permanent and irreparable lesions in the social fabric. However, if you consider the catastrophic housing conditions of industrial workers during the first half of the nineteenth century – and for long after – you might conclude that for most of the urban population of that world the very notion of "home" might have been inconceivable. Yet I think you would be wrong. A memoir by Frank McCourt, *Angela's Ashes*, describes the most abject condition of the industrial poor in Northern Ireland before the Second World War; McCourt does not gloss over any of the squalor or the miseries of his childhood, nor does he show any of the exile's desire to return. Yet the very precision of his account witnesses to a perverse attachment of the author as a child to the home town in which he lived in conditions not unlike those described by Engels in *The Condition of the English Working Class* in 1844, a century earlier.

Industry did, in the end, also bring many benefits, especially to the countries in which it began. To us who live through it, the benefits promised as a result of globalization are less evident than its present disadvantages. However, what has been done cannot be unmade – the journey through time is one-way. For all that, I want to draw out the implications of the distinction I have been at some pains to historicize, the contrast between *chora* and *topos*. It seems to me to be worth making, because there has been, in the wake of the work of some French colleagues, particularly that of Henri Lefebvre and his followers in the English-speaking world, much talk of space as a social product. I want to emphasize the word "product," because it seems to me to have several implications for the study of history, especially urban history. Against this notion of space as a "thing" that has been produced by social and economic forces, I would like to propose a somewhat different conception of it which I owe to another French thinker, Maurice Merleau-Ponty, who has pointed out that

> our field of perception is made up of "things" and of the voids between things . . . at first I see as things the objects which I have never seen in motion: houses, the sun, mountains . . . if we consider as "things" the intervals between them, the outlook on the world will be appreciably

altered . . . This would mean that it is made up of the same elements, differently interconnected, the same sensations differently associated . . . (Not) the same material in a different form – but a different world altogether.[12]

Although Merleau-Ponty does not elaborate on this pithy statement, yet it seems to me to suggest that what he called "space" is constituted of what perception can touch – that the space of which he speaks is very much like a kind of *chora*, a container – and this returns me to Claudius Ptolomaeus' distinction between the intricate *chora* of qualities and the wholly matter-of-fact and measurable *topos*. Any account of the space we humans inhabit therefore, and of our working on it, our ability to transform it, must be in terms of *chora*.

Yes, we have suffered in the late capitalist period the alienation of the perceiving subject of which Lefebvre makes so much, but as a result, the quantifiable aspect of spatial experience is more accessible to the student than the subtler one suggested by *chora*. Moreover, when we consider space as a product, it does become that "thing" against which Merleau-Ponty warned us – and is a "thing" so vast and intangible that it precludes any possibility of direct intervention or manipulation. The implication of such a reading is that it absolves us from our direct responsibility for the shaping of things which are the object of our primary perception. Shaping, of course, implies forms of regulation and "design," of giving the objects that arrest our gaze and our touch defined shape and so distinguishing radically the bitty and willed (and therefore also rationally determinable) experience of social practice from the smooth, continuous and automatic – or at any rate amoral – operations of those quasi-natural socio-historical forces, the producers of space.

It seems to me that the distinction is particularly relevant now that any account of urban development (and of urban theory) is dominated by two tendencies, both of which appeal to a crypto-Marxist view of history. The first demands that historians who identify the principal motors of the socio-economic dialectic, as well as the politicians and other activists who make use of (or apply their studies to) current situations, recognize the unalterable power of such forces. The more extreme advocates of such a view used to maintain that when social conflict was no longer bearable, the revolution this would provoke would – inevitably – resolve environmental problems. Since various revolutions have repeatedly failed to deliver that solution, the advocates of such a reading now look to something even less definite – the creation of new urban space in which he or she can be "a polyvalent, polysensorial, urban man capable of complex and transparent relations with the world."[13] A space which reflected these qualities would be ungendered and quite uninflected by race or class, of course. This reading of the city as a "space of heterogeneity" is mirrored by another approach that relies on the image of the economy being modelled on the unpredictable but unavoidable forces of nature.

The free market, we are often told, is uncontrollable by definition – and we can therefore read the market data in the same spirit as we read the weather forecasts. Our choices in how to deal with either market or weather are strictly limited. The weather may still condition the most ambitious technological enterprise

– say, the launching of a space probe – but the free operation of market forces determines the prosperity of any city. Regulatory constriction can only stunt the free growth of the market as any constriction of roots or branches can stunt the growth of a plant. Over-regulation will make us all poorer and our cities with us. Tampering with the forces of history and those of the market is likely to land us in problems of an almost ecological nature. On that showing, the city can be considered an aspect of that quasi-natural production of social and economic circumstance, and its fabric a secretion of society, like the shell is a smooth secretion of the snail. This is obviously not true – the city works quite unnaturally by jumps and fits and starts whose erratic ways it is the business of the historian not only to chronicle but also, as far as he or she can, to motivate.

Both schools, the left-wing libertarian or the neo-liberal, though diametrically opposed politically, have a neo-Marxist substructure, and both are only marginally concerned with the physical fabric of the city, never mind any complex perception of it suggested by understanding it as *chora*. To both groups, urbanists or architects can only be interesting in so far as they externalize the hidden and powerful forces operating on the infrastructure at the visible surface. I wish, on the contrary, to advocate a more micro-historic approach to any account of the urban fabric by assuming that the vast and seemingly impersonal historical and economic forces shaping the city have always been the aggregate product of choices made by individuals – and these choices are metaphorically exemplified by the forms of "things." I would therefore suggest that if you wish to understand and operate effectively on the urban fabric, you will have to abandon the notion of space as a product.

If you think of any historical process in such graphic terms, as the vector resulting from any number of forces acting – sometimes – in different directions, you will see that the smallest alteration in alignment will deflect the angle of the vector. That is where the motives of all the agents – developer-investors, administrators, politicians who manipulate the urban fabric – must be examined critically, and censored if need be. Even when they seem to be quite rational, nay calculating, they nevertheless often turn out to be obscure and quite wilful, nor can these agents always articulate them explicitly. The shrewd, logical, sober desire for profit and/or power may be balanced by much less rational machinations for prestige and status which can also be tempered by social responsibility and even genuine, disinterested benevolence. Moreover, the most carefully and cunningly calculated actions may turn out to have results which completely betray the intentions of their initiators. Each one of us has a measure of freedom to weigh his or her motives against the constrictions of circumstance – and therefore to act in a particular way, but also to act otherwise.

Irrationality and miscalculation are as much an inescapable part of the history of urban development as they are of the history of banking or of the industrial economy, or (even more explicitly), of any trading in stocks and futures. However inept or shrewd the calculation, the consequences of my action may be what I wanted or foresaw, but they may also turn out to be quite different from what I or anyone else could predict. As we make our history or even history *tout-court*, Marx pointed out, we do not choose the circumstances in which we do so, since the past always conditions our present as it determines the patterns of our thinking and feeling.

A risk of miscalculation and failure attend on freedom – and freedom, as politicians remind us constantly, presupposes responsibility. Although no town or city I live in can possibly be exactly as I wish it – even in the best of all possible worlds – yet the way it looks and works has been determined by people like myself, not by impersonal forces. The citizens' view of their own city can be discussed in terms of the success (or failure) of sports teams, the growth or fall of the crime rate, royal or presidential visits and other press-worthy events, but any accounting for its visible fabric in terms of its economic success or failure is often considered "aesthetic" and without real impact on its fate. And yet everyone knows that his or her face has certainly had an effect on fate – since fate and face are linked in a constant two-way process.

Some of what I have written above may seem self-evident. If I have taken the risk of being over-explicit, it is to insist on something much less obvious, which nevertheless seems to me to follow on my more self-evident remarks. If my truisms are indeed true, then the whole argument which makes the city and its social frame-work the producer of space can be intellectually (as well as) politically dangerous because it seems to deny the citizen any responsibility for the fabric of his or her city. In fact space, unlike place, is not a thing that can be instrumentalized (never mind reified) and therefore shaped. Since I am primarily concerned with form as well as responsibility, it seems to me, both as a historian and as an activist, mistaken to consider space as the determining urban product.

This abrupt and uneven jigsaw of circumstance, of conscious and unconscious workings is what I have always found so fascinating. In that jigsaw *philochoria* must play an essential role: the relation of the exile to his home, sometimes characterized by his love for it, nostalgia, a longing for return; at others (as that of Oedipus to Thebes) it may be repulsion, even loathing. Either feeling will always be a powerful factor in the constitution of city form. I would even like to generalize from this that any history of place must be primarily one of *choros*. Of course, the word has been dropped from modern parlance for many reasons. *Topos* is now the Greek word left to us to signify "place" and has taken over the meaning which Claudius Ptolomaeus reserved for *chora*. That I think is the real justification of inventing the words *topophilia* and *topophobia* which may seem barbarous to some purists.

Notes

1 Aeschylus, *Eumenides*, line 292, αλλ' εΠτε χὅρας εν τΈποις λιβυστικο ϼϛ . . . εΠτε φλεγραίαν πλακα.

2 Lines 3 ff., 37 ff. τινας χωρους, αφιγμενΘ' η τινων ανδρων πολιν. The play seems to have been first produced after Sophocles' death, in 401 BC. I have used (but adapted) Robert Fitzgerald's translation in David Greene and Richard Lattimore (eds), *The Complete Greek Tragedies*, Chicago: Chicago University Press, 1954.

3 *Timaeus* 51 e, 52, εν τινι τοπω και κατεχον χωραν τινα, (52 b). I have used Francis Macdonald Cornford, *Plato's Cosmology*, London: Kegan Paul, 1937, pp. 185 f.; (but see also pp. 200 ff.); Platon, *Œuvres Complètes*, vol. X (ed. Albert Rivaud) pp. 170 ff. Paris: Les Belles Lettres, 1925;

Edith Hamilton and Huntington Cairns, *Plato: The Collected Dialogues*, New York: Pantheon Books, 1961, pp. 1178 ff.

4   Claudius Ptolomaeus, *Geographias Synthesis/Iphigisis*, Book I, section 1, paragraph 6.

5   This distinction is discussed earlier in *Timaeus*, 49 a, ff.

6   "Religio Medici," in *Works*, Chicago: The University of Chicago Press, 1964, p. 82; Samuel Johnson, J. Johnson and others, *A Dictionary of the English Language*, London, 1799, (unpaginated), s.v.

7   Shalmaneser III and Sargon, II Kings xvii, Nebuchadnezzar. II Kings xxiv, 10 ff., II; Chron. xxxvi, 6 ff.; Jer. xxiv ff.

8   Psalms, 136.

9   Esdras I, 1 ff.

10 Jean Babelon, *Alcibiade*, Paris: Payot, 1935, pp. 132 ff.

11 *Crito* 44 b, ff. Laws IX, 877 a ff, 881 c, ff.

12 Maurice Merleau-Ponty, *La Phénoménologie de la Perception*, Paris: Gallimard, 1945, p. 23 (my translation), in more detail pp. 281 ff. Against this see Henri Lefebvre, *The Production of Space*, Oxford: Blackwell, 1991, pp. 80 ff.

13 Henri Lefebvre, *Writing on Cities*, Oxford: Blackwell, 1996, p. 149; quoted by David Harvey in "The Right to the City," in *Divided Cities*, ed. Richard Scholar, Oxford: Oxford University Press, 2006, p. 90.

2

Time, Space, and Architecture
Some Philosophical Musings

Yi-Fu Tuan

We live in place, move through space, and we are temporal beings, by which I mean not only that we live in time, as of course all living things do, but that we humans are naggingly conscious of time. What does this entail, experientially, in a built environment? How do the arrangements in a built environment, from those in an individual house to those in the city, reflect and enforce our time consciousness, whether this be the diurnal and seasonal cycles, the stages of a human life, or directional and progressive as in much modern experience and thought?

Awareness that time ceaselessly propels us forward makes us yearn for stability – for time to stand still so that we can make sense of and savor what is around us. The spiritually inclined yearn for more – a sense of the eternal. Religion and its architectural expressions have historically catered to these yearnings. This is no longer quite the case. Religion as a calling that engages the best minds has retreated before modern secularism. As for architecture, in booming cities such as Beijing and Shanghai, buildings sprout up that, in their metallic brightness, seem designed to defy time and corruption. Yet they may turn out to be disconcertingly mortal, for, unlike great buildings of the past, they are highly sensitive to aesthetic fashion and to innovations in technology.

Dizzying Change

Technological innovations capable of changing the face of the earth almost overnight are a fairly recent phenomenon. When I was born, in 1930, most of the world's population still lived in villages and small towns, and civilization remained essentially agricultural, with ways of living and notions of the good life that have altered little from those of the past. As for change in the lifetime of a 30-year-old, the pace is even more remarkable. Just consider the fact that at the time of his birth, a silhouette of densely packed skyscrapers could only be Manhattan, New York. Now it can be any one of a dozen cities.

What was it like to live in an agricultural civilization, our recent past? Efficiency was not then all demanding. At home, people no doubt tried to do their chores well, that is, efficiently, but this desire had to confront and was quick to give way to home's messy biosocial intimacies and urgencies. In commerce and manufacture, efficiency no doubt had greater relevance and spaces were so arranged to promote it. Governmental functions needed to be efficient too, but the buildings that housed them also had to project other values, such as legitimacy and power. As for buildings devoted to religion, whatever values they embodied, it was not simply getting through procedures with maximum economy. The fact that in an agricultural civilization religious beliefs and practices penetrated, in some form or other, nearly all spheres of life can be taken to mean that efficiency was not a pervasive concern.

By contrast, technological civilization dotes on efficiency. It is understandably the guiding principle in commerce and industry, but it infiltrates other areas of life as well, including even life in the church, with its ever burdensome need to juggle a wide range of activities and to balance the budget; and life in the home, with its lab-like kitchen and an electronic monitoring system to ensure that everything is in place and every activity is on time. No one has yet called the church "a machine for producing saints," but Le Corbusier did famously call the home "a machine for living in." A machine is designed for efficiency. So of the home, one might well ask, "Efficiency for what – for what end?"

I would like to take up these questions and see what illumination can be given them in the context of three broad facts. First: the values of civilization were, until recently, grounded on the requirements of food production. Second: from the start, there existed a rival set of values based on commerce, money, and mobility. And third: from the nineteenth century onward, a technology supported by basic science has given us humans so much power that we have become a threat not only to external nature – the environment – but also to our own nature. So conscious are we of our potential to make and build that we are in danger of losing our sense of limitation.

Agricultural Civilization and Ambivalent Nature

One major civilizational shift in the past hundred years is the disappearance of almost all agricultural activities from the city. Even in the nineteenth century, in rapidly industrializing England, no city had severed itself from its rural connections, according to Dyos and Wolff; and by "rural connections" they meant not just "half-a-dozen hens in a coop of soap boxes," but rather "extensive backyard agriculture."[1] As for China, I can draw on my own childhood experience of approaching a city wall and entering a gate expecting to find bustling urban life, and encountering farms and villages instead. Walled cities in China, in my childhood, contained much agricultural land. This now makes sense to me, for the traditional Chinese city, being a cosmos, necessarily included not only built-up areas but also their ultimate means of support – farming.

Farming weds us to nature. Yet the very existence of the farm and the hard work necessary to maintain it remind us that nature is not wholly accommodating. Understandably, we feel a certain ambivalence toward it. To take the positive side first, a recurrent question, even when we live in a consumer's paradise, is this. What better life is there, in a deep sense, than to live close to the earth with its endearing odors, sounds, and sights? What greater sensual satisfaction is there than cool water to quench thirst, wholesome food to relieve hunger, and a couch on which to slump in well-earned sleep? Both in the East and in the West, the elites of society have praised life on the farm, and they did so not only because it was the material basis of their wealth and power; for, even if gentlemen-farmers didn't actually put their shoulders to the plow, they could not help knowing from day-to-day engagements with farm life that it offered the keenest sensory rewards.

Against this idyllic image is the dark side of back-breaking labor and uncertainty. Nature may be fertile, but the fertility has to be coaxed – it requires labor. And nature is Janus-faced in that anytime its smile can turn into a frown, its serenity into rage. For this reason, it is personalized, treated as beings whose unruly power is tempered by a certain responsiveness to human deference and self-abasement, expressed in prayers and offerings. If by topophilia we have these gestures of deference in mind, the conclusion is unavoidable that its psychological base is actually topophobia – the *dread* of nature. To the question, What is more deeply rooted in human experience? the answer might well be anxiety and fear rather than delight and appreciation.

The Cosmic City

A landscape of farms is an achievement, an affirmation of our need for order and predictability. But it is not yet an architectural achievement, for architecture has come to mean something more formal and ambitious; it proclaims, with a touch of hubris, that humans are not totally earthbound. Inspiration for architecture is, historically, heaven and its stars – their grandeur and regularity. The anxiousness and uncertainty that are inescapable parts of being human can be assuaged by building a cosmic city, anchored on the North Star, with walls aligned to the cardinal points. Cities of this type were fairly common in various parts of the ancient world. In China, the earliest example dates back to the second millennium BC, and among the most recent is Beijing, a city that retained its cosmic template until the middle of the twentieth century.[2]

Chinese ritual books prescribe that the city should be rectangular and properly oriented, that its walls be pierced by twelve gates to represent the twelve months, that it should have an inner enclosed square to contain the royal residences and audience halls, a public market to the north of the inner enclosure, a principal street that runs from palace to the south gate, a royal ancestral temple and an altar of the earth on either side of the principal street. So conceived, the city is clearly not just a plan, but also a timepiece that registers the daily and yearly courses of the sun.[3]

The Diurnal Cycle

The sun's daily course dictates periods of wakefulness and sleep, activity and rest. Awake, we follow a countless number of circular paths, from tiny ones in the house and workplace, to larger ones from the house to the workplace, returning in each case, as the sun sets, to the point of departure that is called home. All these paths occur within the city. To follow a path beyond it for any distance would break the daily round that begins and ends in the home, and so offers a different kind of experience – the experience of the traveler.

Within the city, each pause in the circular path is a place, be it small, such as the bed we sleep in and the workbench we sit on, or larger, such as the rooms built for various purposes, or larger still, such as a neighborhood, a marketplace, a street. To most of us, home is a special place, and it is so for a number of reasons, including the fact that it anchors the round trip; also, home is where we spend the most time, experiencing it – unlike other places – during a good part of both day and night; and, importantly, home is where we rest to regain the energy on which all activities depend.

These small round trips become routine and so barely register. Nor do we take particular notice of the places at which we pause during each trip; they too become routine and fade from awareness. Much of life is reassuringly repetitious and unmarked. Even in the traditional walled city, the daily cycle and its routines are not marked by any special ceremony, a major exception being perhaps the opening and the closing of the city gates, the one initiating social and economic life, the other re-entry into the primordial world of darkness, sleep and animal ease. The numerous practical tasks and routines of the day require, of course, an elaborate infrastructure of houses and streets, but these, however imposing in the aggregate, are seldom grand or distinctive individually. They may become so, however, when they are the setting for the larger seasonal and annual cycles, and when they commemorate special events.

The Seasonal Cycle

In an agricultural civilization, the seasonal cycle has a number of critical transitional moments that call for observation and ceremony, and these in turn may call for an appropriate stage. I have noted that the cosmic city is itself such a stage: it is both monumental architecture and monumental timepiece. Its massive walls are so oriented that each side evokes a season: thus east is spring, south is summer, west is autumn, and north is winter. The cardinal points and the center are also in synesthetic and metaphoric correspondence to a host of other traits and qualities, including – in the Chinese case – the five elements, the five colors, the emblematic animals, human roles and functions. Together they make up a complex but orderly universe that is far different from the uncertainties that people know on earth, whether they be caused by human passions and turmoil, or by the intemperances of nature.

Commerce and Merchants: The Marginalized

An orderly universe enjoys another advantage from the traditionalist point of view. It is well suited to a hierarchical social order of emperor, scholar-officials, merchants, artisans, and farmers. Farmers may occupy only a modest place in such an order, yet they command respect because, in a sense, the entire cosmos – the architecture and its rituals – is set up to ensure their way of life. Marginalized are people who do not own land and do not till the soil: they are the craftsmen and tinkers, and, above all, traders and merchants, for they tend to be the most rootless, the most mobile. In the paradigmatic cosmic city, quarters are set aside for commerce behind the palace compound, on the north – the dark or yin – side of the world. Seldom, however, can this ritually appropriate location be made actual. Likewise, although officialdom makes every effort to regulate commerce and discourage it from spilling over to the residential compounds, this is almost never successful in a rapidly growing city.[4]

As trade prospers, some merchants may become very wealthy, but their status remains modest. The only way for them to gain prestige is to acquire some of the trappings of officialdom, and this includes Confucian manners and erudition, land ownership, and living in courtyard houses. Note that the layout of these courtyard houses derives its symbolic import from an agricultural cosmology, and is therefore at odds with the merchant's own way of life. For all its large impact on the world, commerce fails to generate potent myths. Its engine is money, and money is number, not the small ones of symbolic resonance but large ones – abstractions – that do not demand expression in distinctive rituals and architecture. An architectural aesthetic that owes nothing to nature's cycles comes much later. It has to wait for a high technology that frees the imagination from everything but the most fundamental laws of physics and engineering.

Europe

The sketch I have given applies to China. Europe is different. Though it too is an agricultural civilization, its dependence on the cycles of nature and their symbols is complicated by a view of time that is historical and directional. I refer here to the Judeo-Christian view that time has a beginning, a middle, and an end, that the human story begins with creation and ends with consummation. In Europe, a conception of space anchored in symbolically resonant cardinal points certainly existed: witness the post-Doric east–west orientation of Greek temples and the customary east–west alignment of Christian churches with the altar placed at the eastern end; witness also the rituals in the church calendar that were and are calibrated to accord with the passage of the seasons. But such evidences of spatial cardinality in Europe are inconspicuous compared with Chinese space at all scales from the walled city to courtyard residences, to farm houses that open to the south, and to the very tile used on the roof of certain important buildings.[5] So, rather than pursue this line of thought further, I would like to turn to directional time – to time marked by a sense of past, present, and future.

Directional Time

A basic and elementary sense of directional time is given by our body's asymmetry – the fact that it has a front and a back, and the fact that we have projects – that we live forward. What I see in front is the present and, possibly, the future. The back is the past, not visible to the eye and, so, in this sense, it is also darkness. Such experience inclines us to assign certain social values to "front" and "back." It is, for example, rude to turn one's back on a person, since doing so makes them invisible and no longer of present concern. In most societies, a person's back and the space behind are considered profane and dark, set aside to serve the body and other private needs. By contrast, their front and the space ahead are orderly, social, and may even be sacred. Values that owe their origin to the body are then transferred to the larger space and to buildings.

China's cosmic space provides an example. There, the emperor on his throne faces south and the noon sun. His back is turned toward darkness and a space prescribed for the transactions of commerce. The typical Chinese courtyard house, a richly symbolic microcosm, is also divided into front and back, with contrasting values. As for the Western world, the distinction between front and back – the one formal and prestigious, the other informal and profane – is even sharper in the older public and private buildings. Guests enter through the front, servants and tradesmen enter through the back.

Directional time so derived is, however, muted, not something we are conscious of or worry about. More intrusive on our consciousness and worrisome is directional time that is given by our life's path from birth, through childhood and maturity, to death. This path and its stages are sometimes called a "cycle," but "cycle" is a misnomer, for old age, euphemistically labeled "second childhood," is not a return to childhood, but is rather the antechamber to death. We move forward in unacknowledged dread toward death. Moreover, the end can come at any moment, inflicted by the violent forces of nature or by hostile human beings. Houses, for all their aesthetic flourishes, are first of all shelters that protect us against these external threats. But our body is also nature, subject to pain, disease and decay, and a source of anxiety. Against this threat, which seems to attack us from within, we respond with medicine, medical skills, and prayers; and we raise specialized buildings – hospices and hospitals, temples and churches – to accommodate them. All these measures are, however, temporary; they can postpone but not erase death.

Balms to Transiency

Transiency may be the human condition, but this does not mean that we are resigned to it. To the contrary, our nature impels us to seek consolations or balms. One balm is lineage – the idea that though an individual's life is short, lineage continues from remote ancestors to distant posterity. Another is to find permanence in such natural features as hills, valleys, forests, and the land itself. Their enduring presence – their restfulness – are a major reason for our deep appreciation of them. By comparison, a humanly made landscape of crops and houses does not last – or it lasts only when it is laboriously maintained, rather in the way that our body lasts only when it is maintained. If architecture has prestige, one reason lies in the edifice's air of perma-nence, projected by the solid building materials and sheer size. If the edifice is also symmetrical, built in the form of a circle, square, or polygon, it is making a claim to being atemporal – eternal. Not having a front or back in itself suggests that the building is beyond the human need for orientation and movement, that it transcends the pettier human divisions of time and their projects.

In an increasingly secular age, the well-educated among us no longer find much consolation in religious doctrine and ritual, sacred objects and sacred archi-tecture, in lineage, or in a reputation so firm that it endures long after our own demise. How then do we struggle against the fact that one day we die? We struggle with the help of technology, which enables us to prolong life, and also to make life so enter-taining and fast-paced and so packed with bright art objects, including architecture, that we can forget our mortality.

Technology: Extending Daylight and Height

One way to prolong life is to stay awake and engaged with the world long after dark. But that is only practical on a broad scale with the invention of gaslight, and then electric light, at the end of the nineteenth century. I still find it surprising that, even in the 1850s, a great city's cultural and social activities must draw to a close as the sun sets, and that they are as obedient to nature's daily cycle as are activities in the countryside. Turning night into day is highly unnatural, and may be counted among the most ambitious efforts to transcend our biological limitation. The success of the modern city in this regard is remarkable. Architecturally undistinguished during the day, in the evening the city turns into a glittering magic carpet. This magic carpet is by now a thoroughly familiar part of our urban environment; yet, such is the force of habit, we still tend to see the city as a phenomenon of broad daylight.[6]

Distancing ourselves from nature may also be accomplished by elevation – by rising as far above the earth as is practical, and so deny our status as creatures that crawl at its surface, that eat and excrete, that depend on nature's abundance or on our own sweaty labor. From the earliest times, height implied prestige. The taller the building, the more platforms it stood on, the more powerful was the message that man aspired to being godlike. There were exceptions, of course: courtyard houses in both Europe and China had greater prestige than high-rise tenement houses, the reason being that tall buildings were unsafe, liable to collapse, and their upper floors had no amenities. This was true even through much of the nineteenth century. In Paris, for example, the best apartments were on the first floor, immedi-ately above the shops. There the bourgeois lived. At the next level, the rooms were smaller, the residents poorer, and so on until one reached the top floor, the attic, where indigent students and Bohemian artists huddled in unheated and waterless rooms.

Within brief decades, extraordinary innovations in technology reversed the prestige of the floors. The higher one's living quarters are located, the greater is the prestige, until at the top of the building, where the penthouse sits, we have – as the advertising slogan goes – "the world at [our] feet." Skyscrapers compete with one another in height and elegance. They have sprung up and continue to spring up at an ever frantic pace in periods of economic boom. What do they mean? What do they say about human aspiration? Or should I say, human desperation? Or is it both?

Skyscrapers: What Do They Say?

Perhaps it has always been both. We human beings want material sufficiency, if not plenty. However, even material plenty is seldom enough to plug the yawning need to be exempt from the ravages of time – from corruption. In a small but significant way, architecture answers this need. The cosmic city is itself an outstanding example of a creation that transcends the routines of biological and social life, that directs people's attention heavenward. But both ritually and in architecture, the city is still geared to the cycles of nature. As for the Western world, until well into the twentieth century, the silhouette of a city is one of towering church spires. Church spires point to the sky, reminders that our destiny is not confined to this world, that we follow a path – a directional time – that begins with the earth but ends in heaven. Inside the church, however, services continue to cater to life's biological and social stages, and rituals are conducted to conform with nature's cycles.

In a modern city, glass-and-steel towers completely overshadow church spires. These new verticals barely recognize our standing as natural creatures. They deliberately cover up, as does the entire downtown area itself, evidences of down turn in the human cycle: injury and pain, corruption and death. Not only does a city dweller almost never see a human corpse, even dead squirrels and dead leaves are quickly removed from his eyes. In the hospital itself, shining surfaces of hygiene and efficiency hide the pathos of suffering and mortality. Few health and official buildings are, in fact, cloud-piercing skyscrapers. Work devoted to the body and to the running of government seem to require a feeling of stability and *gravitas* that is best projected by low-lying buildings. Very tall buildings in today's skyline mostly cater to the needs of business and finance, which are directed to goals of abstract wealth that have no limit. And so an eye-catching architecture emerges in the landscape that, for the first time in the history of civilization, owes nothing to the template of a rotating cosmos.

Even people repelled by capitalism and great wealth must acknowledge that the tall buildings raised by famous architects in just the last decade are a feast for the eyes, a lilt to the spirit. The uprights and cylinders of an earlier time – pictures of rectitude – will soon be outnumbered by skyscrapers that curve and gyrate in daring freedom. For the first time in history, architects feel free to disregard lay people's intuitions of structural soundness and stability, or the need to adapt to either local topography or the stars in a readily discernible way. Some cities are beginning to look like gigantic sculptural gardens. The buildings in them are competing works of art, to be seen and admired, rather than places that mature into happy, eupeptic habitats. Do these daring buildings achieve greatness? Can there be greatness without grounding in our biological nature, some clear reference to the cosmos, or a religious foundation?[7]

Endurance: Buildings As Art

I have no answer except to say that one test for greatness in art is whether it endures. And here I have a troubling thought. In premodern times, buildings were not taken to be art. The more important ones – shrines, temples, churches, and the cosmic city itself – were religiously inspired. In the nineteenth century, commerce needed architectural showpieces to house its merchandise and, even more importantly, to advertise its newfound power and glory. World arts and industrial expositions and the buildings in them, such as the Crystal Palace and the Eiffel Tower, served that purpose. They were, however, subject to criticism from an aesthetic point of view, as religious buildings of an earlier age were not. The Crystal Palace and the Eiffel Tower survived the criticism, and the Eiffel Tower stands today as a proud symbol of French achievement and as a tourist attraction.

But that was the nineteenth century. In our time, criticism is more influential and potentially far more damaging. It is so in at least two ways: one, it has gained enormously in power by riding on the back of popular media and, two, it is sensitive to fashion and technological innovation as never before. What if, after spending five hundred million dollars on a building, it is trounced as bland or kitschy by powerful critics, in the same way that a heavily financed film may be so trounced, ending in financial disaster? A half-empty movie palace eerily prognosticates the future of a skyscraper, one that is new and only half-occupied, but one that already shows water stains and exudes plugged-drain odor – intimations of mortality that it bravely denies in its bright sheaths of steel and glass.

Fashion in buildings is not, however, just a matter of aesthetic taste; it is also a response to the pressure of advances in material science and engineering. If, thanks to such advances, upright surfaces can bend and twist, so they will bend and twist; moreover, tall buildings themselves may become dated, as they are complemented, if not displaced, by spheres and Möbius strips. What this means is that monumental architecture no longer spells permanence – something that we humans, in our frailty and transiency, can hang on to and say, "Yes, but we have buildings of power, beauty, and character that defy time."

Notes

1   H. J. Dyos and Michael Wolff, "The Way We Live Now," in H. J. Dyos and M. Wolff (eds), *The Victorian City: Images and Realities*, 2 vols, London: Routledge & Kegan Paul, 1973, vol. 2, p. 899.

2   Paul Wheatley, *The Pivot of the Four Quarters*, Chicago: Aldine, 1971; Kwang-chih Chang, *The Archaeology of Ancient China*, New Haven, CT: Yale University Press, 1963, p. 157.

3   "Code Book of Works," preserved in *Li Chi* (Book of Rites); Arthur F. Wright, "Symbolism and Function: Reflections on Changan and Other Great Cities," *Journal of Asian Studies* 24(4), August 1965, 667–679.

4   Étienne Balazs, *Chinese Civilization and Bureaucracy: Variations on a Theme*, New Haven, CT: Yale University Press, 1964, p. 71.

5   Nelson I. Wu, *Chinese and Indian Architecture: The City of Man, the Mountain of God, and the Realm of the Immortals*, New York: George Braziller, 1963, pp. 11–12, plate 1, pp. 32–34.

6   Matthew Luckiesh, *Artificial Light: Its Influence on Civilization*, New York: The Century Co., 1920; John A. Jakle, *City Lights: Illuminating the American Night*, Baltimore, MD: Johns Hopkins University Press, 2001.

7   Antonino Terranova, *The Great Skyscrapers of the World*, Italy: White Star Publishers, 2003; Mark Kingwell, "The City of Tomorrow: Searching for the Future of Architecture in Shanghai," *Harper's Magazine*, February 2005, pp. 62–71.

A condensed version of this chapter has been published before in *Coming Home to China* by Yi-Fu Tuan, published by The University of Minnesota Press, 2007.

3

Topophilia/Topophobia

The Role of the Environment in the Formation of Identity

Neil Leach

"Odi et amo: quare id faciam, fortasse requires
Nescio, sed fieri sentio et excrucior."
"I love and I hate. 'Why?', you might ask.
I don't know. But I feel it happening to me, and it's excruciating."
(Caius Valerius Catullus, *Carmen* 85)

We all know what a significant role the environment plays in our identities. We know how it conditions our everyday lives. We know too how we tend to identify with particular places, and become attached to them. Certain buildings and landscapes feature in our dreams, and frame our very existence. But what exactly is the relationship between environment and identity? By this I do not mean what is often referred to as the "identity" of places – a somewhat confusing use of the term, which has nothing to do with identity as such, but refers simply to the distinctive architectural and geographic features that set one place apart from the next. Rather I am referring to subjective processes in the development of human identity itself. How are we to understand the formation of human identity in relation to the environment? And what role does place play in that process?

The actual process of identity formation is a highly complex one, and it is beyond the scope of this chapter to address it in full. All I want to do here is to interrogate the role of the environment in that process. I wish to suggest that it is through the twin impulses of attraction and repulsion that we can grasp most fully the complex ways in which identity is forged against a backdrop. I shall do so by juxtaposing two seminal texts on the relationship of the organism to its surroundings, "Mimicry and Legendary Psychasthenia," an essay on the behavior of mimetic insects by the French social theorist, Roger Caillois, and "The Mirror Stage," a later essay on the development of identity by the French psychoanalytic theorist, Jacques Lacan.[1] The one exposes the danger of the loss of self that might be caused by an over-identification with the environment. The other describes the way in which identification with the environment overcomes the condition of alienation. Read in terms of the physical environment, the one describes the fear of being "engulfed" by place – *topophobia*. The other sets out the conditions for becoming attached to place – *topophilia*. I wish to argue that it is between these two states, the horror of the undifferentiated self and the horror of the alienated self, that identity is formed, and that place, as an important component of the environment, plays a vital role in the formation of identity.

Mimicry

In "Mimicry and Legendary Psychasthenia," Caillois interrogates the relationship between an organism and its surroundings by interrogating the behavior of creatures that camouflage themselves against the environment by mimicking that environment. Caillois takes a fresh look at many of the received views on mimicry, and challenges the popular assumption that mimicry in animal life is a mechanism of survival. According to Caillois, we do not need to look for some "sophistic" argument to overturn the hypothesis that mimicry is about defence. Animals hunt as often by smell as they do by sight, and visual camouflage is seldom a very effective form of defence. "Predators," Caillois observes, "are not at all fooled by homomorphy or homochromy . . . Generally speaking, one finds many remains of mimetic insects in the stomachs of predators."[2]

Caillois claims that mimicry operates through a form of sympathetic magic, which is ideational in nature. He notes the earlier comparisons of Tylor, Frazer, Hubert and Mauss between the principles of magic and the association of ideas: "To the law of magic – *things that have once been in contact remain united* – corresponds association by contiguity, just as association by resemblance corresponds quite precisely to the *attractio similium* of magic: *like produces like.*"[3] From the primitive onwards there is an overwhelming tendency to imitate, a tendency which survives in modern man, but which can also be detected in animal life while organs remain "plastic" enough to transform themselves. This leads Caillois to conclude: "Mimicry would thus be accurately defined as *an incantation fixed at its culminating point* and having caught the sorcerer in his own trap."[4] Caillois defines this incantation as "prestigious magic" or "fascination." This search for the similar is an intermediate stage in a process whose ultimate objective is "assimilation to the surroundings."

Caillois compares this to the "magical hold" of darkness, which likewise blurs the boundaries between the organism and its milieu. There is a comfort, as Eugène Minkowski observes, in dark space:

> Dark space envelops me on all sides and penetrates me much deeper than light space, the distinction between inside and outside and consequently the sense organs as well, insofar as they are designed for external perception, here play only a totally modest role.[5]

The very seduction of darkness is echoed in the ecstasy of losing oneself in one's surroundings through mimicry. For Caillois, then, mimicry is nothing else than a form of "temptation by space."

This condition becomes problematic when it leads to a collapse of spatial awareness:

LOSS OF SELF

> It is with represented space that the drama becomes specific, since the living creature, the organism, is no longer the origin of the coordinates, but one point among others; it is dispossessed of its privilege and literally *no longer knows where to place itself*.[6]

This confusion is a characteristic of abstract and generalized representational space, which threatens the very foundations of one's personality, and may even prompt a sense of schizophrenia – "I know where I am, but I do not feel as though I'm at the spot where I find myself."[7] This inability to distinguish oneself from the environment – this boundary failure – leads to a condition of crisis:

> To these dispossessed souls, space seems to be a devouring force. Space pursues them, encircles them, digests them in a gigantic phagocytosis. It ends by replacing them. Then the body separates itself from thought, the individual breaks the boundary of his skin and occupies the other side of his senses. He tries to look at *himself from* any point whatever in space. He feels himself becoming space, *dark space where things cannot be put*. He is similar, not similar to something, but just *similar*.[8]

The reason why this condition is problematic is that identity depends on the ability of an organism to *distinguish* itself from its surroundings. He notes:

> From whatever side one approaches things, the ultimate problem turns out in the final analysis to be that of *distinction*: distinctions between the real and the imaginary, between waking and sleeping, between ignorance and knowledge, etc. – all of them, in short, distinctions in which valid consideration must demonstrate a keen awareness and the demand for resolution. Among distinctions, there is assuredly none more clear-cut than that between the organism and its surroundings.[9]

Without this ability to distinguish ourselves from our surroundings, we descend into a condition that Caillois describes as "legendary psychasthenia":

> The feeling of personality, considered as the organism's feeling of distinction from its surroundings, of the connection between consciousness and a particular point in space, cannot fail under these conditions to be seriously undermined; one then enters into the psychology of psychasthenia, and more specifically of *legendary psychasthenia*, if we agree to use this name for the disturbance in the above relations between personality and space.[10]

"Psychasthenia" could be defined as a weakening of the sense of self, that is brought about by an erosion of the distinction between the self and the environment. Caillois illustrates this by way of Gustave Flaubert's *The Temptation of Saint Anthony*. Here St Anthony himself succumbs to the mimicry present in nature where "plants are now no longer distinguished from animals . . . Insects identical with rose petals adorn a bush . . . And then plants are confused with stones."[11] As a result, St Anthony finds himself "dissolving" into space. Caillois refers to this process as a "descent into hell."[12]

Importantly, then, Caillois locates assimilation to the environment at the root of problems of psychic identity. For assimilation is precisely an *overcoming* of the distinction between the self and the environment. The net result of this assimilation is a form of depersonalization, akin to a schizophrenic "stepping out from the self." Assimilation is therefore about a loss of self. It is accompanied, as Caillois puts it, "by a decline in the feeling of personality and life."[13] This leads Caillois to reappraise the traditional assumption that the purpose of mimicry is about self-preservation. For it seems to him that mimicry is about exactly the opposite – a relinquishing of our life force, and a surrendering of our sense of self. Alongside the instinct for self-preservation, Caillois therefore sees a corresponding "instinct for renunciation" – a loss of *élan vital* – at the heart of mimicry. Through mimicry, remarks Caillois, "life takes a step backwards."[14]

Although Caillois analyses the behavior of mimetic insects and creatures, he is not really concerned with insects and creatures themselves. Essentially he is addressing the question of *human* behavior. Caillois's quest is to interrogate how humans relate to their habitat, and, by extension, to understand how identity itself operates. What concerns Caillois is not the failure to identify with our surroundings, but the failure to distinguish ourselves from them. This may prove even more dangerous than the alienation that might result from the opposite condition. For the failure to distinguish the self may lead, either, at the level of the individual, to a psychotic condition, *psychasthenia* – a "descent into hell" – or, at a collective level, to something altogether more sinister – potentially uncontrollable mass movements. It is perhaps no coincidence that Caillois wrote his article in a Europe that was about to be engulfed by fascism.

The Mirror Stage

In "The Mirror Stage," Jacques Lacan sets out the corollary to Caillois's condition of psychasthenia – the condition not of loss of self, but of the discovery of the self. Here he refers specifically to Caillois's essay:

> But the facts of mimicry are no less instructive when conceived as cases of heteromorphic identification, in as much as they raise the problem of the signification of space for the living organism – psychological concepts hardly seem less appropriate for shedding light on these matters than ridiculous attempts to reduce them to the supposedly supreme law of adaptation. We have only to recall how Roger Caillois . . . illuminated the subject by using the term "legendary psychasthenia" to classify morphological mimicry as an obsession with space in its derealizing effect.[15]

This reference to "heteromorphic identification" implies an identification with something that is "other", and points to Caillois's interest in the principal of "distinction" between the self and the other, whereas Lacan's primary concern is for "homeomorphic" identification – identification, that is, with something that is similar. For Lacan, this "homeomorphic identification" explains how, for example, various animals develop behavioral patterns by viewing others of their own species.[16] But like Caillois, Lacan is interested not in animal life, but in human life. He traces the urge for identification back to an early stage in human development.

In his essay on the mirror stage, Lacan describes the moment when a child recognizes the reflection of its own image:[17]

> This event can take place, as we have known since Baldwin, from the age of six months, and its repetition has often made me reflect upon the startling spectacle of the infant in front of the mirror. Unable as yet to walk, or even to stand up, and held tightly as he is by some support, human or artificial . . . he nevertheless overcomes, in a flutter of jubilant activity, the obstructions of his support and, fixing his attitude in a slightly leaning-forward position, in order to hold it in his gaze, brings back an instantaneous aspect of the image.[18]

The stage marks an important development in the subjectivity of the individual.[19] It describes the formation of the ego by a process of an imaginary identification with the specular image, which is later supplemented by symbolic identification, accessed through language.[20] Up until that moment the child had been "informed" affectively through interaction with the mother. Indeed, it had failed to distinguish itself properly from the mother, in that the mother's breasts had always been available to it. Now it comes to recognize itself in visual terms through its specular image.[21] The child begins to model itself on that image, and identify with it. In so doing the child achieves a degree of autonomy. It is no longer lost within an "undifferentiated sea of sensations" but comes to perceive itself for the first time as a separate being, clearly distinguishable from the mother. In so doing, it also introduces a sense of alienation which sets the subject apart from the world through a process of "objectifying identification." It is precisely because the subject knows itself as an object through its reflection in a mirror that the subject can be understood as "an object within a world of objects."[22]

As a result, the mirror stage marks the moment when the subject can begin to identify constructively with the world. Although it constitutes a form of "alienating" identification, in that the subject now identifies with itself objectively as an *imago* – it sets the scene for potential secondary identifications. For without the initial alienation of the mirror stage, there could be no secondary identifications. These secondary identifications are significantly different from primary identifications. Whereas with primary identifications the subject has yet to distinguish its identity from that of other objects, with secondary identifications the subject is able to identify with another object as a separate entity.

Implicit within this model there is a tension between early childhood and adult life. Secondary identifications represent the urge to return to a childlike state of oneness. Adult life, by contrast, is premised on individuation – on separation from the outside. This dynamic remains at play throughout subsequent life, such that in moments of creative identification – in viewing representations of any kind, photographs, models, drawings, and so on – we need to adopt a childlike mode of engagement in order, as it were, to transport ourselves into the original. This is the principle of regression that can be used creatively to temporarily restore a childlike oneness with the world. As Freud himself comments: "The primitive stages can always be re-established; the primitive mind is, in the fullest meaning of the word, imperishable."[23]

This "alienating identification" in which the child is forced to accept its own autonomy, allows the child to develop a distinct – if not necessarily coherent – sense of identity, and a degree of motility by recognizing itself as a co-ordinated entity. As Dylan Evans observes:

> The baby sees its own image as a whole, and the synthesis of this image produces a sense of contrast with the uncoordination of the body, which is experienced as a fragmented body; this contrast is first felt by the infant as a rivalry with its own image, because the wholeness of the image threatens the subject with fragmentation, and the mirror stage thereby gives rise to an aggressive tension between the subject and the image. In order to resolve this aggressive tension the subject identifies with its own image; this primary identification with the counterpart is what forms the ego.[24]

It thereby allows the child to identify with other "objects" in its world, thus inaugurating the possibility of seeing itself reflected in its surroundings, and establishing a relationship with place.

Lacan hereby introduces a vital dynamic into the formation of identity. For he recognizes that identity is articulated as much through distinction as through connection. Identity is born of an interaction between the self and the other, as a continual process of attraction and repulsion. Kristeva describes identification as an open-ended, fluid process, a transference between the body and its "ever-evolving" psychic apparatus with an *other*.[25] Identification therefore remains a compromised activity, doomed to failure, yet posited in opposition to attempts to remain autonomous that will never succeed. As Kristeva describes it:

> If I concede that I am never ideally One under the Law of the Other, my entire psychic experience consists of failed identifications as well as my impossible attempts to be an autonomous being, attempts that circumscribe narcissism, perversion, and alienation.[26]

Attraction and Repulsion

Implicit within Lacan's model of the mirror stage there seems to be a dialectics of connection and separation, of attraction and repulsion. For identification with the external world can only take place after the crisis of alienation of the mirror stage itself, and the alienation of the mirror stage can only take place after the lack of differentiation that precedes it. Likewise, while of course there can be "pure" attraction or repulsion, we should also recognize a potential repression that might operate within these very processes, in that repulsion may often be the result of a repressed attraction for some object, while attraction might equally be the result of a repressed repulsion.[27]

This might cause us to revisit Caillois's article and interrogate it further. For, if there is a weakness in Caillois's powerful critique of the problem of identification, it is his failure to address sufficiently the dialectical nature of this operation. There is, for Caillois, a primary urge to distinguish the self. Yet mimicry, it could be argued, does not consist of a dissolution of the self, so much as a reinforcement of the self. The purpose of mimicry, as Lacan reminds us, is not to blend in with, but to remain distinct from the background:

> Mimicry reveals something in so far as it is distinct from what might be called an *itself* that is behind. The effect of mimicry is camouflage, in the strictly technical sense. It is not a question of harmonizing with the background but, against a mottled background, of becoming mottled – exactly like the technique of camouflage practised in human warfare.[28]

Furthermore, in order to respond to the urge for distinction, we need to have a sense of its opposite: connection. Without an initial connection there can be no distinction, just as without distinction there can be no connection. The one, as Georg Simmel observes, is always a presupposition of the other.

> Only to humanity, in contrast to nature, has the right to connect and separate been granted, and in the distinctive manner that one of these activities is always the presupposition of the other. By choosing two items from the undisturbed store of natural things in order to designate them as "separate", we have already related them to one another in our consciousness, we have emphasized these two together against whatever lies between them. And conversely, we can only sense those things to be related which we have previously somehow isolated from one another; things must first be separated from one another in order to be together. Practically as well as logically, it would be meaningless to connect that which was not separated, and indeed that which also remains separated in some sense . . . In the immediate as well as the symbolic sense, in the physical as well as the intellectual sense, we are at any moment those who separate the connected or connect the separate.[29]

Identity, then, can only be secured by first having established a relation with our surroundings. Yet, equally, identity depends on the ability to distinguish ourselves from those surroundings. In order to distinguish ourselves from the world around, we need the capacity to relate to it, and in order to relate to it we need to have the capacity to distinguish ourselves from it. Identity is based on separation, but separation presupposes and generates the capacity for further identification. We should therefore question Caillois's somewhat negative stance towards the question of assimilation. For assimilation, it would seem, is also that which helps to *establish* an identity.

A further way to reflect on the dynamics of identity is to consider the importance of "loss" or "separation" in consolidating an identity. Psychoanalysis tells us that the development of the identity of an individual is founded on the principle of loss and distinction, such as separation from the mother. As Julia Kristeva puts it: "Psychoanalysis identifies and relates as the indispensable condition for autonomy, a series of separations: birth, weaning, separation, frustration, castration. Real, imaginary or symbolic, these processes necessarily structure our individuation. Their nonexecution or repudiation leads to psychotic confusion."[30] Such a process is an essential part of the development of the subject. Kristeva notes:

> It is well known that the so-called "depressive" stage is essential to the child's access to the realm of symbols and linguistic signs. Such a depression – parting sadness as a necessary condition for the representation of any absent thing – reverts to and accompanies our symbolic activities unless its opposite, exaltation, reappropriates them.[31]

What this suggests is that loss, whether actual or imaginary, or experienced vicariously, can serve to reduce this confusion and reinforce an identity.[32]

The notion that identity depends on loss clearly extends to whole communities. In psychoanalytic theory, as the Slovenian theorist, Slavoj Žižek, has observed, even the identity of a nation is based on the "theft of its Enjoyment."[33] If a nation perceives itself in terms of a nation Thing – as a community of individuals who organize their Enjoyment around a certain concern – as opposed to those others who fail to appreciate that concern and are therefore a threat to it, the very being of a nation is based on the "possession" of a certain sense of Enjoyment. Or, put another way, that very being of a nation is defined by the threat to its Enjoyment. If the "other" is a threat to the collective self, the potential threat to the Enjoyment of the collective is effectively that which articulates and constitutes the "other" – the way that the "other" organizes its own "perverse" Enjoyment.[34]

Not surprisingly then, a nation is defined most clearly when it is at war and its very "way of life" is under threat. But this extends beyond moments of actual conflict to periods of peace when, in order for some sense of national identity to be preserved, a new threat has to be imagined.[35] Nothing will therefore foster a sense of national identity more than a perceived external threat, whether actual or imaginary. For a threat need not be an actual threat. Just as communities are always "imagined" communities, so too threats to those communities can be "imagined" threats.[36] And it is around the victims of this threat – the lost heroes and martyrs – that a kindred sense of identity is forged. It is important to recognize that national identity depends on opposition. And the same applies to sport. The logic of nationalism follows closely the logic of sport. A team is forged around competition. A nation comes together when under threat.

This introduces a new dynamic into our understanding of identity. For it begins to suggest that identity, although born of identifications, is consolidated precisely when those identifications come under threat. Freud's insightful description of identity as a "graveyard" of lost lives and former identifications can be linked to Caillois and Lacan's concern for the need for distinction from the environment. What begins to emerge is a scenario in which the environment – including the physical environment – plays a crucial role in the forging of an identity. An initial identification with that environment must first be established, but it is as that identification comes under threat that identity itself is consolidated. And yet that identity is always in flux, and never reaches a point of stasis.

The Role of Place In Identity

Identification always involves a process of seeing the self in the other. This urge is a deeply strategic one. It concerns a broadening of horizons and an opening up to the world. It amounts to an overcoming of a condition of melancholic introspection that might otherwise isolate an individual. It establishes connections. It serves to counter the *horror vacui* of a depersonalized, atomized self in a society of increasing alienation.

Yet the opposite tendency, the urge to distinguish the self from the other, and overcome the horror of the undifferentiated self, can itself be a product of an over-invested engagement with the other. Both the *horror vacui* of the alienated self and the horror of the undifferentiated self are potentially nihilistic conditions. The failure to engage with the world may lead to self-absorption, while an over-invested engagement may lead to an uncritical absorption into the other. In this respect, identity operates between two extreme states of the melancholic withdrawal into the self and the potentially fascistic loss of self in the other.

The condition of identity is never a static one. It resides neither in the state of being connected, nor in the state of being distinct. Rather it involves a continual shuttling between these two conditions, a keeping alive of the very possibility of change. Identity should be viewed as an interactive process of becoming – of becoming one with the world, and of becoming distinct from that world – where both states are locked into a mechanism of reciprocal presupposition, and are interdependent. It is only by becoming similar that a sense of distinction can be envisioned, while it is only by becoming distinct that a sense of connection can be postulated. The two tendencies operate as a form of *gestalt* formation – as a figure/ground relationship. Identity is ultimately a question of foreground and background. It is a matter of defining the self against a given environment.

The environment, then, consists of a reservoir of impulses that condition human existence. "The rhythm of streetcars and carpet-beating," noted Walter Benjamin, "rocked me in my sleep. It was the mold in which my dreams took shape."[37] These impulses are made up of a complex spectrum of material and social factors. But if we were to highlight the role of the physical environment within that regime, we could perhaps point to a range of iconic buildings and geographic formations that feature prominently in the national psyche, to those of less significance that nonetheless structure our everyday lives. It is here that we can recognize the potential of "place" as a register of indexical markers that condition personal identity.

It is important, however, to understand "place" beyond the limitations of any discourse of form alone. For place, like any cultural formation, is comprised not only of a system of objects alone, but also of the narratives that imbue those objects with meaning.[38] It is not that the physical environment has any intrinsic meaning in itself, as those who argue for the "identity of place" might claim. Rather the physical environment is essentially "inert," and has meanings "projected" on to it. The physical environment thus operates as a form of "screen." It serves as a repository of meanings that come to be identified with it, as though they were a property of that environment.

If identification is always specular – if it is always a question of recognizing the self in the other and the other in the self – then that "screen," invested as it now is with layers of personal associations, will take on the role of a mirror, in which those who have identified with it will see themselves reflected.[39] And it is as a mirror that place contributes to a sense of personal identity, echoing the mechanisms of the mirror stage itself.

The self is therefore formed through a direct identification with the environment – a form of *topophilia*. At the same time, however, there is a need for the opposite tendency – a form of *topophobia* – the urge to distinguish the self from that environment. In terms of our social development, the former tendency could be understood as the desire to return home, and to seek the solace of a familiar environment, and the latter tendency could be understood as the urge to "flee the nest," and to establish an autonomous identity. Indeed, if maturation is perceived as the reinforcement of a sense of self by an increasing distantiation of the self from the other, identity could be perceived as a process of individuation that challenges – but equally depends upon – that previous moment of identification. In other words, we need first to identify with our background environment and then distinguish ourselves from it. Yet this process of distinction is never complete, in that at times we will revert back to conditions of close affiliation.

This principle would extend to national identities. These collective identities are reinforced by the same mechanism of distantiation. For, if identity is forged against a backdrop, such that the physical environment comes to comprise a vital component in any form of national identity, a threat to that backdrop would amount to a threat to national identity itself. On the one hand this would help to explain the urge to destroy buildings and ravage the land in times of war as a way of attacking the enemy itself. For to attack an enemy's possessions is not only to symbolically attack the enemy. It is also to attack the very root of its self-definition as a community.[40] On the other hand, this would also explain how it is that, precisely when such features within the environment are destroyed, a sense of national identity is further consolidated.

The environment in which we have been brought up will always play a prominent role in our identities – both individual and collective – as a form of backdrop against which those identities are forged through a process of attraction and repulsion. And if we are to understand place itself as an important physical component within that environment, we can recognize how those identities are in part constructed through the complementary, yet opposite urges of *topophilia* and *topophobia*.

Notes

1 Roger Caillois, "Mimicry and Legendary Psychasthenia," trans. by John Shepley, *October* 31, 1984, 16–32, reprinted in *October: The First Decade, 1976–86*, Cambridge, MA: MIT Press, 1987, pp. 58–74; Jacques Lacan, "The Mirror Stage," in Jacques Lacan, *Écrits: A Selection*, trans. by Alan Sheridan, New York: W. W. Norton & Company, 1977, pp. 1–7.

2   Caillois, "Mimicry and Legendary Psychasthenia," pp. 66–67.

3   Ibid., p. 67.

4   Ibid., p. 69.

5   Eugène Minkowski, as quoted by Caillois, p. 72.

6   Ibid., p. 70.

7   Minkowski, as quoted by Caillois, p. 72.

8   Ibid.

9   Ibid., p. 59.

10 Ibid., p. 70.

11 Quoted by Caillois, p. 73.

12 Ibid., p. 73. Interestingly, Caillois also cites the works of Salvador Dali, which, he notes, "are less the expression of ambiguities or of paranoiac 'plurivocities' than of mimetic assimilations of the animate to the inanimate." Caillois is perhaps unaware of Dali's own obsession with mimetic insects, but this obsession may well explain the constant refrain within Dali's œuvre, in which either human beings dissolve into their environment, or the environment reconfigures itself into the form of human beings.

13 Ibid., p. 72.

14 Ibid.

15 Lacan, "The Mirror Stage," p. 3.

16 The maturation of the gonad of the female pigeon, he notes, depends upon the pigeon seeing another, while the migratory locust develops patterns of social behavior when exposed to animated movements that mimic that of its own species.

17 In effect, Lacan rethinks the question of identification by combining the psychologist Henri Wallon's examination of the mirror with Freud's narcissism and Hegel's dialectic. On this, see Mikkel Borch-Jacobsen, *Lacan: The Absolute Master*, trans. by Douglas Brick, Stanford, CA: Stanford University Press, 1991, p. 46.

18 Lacan, "The Mirror Stage," pp. 1–2.

19 The stage remains throughout adult life, and characterizes the relationship between the subject and its image. The mirror stage, as Lacan observes,

> is a phenomenon to which I assign a twofold value. In the first place, it has historical value as it marks a decisive turning point in the mental development of the child. In the second place, it typifies a libidinal relationship with the body-image.
>
> (Lacan, as quoted in Dylan Evans, *An Introductory Dictionary of Lacanian Psychoanalysis*, London: Routledge, 1996, p. 115)

20 We need to distinguish here between imaginary and symbolic identifications. Imaginary identifications come into operation during the mirror stage, and relate to the formation of the ideal ego. Symbolic identifications, on the other hand, allow for the formation of the ego ideal. As forms of secondary identification which nonetheless partake of the imaginary, they serve to stabilize the subject by transcending the aggressivity of the mirror stage. They also mark the transition into the symbolic order. Žižek characterizes the distinction as follows:

> Imaginary identification is identification with the image in which we appear likeable to ourselves, with the image representing "what we would like to be", and symbolic identification, identification with the very place from where we are being observed, from where we look at ourselves so that we appear to ourselves likeable, worthy of love.

From this perspective the imaginary identification associated with the ideal ego is one of a "constituted" identification, while the symbolic identification associated with the ego ideal is "constitutive." Put another way, as Žižek remarks:

> In imaginary identification we imitate the other at the level of resemblance – we identify ourselves with the image of the other inasmuch as we are "like him", while in symbolic

identification we identify ourselves with the other precisely at a point at which he is inimitable, at a point which eludes resemblance.

(Žižek, *The Sublime Object of Ideology*, London: Verso, 1989, p. 109)

There is always a gap – a "leftover" – between these two operations, a gap which Žižek associates with the figure of "desire."

21 The mirror stage constitutes a form of "recognition" which is at the same time a form of "misrecognition." This is not because the subject identifies with an image, which must necessarily be an inverted image of the self, and hence a false representation of the self. Rather, it is because by identifying with an object exterior to the self, the subject fails to grasp certain characteristics of the self. This "misrecognition" embodies the illusionary nature in our engagement with "reality," that characterizes Lacan's whole philosophy.

22 Borch-Jacobsen, *Lacan*, p. 58.

23 Freud, as quoted in J. Laplanche and J.-B Pontalis, *The Language of Psycho-Analysis*, trans. by Donald Nicholson-Smith, New York: W. W. Norton & Company, 1973, p. 387.

24 Evans, *An Introductory Dictionary of Lacanian Psychoanalysis*, p. 115.

25 Julia Kristeva, *New Maladies of the Soul*, trans. by Ross Guberman, New York: Columbia University Press, 1995, p. 173.

26 Ibid., p. 177.

27 A common manifestation of repulsion as a repression of fascination would be homophobia, which is often understood as an externalization of desires that a homophobic individual does not want to acknowledge. By projecting them on to the external world so as to criticize them, the homophobe comes to mask and repress his/her own gay identity.

28 Jacques Lacan, *The Four Fundamental Concepts of Psycho-Analysis*, London: Penguin, 1994, p. 99.

29 Georg Simmel, "Bridge and Door," in Neil Leach (ed.), *Rethinking Architecture: A Reader in Cultural Theory*, London and New York: Routledge, 1997, p. 66.

30 Julia Kristeva, "Holbein's Dead Christ," in Michel Feher (ed.), *Fragments for a History of the Human Body, Part One*, New York: Zone Books, 1989, p. 261.

31 Ibid.

32 To some extent these mechanisms are replicated in conventional religion. It is the sacrifice of Christ, Kristeva would argue, that gives Christianity its force. The death of Christ offers Christians a vicarious mechanism of loss. The Christian need not experience that loss directly, but by identifying with Christ's own suffering, may empathize with that suffering, and benefit from the sense of loss that it evokes. In this respect the success of Christianity lies largely in acknowledging the necessity of loss or rupture and recognizing that this may be acted out within the realm of the imaginary through an identification with Christ. As Kristeva notes:

On the basis of that identification, one that is admittedly too anthropological and psychological from the point of view of a strict theology, man is nevertheless provided with a powerful symbolic device that allows him to experience death and resurrection even in his physical body, thanks to the strength of the imaginary identification – and of its actual effects – with the absolute Subject (Christ).

(Ibid., p. 262)

33 Slavoj Žižek, "Eastern Europe's Republics of Gilead," *New Left Review*, 183, September/October 1990, 50–62. "Enjoyment," here, as Žižek notes, is not to be equated with pleasure: "enjoyment is precisely 'pleasure in unpleasure'; it designates the paradoxical satisfaction procured by a painful encounter with a Thing that perturbs the equilibrium of the 'pleasure principle'. In other words, enjoyment is located 'beyond the pleasure principle'." Ibid., 52.

34 As Žižek observes:

What is therefore at stake in ethnic tensions is always the possession of the national Thing. We always impute to the "other" an excessive enjoyment; s/he wants to steal our enjoyment (by ruining our way of life) and/or has access to some secret, perverse enjoyment. In short, what really bothers us about the "other" is the peculiar way it organizes its enjoyment: precisely the surplus, the "excess" that pertains to it – the smell of their food, their "noisy" songs and dances, their strange manners, their attitude to work (in the racist perspective, the "other" is either a workaholic stealing our jobs or an idler living on our labour; and it is quite amusing to note the ease with which one passes from reproaching the other with a refusal of work, to reproaching him for the theft of work).

(Ibid., pp. 53–54)

35 Thus, for Žižek, in Eastern Europe, following the collapse of the Cold War and the removal of the West as an effective form of threat, a replacement threat had to be found. Inevitably according to a logic of the soil, or of the community, it is the outsiders – Jews, gypsies, wanderers, anyone not bound to the soil – who are perceived as a threat, fluid insurgents that cannot be controlled. Jews, meanwhile, become the scapegoats in Eastern Europe even if there are few Jews to be found there any longer.

36 On "imagined communities," see Benedict Anderson, *Imagined Communities: Reflections on the Origin and Spread of Nationalism*, London: Verso, 1983.

37 Benjamin, as quoted in Shierry Weber Nicholsen, "*Aesthetic Theory's* Mimesis of Walter Benjamin," in Tom Huhn and Lambert Zuidervaart (eds), *The Semblance of Subjectivity: Essays in Adorno's Aesthetic Theory*, Cambridge, MA: MIT Press, 1997, p. 60.

38 On this see Homi K. Bhabha, "Introduction: Narrating the Nation," in Homi K. Bhabha (ed.), *Nation and Narration*, London and New York: Routledge, 1990, p. 3.

39 The mechanism by which identification takes place is a complex one. It may be understood as a process of "mirroring" based on the psychoanalytic concepts of "introjection" and "projection." "Introjection" could be described as the absorption of the external world into the self. It is as though the body operates as a form of recording surface, registering the various sensations of certain places. So it is when we revisit a place which we have previously visited, a "mirroring" occurs as our experiences of the place match our earlier experiences of it. "Projection" occurs as we project something of our own intentionality on to the external world over time. Thus, for example, we come to invest personal possessions – or even public objects which we use frequently, such as a park bench – with something of ourselves. In either case – whether through "introjection" or "projection" – mirrorings occur. We come to see ourselves reflected in the external world, and the external world within ourselves. Repetition serves to reinforce these experiences and thereby consolidate identification with the external world. For a more detailed discussion of this process of identification, see Neil Leach, "9/11," in Mark Crinson (ed.), *Urban Memory: History and Amnesia in the Modern City*, London: Routledge, 2005, pp. 169–191; Neil Leach, "Belonging," London: Postcolonial City, *AA Files* 49, 2003, 76–82.

40 In psychoanalytic terms, to attack an enemy's possessions is to undermine the very Thing around which the enemy has organized its own Enjoyment, and therefore through which it defines itself as a community.

4

Heterotopias and Archipelagos

The Shape of Modern Topophobia

Jean-Louis Cohen

One of the main attitudes of designers involved in the modernization of architectural and urban culture in the twentieth century was to dissolve the connection with the continuous city inherited by history, and to propose the alternative figure of an open space punctuated by free-standing buildings. This sort of conspiracy has now been clearly documented.[1] Haussmann's Paris was still a completely continuous city, even if the street network had been broadened, at the expense of many elements of the former topography and of numerous traces of the city's long history. But Le Corbusier's "Contemporary City for Three Million Inhabitants" (1922) (Figure 4.1), Ludwig Hilberseimer's "Vertical City" (1924) and, thirty years later, Lucio Costa's "Plan Piloto" for Brasília (1956) were conceived as continuous open landscapes, in which buildings stood out as lonely objects and in which the character of their sites was dispensed with. Only in the Planalto area of the Brazilian capital would Costa take altitude and views into consideration.

One could contend that the objective process of modernization and the cultural strategy defined as Modernism, indeed a rather loose notion – using in this instance the term "Modern Movement" would not help very much, as this slogan-like construct plays down the conflicts that have fraught the emergence of the new ideas – have led to the shaping of "generic spaces" that are now repeated throughout the entire world. This notion was introduced in 1995 by Rem Koolhaas in his provocative book *S, M, L, XL*.[2] But harsh critiques predated this interpretation by some thirty years. For instance, if we look closely at Jacques Tati's 1967 film *Playtime*, for which Tati built an extravagant set in Nice, with reproductions of buildings moved around on wheels, constantly changing the "urban" landscape, we perceive how he mocked the repetitive character of the Modernist urban landscape, shaped by similarly looking edifices used for all types of purposes, from housing to offices and public programs (Figure 4.2).[3] Jean-Luc Godard's almost contemporary film *Alphaville*, released in

1
e Corbusier,
Contemporary
ity for Three
lillion
habitants," 1922
Fondation Le
orbusier, Paris)

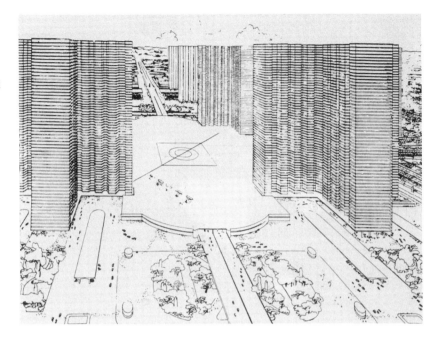

1965, goes in the same direction, by presenting the Paris high-rise business suburb of La Défense, which was being built at the same time, as a collection of buildings, decks and underground parking lots that could have been assembled anywhere.[4]

It is true that the great figures of Modernism tried to define systems meant to be implemented in many different contexts, that is, in a certain manner – indifferent to place. Le Corbusier's most significant urban scenes oscillate between nearly abstract ones, such as his "Voisin Plan," aimed at transforming the center of

4.2
Jacques Tati,
a city view in
Playtime, 1967
(Tati estate,
c/o Jérome
Deschamps)

Paris into a city of towers (1925) or his reconstruction plan for Saint-Dié (1945), and solutions based on a thorough observation of place, even if they break completely with the existing building patterns, such as the plans for Rio de Janeiro (1929) and Algiers (1932). In both series of plans, homologous urban components are featured, such as the business center, promoted in Moscow in 1930 as the "headquarters of the Five Years Plan."[5] At the same time, Berlin architect Ludwig Hilberseimer was proposing an even more radical view of the city of high-rise buildings, one in which a thorough segregation of traffic levels would take place, extending imaginary projects published in North American magazines before the First World War. In the case of his 1924 "Vertical City," the functional segregation of the buildings was achieved by the superimposition of underground offices and emerging residences.[6]

The idea of adapting the city to the industrial age led to many types of projects that were intended to be implemented in terrains considered as quasi-neutral, in which the productive layout of factories would be reproduced. Bolshevik bureaucrat Nikolai Milyutin derived from Henry Ford's conveyer belt, as developed for his Detroit plants, and from Arturo Soria y Mata's Ciudad Lineal, the concept of the industrial linear city, with a zoning based on parallel specialized ribbons (Figure 4.3). Entire cities were structured as mirror-like extensions of the mammoth plant to which their existence was related. Frank Lloyd Wright's Broadacre City, conceived between 1932 and 1935 as an alternative to both the density of the metropolis he hated and the isolation of the country, meant to distribute evenly over the United States houses and places of production, thus blurring the differentiation between the city as a place of socialization and the rest of the territory.

Since the mid-twentieth century most generalizing historical narratives have focused on this collection of theoretical projects in their propagandistic discussion of modernist urbanism, and have privileged the study of "new towns" over the investigation of the methods through which existing towns have been modernized. I am referring, for instance, to Leonardo Benevolo's *History of the City* or to

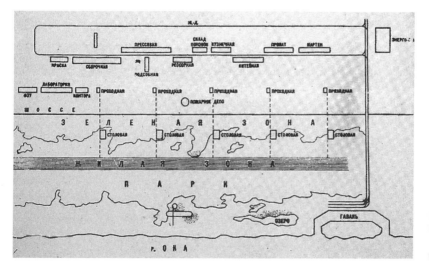

4.3
Nikolai Milyutin, linear scheme for Nizhny Novgorod, 1930 (All rights reserved)

Edmund Bacon's *Design of Cities*, two influential books written between 1965 and 1975.[7] Yet, many new interpretations have appeared that follow different avenues. They allow us to understand with an increased subtlety the cultural changes that have taken place in the making of cities, also highlighting implicit or hidden patterns of continuity in respect to anterior historical moments.

It is true that the response to local situations sometimes characterized the designs of the most provocative modernists. Such was the case with Le Corbusier's abovementioned project for Algiers, in which he flexibly adapted the system of freeways and high-rise housing previously imagined in his theoretical schemes to the extraordinary seaside site of the city. Clearly more site-specific than his previous proposals, this project nonetheless treated with the utmost brutality the pre-colonial Casbah.[8] Critics and historians have often understood Modernism as a utopianism, and inserted the work of Le Corbusier and others in a series of social and political projects rooted essentially in the utopian discourse. Indeed, this is one of the most abundant literary strategies of modern times: Riot-Sarcey has identified more than 1500 books published between Thomas More's paradigmatic *Utopia* of 1516 and the late nineteenth century which can be considered as utopian.[9]

Many of these narratives could be defined as a specialized branch of what Gaston Bachelard defined as "topophilia" when he delineated the purpose of his *Poetics of Space*:

> the images I want to examine are the quite simple images of *felicitous space*. In this orientation, these investigations would deserve to be called topophilia. They seek to determine the human value of the sorts of space that may be grasped, that may be defended against adverse forces, the spaces we love. For diverse reasons, and with the differences entailed by poetic shadings, this is eulogized space.[10]

According to Michel Foucault:

> Utopias are sites with no real place. They are sites that have a general relation of direct or inverted analogy with the real space of Society. They present society itself in a perfected form, or else society turned upside down, but in any case these utopias are fundamentally unreal spaces.[11]

Such "sites with no real spaces" have shaped the reflection leading to Modernist models, but utopias have also been understood by scholars such as Louis Marin or Françoise Choay primarily as narrative strategies.[12] Utopias have perhaps never shaped a "real space," but they have provided a stimulus to conceive of imaginary buildings and built territories. Such was the case of French utopian Socialist Charles Fourier's concept of a Phalanstery, a building resembling the palace of Versailles meant as the frame for a new type of social organization corresponding to a certain stage on the way to "universal harmony." Another utopian thinker, the Scot, Robert Owen, imagined "villages of harmony and cooperation" that were not specifically intended to be built in Scotland, but would also be designed for the vast plains of Texas, where the experiment failed. In 1824, Thomas Stedman Whitwell gave the best graphic representation of these enclosed settlements surrounded by agricultural land. The making of twenty new towns extended this attitude in which space, or rather place – I shall return to this differentiation – was a secondary concern.

Of course, projects for the new capitals of the twentieth century have a location, they might even have a topography, but they are inscribed in a narrative tending to the shaping of perfect society. In Chandigarh, as designed by Le Corbusier, who recycled the previous project of American architect Albert Mayer, the perfect society is one of careful distribution of social groups in an orderly space (Figure 4.4).[13]

4.4
**Le Corbusier,
Chandigarh new
town, view of
a housing area
(Photo: Jean-Loui
Cohen)**

4.5
**Lucio Costa,
Brasília, view of
a "Superquadra"
(Photo: Jean-Louis
Cohen)**

Thousands of kilometers away, Brasília was meant in the mid-1950s to be a city inhabited by political rulers and diplomats, with the bulk of the population active in the bureaucracy. Lucio Costa's "Superquadras" housing neighborhoods were conceived for an emerging middle class and no one expected the massive onslaught of workers that took place with the building campaign (Figure 4.5). Yet these workers never left and unplanned "satellite towns" such as Planaltinha or Taguatinga now house the major part of the population, and with a much more conservative network of roads and squares than Costa's own "Plan Piloto."[14]

I will here try to develop a different set of ideas. Rather than interpreting the history of Modernist planning and architecture as a series of failures to implement innovative schemes of a utopian nature, the way critics celebrating Brasília and scorning its spontaneous suburbs would do, I will propose two hypotheses. The first one is an invitation to consider the body of *heterotopias* imagined and produced as more significant than the body of utopias on which historical narratives have focused. The second one is an invitation to consider cities overlooked in planning histories because they have no clearly identified master plan or master composition. I would call them *pragmatic* new cities and oppose them to the dogmatic textbook new towns.[15]

Rather than only shaping utopias, Modernism and modernization have in fact determined an extremely broad spectrum of heterotopias, a concept proposed by Foucault. Initially, Foucault related the notion to pre-modern structures, when he discussed the architecture of jails in his seminal book *Discipline and Punish*, originally published in 1975, beginning with an analysis of Jeremy Bentham's Panopticon of 1791, an enclosed building completely regulated by the strategy of surveillance, with a central observation point.[16] In a text published, interestingly enough, in 1984 in the French architectural journal *Architecture, mouvement, continuité*, but already given as a lecture as early as 1967, Foucault, who had worked on the layout of hospitals together with the architect Bruno Fortier, extended his consideration of prisons and healing establishments to what he called "other spaces." In a certain manner, these spaces are precisely the ones Bachelard refuses to consider, affirming that "the space of hatred and combat can only be studied in the context of impassioned subject matter and apocalyptic images."[17]

The late eighteenth-century projects for the reconstruction of the Hôtel-Dieu, the oldest and most central hospital in Paris on a new, open territory west of the center is one of the "counter-sites" analyzed by Foucault (Figure 4.6). He contends that

> there are, probably in every culture, in every civilization, real places – places that do exist and that are formed in the very founding of society – which are something like counter-sites, a kind of effectively enacted utopia in which the real sites, all the other real sites that can be found within the culture, are simultaneously represented, contested, and inverted. Places of this kind are outside of all places, even though it may be possible to indicate their location in reality. Because these places are absolutely different from all the sites that they reflect and speak about, I shall call them, by way of contrast to utopias, *heterotopias*.[18]

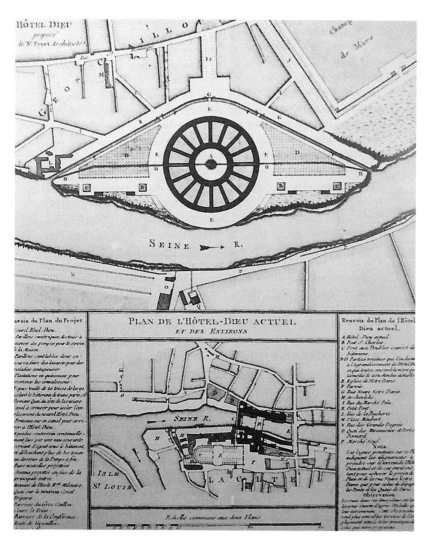

Much more than by large plans, the transformation of space has been based since the eighteenth century on partial attempts at rationalization, focused on self-centered entities or islands. Under the converging effects of the Industrial Revolution and the Enlightenment, the construction of modern nation-states and the implementation of colonial policies have crystallized in archipelagos, collections of islands devoted either to productive serfdom or to relative emancipation from the direness of existing cities. The production of these enclaves has never been the exclusivity of civilian or military state machines. Their creation has resulted, on one hand, from the action of organizations, of reform-oriented groups, even cults in some instances and, on the other hand, of commercial policies. The present "gated communities," which appear as a surprise for many ill-informed observers, can be seen in the end as a recent manifestation of the residential enclaves in which ruling classes have enclosed themselves since the Middle Ages, while sometimes also segregating the popular classes or specific social groups in other types of enclaves.

There are a large number of heterotopias, produced by various social agents and with extremely different goals. The more generous ones were probably generated by utopists such as Charles Fourier, whose Phalanstery was as autonomous as the Versailles château that inspired it (Figure 4.7), or Robert Owen's "Village," an enclosed entity in the middle of agricultural land. Prisons and detention camps were of course the most obvious spaces in which a rigorous rule was applied, and in which the cellular principle was literally implemented. The organization of punishment led to a vast spectrum of facilities, some of them allowing for seclusion in the open, in the manner of penitentiary colonies. The military have also been extremely active for centuries in creating their own archipelagos of barracks, camps, testing grounds, factories and arsenals, both inside and outside cities, and their indefatigable production of enclosed spaces deserves more attention from this point of view. Many programs related to modernization within enclosed precincts have recycled these military infrastructures, as the army has also constantly functioned as one of the most conservative institutions in protecting its own territorial heritage.

The extension of healthcare and hygiene has allowed for the modernization of an old building type, the hospital, into full networks of sanitary institutions devoted to the containment of the physically or the mentally ill. In Paris, the fortress-like Hôtel Dieu, built by Gilbert in 1865 on the Île de la Cité, a solid block opposite the church of Notre Dame and the Police Headquarters is a good example of an inner-city sanitary enclave, built as a conclusion to a problem set 90 years earlier.[19] Developing the medieval type of the scholarly college, which existed inside large cities in the Italian or French tradition or in small towns, in the English or German manner, university campuses have also proliferated, shaping self-centered entities, sometimes in dire conflict with their surroundings. The 1968 students' uprising at Columbia University in New York was in part triggered by the students' discontent

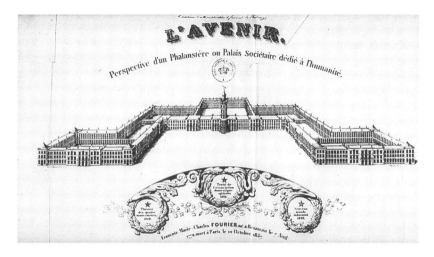

with the profitable university's real-estate investments in nearby blocks of African-American Harlem.

Schemes devoted to the housing of popular classes in Europe have often taken the shape of heterotopias. The incredible project conceived for sheltering all the urban poor of Genua in the massive structure of the "Albergo dei Poveri" led to the creation in the second half of the seventeenth century of one of the most extreme of these structures, one that would still feature as an example in Julien-Azaïs Guadet's *Eléments et théorie de l'architecture*, the main design handbook at the Ecole des Beaux-Arts in the early twentieth century.[20]

The first steps in the making of workers' housing were sometimes directly derived from the Phalanstery, but without its critical content. Jean-Baptiste Godin's Familistère, built in the northeastern French town of Guise, beginning in 1859, was centered on industrial labor, as opposed to the free association of skills suggested by Fourier. Then working-class housing started as purely factory-bound settlements contained within specific entities, such as the villages for the workers of the Menier chocolate factory near Paris (Figure 4.8) or the Krupp Siedlungen in Essen.[21] These man-made paradises were meant for the salvation of particular social groups. Only in several instances did industrialists merge forces in the nineteenth century to create joint estates where workers from competing factories would be settled. Such was the case in the Southern Alsacian city of Mulhouse, where a sort of counter-city meant for the labor force of the textile factory and facing the bourgeois town was erected.[22]

The most significant enclosed environments were not developed in the sphere of what Karl Marx called reproduction, but for production itself, as in the ideal city of Chaux designed by Claude-Nicolas Ledoux in the late eighteenth century. Developed initially from military arsenals, the industrial factory became an enclosed

4.8
Housing for the Menier chocolate factory near Paris, c. 1880 (Photo: Jean-Louis Cohen)

.9
Giacomo Mattè
Trucco, Fiat
actory, Turin,
917–22 (Photo:
ean-Louis Cohen)

space ruled by the specific rhythms and measurements related to the movement of materials and goods, and under the effects of Taylorism and Fordism to the organization of the assembly line. Factories were actual infernos of violence, in reality as well as in fiction. They inspired enquiries such as the one Upton Sinclair led in Chicago's Packingtown and published in *The Jungle* or narratives such as Jules Verne's *Les 500 millions de la Bégum*, in which he depicts the devilish city of Stahlstadt, modeled after the factories of Krupp. Modern factories also became fortresses, sometimes coupled with experimental devices such as the roof track designed by Giacomo Mattè Trucco for the Fiat factory in Turin (Figure 4.9). Finally, entire industrial cities developed as completely heterotopic environments. This was the case of the Bata shoe factory and related town in Zlín, Czechoslovakia, built in the 1930s, perhaps the most extraordinary example, and one that was exported to many countries of Europe, Canada and as far as India.[23]

War is a major overlooked issue in the history of modern architecture and urbanism. Yet in this discussion, it played a fundamental role. Factory architecture took a new meaning with the diffusion of the blackened-out factory in the United States during World War II. The completely sealed box, with air conditioning and fluorescent lighting, which came out of the war effort and was refined on the drawing boards of offices like Detroit-based Albert Kahn & Associates, is perhaps as typical of modernization in architecture as the skyscraper.[24] Large bureaucratic schemes related to defense, such as the Pentagon in Washington, DC, are also obvious heterotopias, devoted to the circulation of information, in this case among some 30,000 white-collar workers. The Pentagon is not significantly different from the skyscraper, and has even been called a horizontal skyscraper. Devoted to clerical work, completely sealed and related sometimes directly to the subway underneath, office skyscrapers have risen as heterotopias, autonomous from each other and containing services that guarantee autonomy, if not autarchy.

Other types of heterotopic spaces have emerged in relationship with commerce and the display of goods. The universal expositions aspired to contain the entire world of production and commerce under one roof. Here the heterotopia became a microcosm. Department stores have extended the cyclical temptations of the nineteenth-century's universal expositions and made them permanent. After the first Paris department stores, which provided the model for Emile Zola's novel *Au Bonheur des dames*, many variations on the theme of the commercial beehive appeared in Europe, America and Japan. It is not much to travel from the department stores to Shopper's Paradises of all sorts. Beginning in the 1940s, Victor Gruen's commercial centers institutionalized a building type conceived as a hybrid between the urban facility and the blackened-out factory.[25] Such a type has now universal diffusion and, ironically, is beginning to be subject in the United States to programs of functional recycling into libraries or other cultural programs.

Powerful modern objects such as the ocean liner can be considered as floating heterotopias, often compared to skyscrapers because of their length or, in the case of Le Corbusier, because of their logical spatial structure providing a paradigm for the organization of the city. A static, earthbound companion of the ocean liner, the grand hotel, is also nothing other than a heterotopia, a space freed, protected from the pressure of urban life. Developed in the metropolises of the United States or in relationship with the extension of railroad networks in "hostile" territory, these hotels have led to the emergence of the modern notion of comfort in collective housing. The resorts that have emerged in relationship with tourism are also shaped as autonomous pockets, where hygiene or sport is an excuse for pleasure away from the busy metropolis, and sometimes at a safe distance from the local population, when the discrepancy between standards of living is unbearable.

From the Midway Pleasance at the 1893 Chicago Exposition to Coney Island and, more recently, Disneylands and their many clones, fairs and theme parks are also heterotopias devoted to the commercialized pursuit of enjoyment. These fun-oriented islands are perhaps one of the most significant contributions of twentieth-century urban planning and architecture to the history of the man-made environment. Far from being simple enclaves or fragments, as they do not only deal with morphology, they shape cities made out of distinct, tightly secluded areas of practice.

Heterotopias can be viewed as particular ways of shaping usage, but indeed not of building urbanity. After all, the Charter from Athens published by Le Corbusier in 1943 as a guide to "functional" urbanism was nothing more than the predicament of a collage of heterotopias in the concrete designs it legitimized. The four functions it delineated were in fact in most postwar projects to be the base of segregated parts of cities.[26] In today's cities, the phenomenon of the enclave is not of a fundamentally different nature. Created by a founding act, by duplication or by germination, these islands have sometimes become microcosms. Taking them into account as parts of a unique narrative shapes a very different chronicle of two centuries of territorial transformations in which large urban or regional plans have been in the end less effective on the ground than the creation of invisible networks of autonomous places, that were alternatively malign or magical. Anti-urban and intra-urban versions of these "other" spaces coexist in a saga yet to be written, dealing with the industrialized West, its colonies and with the East.

In real cities, heterotopic islands are only part of a broader picture in which generic and specific solutions are combined. At this point, a second hypothesis has to be formulated. Modern urbanism and urban architecture have often been most innovative and stimulating in cities that I would call pragmatic, i.e. cities not born out of a single, unified design, but out of no particular formal design. In these cities, the issue was not so much design as regulation, sometimes with specific architectural goals in mind, and sometimes not. The opposition introduced by biologist and urbanist Patrick Geddes between U-topia, "impossible to implement anywhere," according to him, and Eu-topia, that is, the careful remodeling of existing cities, is useful at this point.[27] Geddes favors a more perceptive attitude towards city development, a term now banal, but suggested by him in 1915 and based on the careful observation of existing conditions.

Two examples of cities where such non-heroic planning has been implemented come to mind, cities to which I have devoted some attention in the past years: Casablanca and Los Angeles. I could just as well discuss large capital cities such as Paris or London or major scenes of modernization such as New York, where central areas, with clearly established and readable forms, are surrounded by more confused suburban developments. But I want to focus precisely on two places that belong to a series of underscored if not even maligned urban scenes. The main feature Casablanca and Los Angeles share is less the trivial fact that they are located on the same parallel than the relevant one of having had a particular development history, in which the pattern has not been one of growth around a unique center, but one of simultaneous growth of a network of neighborhoods.

Determined by its colonial condition, being ruled by the French from 1907 to 1956, Casablanca is not only a city of juxtaposition but also a city based on exclusion. The new European town was built according to the policies of General Hubert Lyautey alongside the pre-colonial walled city, in which Muslims and Jews lived together with the first European settlers. Urban extension started around 1910 in a far-West like atmosphere, in which the intense real estate market, based in the cafés, determined the development of scores of subdivisions around the denser city core. The complete segregation envisioned for social and ethnic groups never worked, although some heterotopias were designed, such as the Moslem new town meant to recreate a framework for identity. Built between 1920 and 1922 by Albert Laprade, the "Indigenous new town," or Habous quarter, was meant to recreate the illusion of a historic Moroccan town, but was soon to be totally inadequate in face of the afflux of rural migrants (Figure 4.10). Although initially conceived as exclusive entities, the presumably "European" quarters were partially inhabited by Muslim families. The only effective heterotopia implemented would be the part of the Habous quarter earmarked for prostitution, the Bousbir red light district, built inside enclosed walls as a small medina inside the new medina, and discussed in countless literary and travel narratives.

As established by Henri Prost in 1917, the French extension plan was not a rigid grid, like those of most preconceived new towns, but one that acknowledged

existing real estate patterns. The new boulevards were built in such a manner as to avoid excessive land condemnation and to integrate the existing owners into the development process (Figure 4.11). In a city where, in 1914, the ratio of automobiles per capita was higher than in Paris, the principle of rapid connection between the central squares, the harbor and the railway station was fundamental. The squares themselves were open, and sometimes loose, expanses of ground, in which patterns celebrated by Camillo Sitte in his 1889 *Town-Planning According to Artistic Principles*

were echoed. Meant as a sort of compensation to the dense urban blocks on which the Prost plan was based, they generated a genuine topophilia which has survived colonial rule and remains one of the bases of urban practice in today's Casablanca.[28]

At the same time, the tight regulations implemented alongside the new boulevards were not aimed at homogeneity, but rather at the introduction of certain architectural resonances between buildings designed according to diverse languages. Art Nouveau façades of the early apartment blocks built in the 1920s and the streamlined office buildings of the following decade would coexist in a rather friendly manner, as long as they were inserted in the same zoning envelope and followed identical rules for the placement of shopping arcades, cornices and rooflines. This all led to the creation of a rather harmonious urban landscape, in an otherwise ruthless city, where real estate speculation has always been the most popular sport.

If Casablanca's plans, from Prost's initial scheme to the metropolitan system designed in the early 1950s by his follower Michel Ecochard, are featured in the main narrative of planning history, Los Angeles is in contrast the very image of the unplanned city, or was considered as such until the recent investigations dealing with episodes such as the 1930 plan by Frederick Low Olmsted, Jr. and Harland Bartholomew for parkways and recreation areas.[29] It is true that Los Angeles never followed any preconceived design, as far as the general structure of the metropolis is concerned. The city was born out of the adjustment of rural and transportation infrastructure and speculative development, but not without a significant series of regulating patterns (Figure 4.12).

Mario Gandelsonas has revealed in efficient graphic representations the superimposition of grids from the Spanish agricultural pattern to the Interstate freeways. His investigation of form complements historical interpretations that have dealt with the constitution of what Reyner Banham has pertinently called the

4.12
Los Angeles, view
of Downtown
from the East
(Photo: Jean-Louis
Cohen)

"transportation palimpsest."[30] Often identified with the freeways and the motorcar, the city had already reached its extension with the streetcars before World War I, as the pioneering research of Robert Fogelson made clear in the 1960s.[31] Planning never worked at a metropolitan scale in Los Angeles, where at a very early stage the immense area affected by urbanization escaped control, first of all because of the many political conflicts involved. However, schemes such as the Olmsted/ Bartholomew 1930 plan left a lasting impact on the city's structure. Also, the resistance to rules imposed on private property led to amazing zoning patterns in which one-lot deep strips were devoted to retail, cutting through residential areas alongside the main boulevards.

Although not exactly a colonial city – it might indeed be qualified as a postcolonial development – Los Angeles contains many types of heterotopias, from the residential to the commercial, from the leisurely to the industrial. In his *Los Angeles: The Architecture of Four Ecologies*, Reyner Banham earmarked in 1971 what he defined as the "art of the enclave," discussing 1930s shopping centers such as Robert Derrah's Crossroads of the World on Sunset Boulevard (Figure 4.13).[32] Since that moment, the proliferation of controlled entities inside the metropolis has never ceased. Movie studios, amusement parks, residential or commercial enclaves have become perhaps more typical of the city than the freeways that are generally considered the trademark of Los Angeles.

These enclaves can be ordered on a scale ranging from the ones generating a certain topophilia, as they can be linked with "happy" consumption or playful practice, to the ones generating an unquestionable topophobia, when they are linked with the exclusion of non-desired social groups, or individual. The privatization of Los Angeles' generous landscape has led to the paradoxical results of creating islands of engineered – and commodified – happiness and islands of autistic

4.13
Robert Derrah, Crossroads of the World, Los Angeles (Photo: Jean-Louis Cohen)

elitism in a metropolis apparently founded on the ideology of unlimited circulation and access.

In his text of 1960, "The Situationist Frontier," Guy Debord, an acute reader of Bachelard, affirms that "the architecture to be shaped has to shun the obsession of the old monumental architecture for spectacular beauty in favor of topological organizations allowing for a generalized participation," and affirms "we will play on topophobia and create a topophilia." He pleads for a "new architecture, which could start practical exercise by the *détournement* of preexisting 'blocks of affective environment' such as the castle."[33] Through the recycling of all sorts of existing shapes – the castle, as in the case of Disneyland, the village, as in the case of the Crossroads of the World, or streets, as in the case of Universal's CityWalk, Los Angeles seems to have almost literally implemented Debord's vision, albeit in a cynical, commercial manner (Figure 4.14).

The space of modernization is neither purely "specific" nor is it purely "generic," to use epithets introduced by Rem Koolhaas in *S, M, L, XL*. It has been shaped by the constant tension between grand design and built objects. Determined by the enclosed spaces of heterotopias and the loose territories of pragmatic cities, where negotiation is the rule, this tension could also be productive for collective life in the contemporary city, but only as long as the city is not reduced to a collage of heterotopic enclaves and as long as pragmatic interaction moderates the destructive forces unleashed by the market economy.

Notes

1 See, for instance, Bruno Fortier, *L'Amour des villes*, Liège: Mardaga, 1994.
2 Office for Metropolitan Architecture, Rem Koolhaas and Bruce Mau, *S, M, L, XL*, New York: Monacelli Press, 1995.

3   Matteo Porrino (ed.), *La Ville en Tatirama: la città di Monsieur Hulot*, Milan: Mazzotta, 2003.

4   On the interaction between film and urbanism, see Thierry Paquot (ed.), *La Ville au cinéma*, Paris: Editions des Cahiers du Cinéma, 2005.

5   Jean-Louis Cohen, *Le Corbusier and the Mystique of the USSR*, Princeton, NJ: Princeton University Press, 1992.

6   Richard Pommer (ed.), *In the Shadow of Mies: Ludwig Hilberseimer, Architect, Educator, and Urban Planner*, Chicago: The Art Institute of Chicago, New York: Rizzoli, 1988.

7   Leonardo Benevolo, *History of the City*, Cambridge, MA: MIT Press, 1980, originally published as *Storia della città*, Bari: Laterza, 1976; Edmund Bacon, *Design of Cities*, New York: Viking Press, 1967.

8   See the main two interpretations of this radical project: Mary McLeod, "Urbanism and Utopia: Le Corbusier from Regional Syndicalism to Vichy," PhD dissertation, Princeton University, 1985; Jean-Pierre Giordani, "Le Corbusier et les projets pour la ville d'Alger 1931–1942," PhD dissertation, Saint-Denis, Université de Paris 8, 1987.

9   Michèle Riot-Sarcey, Thomas Bouchet and Antoine Picon (eds), *Dictionnaire des utopies*, Paris: Larousse, 2002.

10 Gaston Bachelard, *The Poetics of Space*, Boston: Beacon Press, 1964, pp. 7–8; originally published as *La Poétique de l'espace*, Paris: Presses Universitaires de France, 1958.

11 Michel Foucault, "Of Other Spaces," *Diacritics* 16(1) Spring 1986, p. 24; originally published as "Des Espaces autres," *Architecture, mouvement, continuité* 5, October 1984, pp. 46–49.

12 Louis Marin, *Utopiques, jeux d'espace*, Paris: Editions de Minuit, 1973; Françoise Choay, *The Rule and the Model: On the Theory of Architecture and Urbanism*, Cambridge, MA: MIT Press, 1996; originally published as *La Règle et le modèle, sur la théorie de l'architecture et de l'urbanisme*, Paris: Seuil, 1980.

13 On the early contribution of Mayer, to whom Le Corbusier's plan is deeply indebted, see Thomaï Serdari, "Albert Mayer, Architect and City Planner: The Case for a Total Professional," PhD dissertation, New York University, 2005.

14 James Holston, *The Modernist City: An Anthropological Critique of Brasilia*, Chicago: University of Chicago Press, 1989.

15 Jean-Louis Cohen and Monique Eleb, *Casablanca: Colonial Myths and Architectural Ventures*, New York, The Monacelli Press, 2002, pp. 442–443.

16 Michel Foucault, *Discipline and Punish: The Birth of the Prison*, New York: Pantheon Books, 1977.

17 Bachelard, *The Poetics of Space*, p. 8.

18 Foucault, "Of Other Spaces," p. 24. Italicization by author.

19 Blandine Barret Kriegel, François Béguin, Bruno Fortier, Michel Foucault and Anne Thalamy, *Les Machines à guérir: aux origines de l'hôpital moderne*, Liège: Mardaga, 1979.

20 Julien-Azaïs Guadet, *Eléments et théorie de l'architecture*, Paris: Librairie de la construction moderne, 1901–1904, vol. 2, p. 193.

21 Upton Sinclair, *The Jungle*, New York: Doubleday, 1906; Jules Verne, *The Begum's Millions*, Middletown, CT: Wesleyan University Press, 2005.

22 Stéphane Jonas, *Le Mulhouse industriel: un siècle d'histoire urbaine, 1740–1848*, Paris: l'Harmattan, 1995.

23 A publication conceived in relationship with an exhibition at the Centre Pompidou is still useful to understand these issues: *L'Usine et la ville*, monographic issue of *Culture technique*, 1986.

24 Federico Bucci, *Albert Kahn: Architect of Ford*, Princeton, NJ: Princeton University Press, 1993.

25 M. Jeffrey Hardwick, *Mall Maker: Victor Gruen, Architect of an American Dream*, Philadelphia, PA: University of Pennsylvania Press, 2004.

26 Le Corbusier, *The Athens Charter*, New York: Grossman Publishers, 1973; originally published as *La Charte d'Athènes*, Paris: Plon, 1943.

27 Patrick Geddes, "Civics as Applied Sociology," 1904, in Helen Meller, *The Ideal City*, Leicester: Leicester University Press, 1979, pp. 88–89.

28 Jean-Louis Cohen and Monique Eleb, *Casablanca, Colonial Myths and Architectural Ventures*, New York, The Monacelli Press, 2002 and *Les Mille et une villes de Casablanca*, Paris: ACR, 2004.

29 Greg Hise and William Deverell, *Eden by Design: The 1930 Olmsted-Bartholomew Plan for the Los Angeles Region*, Berkeley, CA: University of California Press, 2000.

30 Mario Gandelsonas, *The Urban Text*, Cambridge, MA: MIT Press, 1991; Reyner Banham, *Los Angeles: The Architecture of Four Ecologies*, Harmondsworth: Penguin Books, 1971.

31 Ralph M. Fogelson, *The Fragmented Metropolis: Los Angeles 1850–1930*, Cambridge, MA: Harvard University Press, 1967.

32 Banham, *Los Angeles*, p. 137.

33 Guy Debord, "La Frontière situationniste," *Internationale situationniste* 5, December 1960, p. 9. In his useful monograph on the Situationists, Simon Sadler has been unable to find an English equivalent for "détournement": *The Situationist City*, Cambridge, MA: MIT Press, 1998.

5

Agreement and Decorum

Conversations within the Architecture of Louis Kahn

Peter Kohane

Topophilia can be associated with the articulation of an architectural or urban space, so that it stimulates the occupants to engage in conversation. They speak to one another in a decorous manner and reach an agreement on topics of common concern. This formulation of a place that is admired, indeed loved, because it brings citizens together, contributed to the work of several influential twentieth-century architects, including Louis Kahn (1901–74). He believed that spaces must be delimited if they are to unite individuals. Although not acknowledged in scholarship on Kahn, his well-known critique of the modern free plan and universal or expansive space was founded on traditional ideas about speech, agreement and decorum. From the late 1950s until his death in 1974, he designed rooms, or room-like spaces, that were intended to talk to each other. A plan for a building could therefore be defined as a "society of rooms."[1] Each interior, along with the overall composition, fosters discussions. Our understanding of topophilia is enhanced by his theory and practice, where the power of speech and moral principle of decorum are attributed to bounded spaces and human beings.

This chapter explores relationships between theoretical statements and buildings. Kahn reflected on recent accomplishments in 1971, when delivering his Gold Medal Acceptance Speech, "The Room, the Street and Human Agreement," and contributing to an exhibition called City/2 (City over Two), held at the Philadelphia Museum of Art.[2] He displayed a group of drawings. In one entitled *The Room*, two seated figures face each other to converse, the result described in the text below the image as a "meeting of vectors" (Figure 5.1). Despite its intimacy, the discussion is relevant to the accompanying drawings of *The Street* and *The City*, which address

the role of buildings within an urban setting and the making of institutions (Figures 5.2, 5.3). These didactic drawings offer insight into Kahn's designs for the Kimbell Art Museum (Fort Worth, Texas, 1966–72), Phillips Exeter Academy Library (Exeter, New Hampshire, 1965–72) and Salk Institute for Biological Studies (La Jolla, California, 1959–65). He took into consideration unique programs and locations. For instance, the interior of the museum at Fort Worth protects and displays precious objects by filtering the harsh external sunlight. The existing brick buildings of the Exeter Academy campus were respected in the exterior of the library. At the Salk Institute, the prominent study towers seem to turn their gaze to the Pacific Ocean. Yet while the three buildings are enriched by particular qualities, Kahn would assume that the topophilia experienced in each depends on a universal theme, in which rooms are composed to promote conversation and agreement.

The conversation in *The Room* is illustrated as a lively activity, but one where the inspiration of the participants is tempered by their desire to reach an agreement. The figure by the fire speaks, while the other leans on the cool window-sill to listen. When conversing, the animated and responsive individuals exercise moderation and decorum. They act appropriately by taking each other into consideration.

The Room endorses the classical analogy between the arts of architecture and conversation. According to this, an architect and orator found their practices on the virtue of temperance and the related human characteristic of decorum. A good building or speech will have a positive impact on citizens, encouraging debate and agreement. *The Room*'s forms were composed like a speech to bring the occupants

5.2
Louis Kahn,
The Street
(Philadelphia
Museum of Art,
Gift of the Artist,
72–32–3)

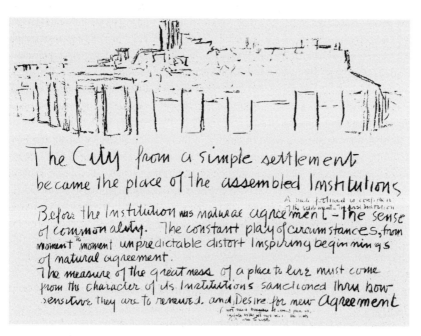

5.3
Louis Kahn, *The
City* (Philadelphia
Museum of Art,
Gift of the Artist,
72–32–2)

together: they turn towards one another and converse. The sketch represents the principle of decorum by connecting the architectural members to the dispositions of the human figures.

Kahn linked *The Room* to the text on *The City*, where he was concerned, even disturbed, by the "unpredictable" nature of human affairs. These are tied to "[t]he constant play of circumstances." Such flux of everyday occurrences was contrasted with the emergence and continued relevance of actions that unite citizens. The text therefore noted the "inspiring beginnings of natural agreement." Kahn stressed that "[b]efore the Institution was natural agreement;" while the "desire for new Agreement" stimulates the ongoing debates that sustain the institutions of a modern culture. These statements from *The City* are pertinent to *The Room*, its conversation illustrating the inspiration and agreement that are essential to the formation and renewal of an institution.

The scales of *The Room* and a walled town, represented as *The City*, are mediated by an urban precinct, depicted in Kahn's drawing of *The Street*. Described in its text as a "Room by Agreement," this external space is delimited by distinct but interconnected buildings. As some are lively in character, others less so, they can be seen to interact in producing a decorous urban ensemble. Buildings in *The Street*, like figures in *The Room*, converse with one another.

In this chapter, the term conversation is defined broadly to include relationships associated with agreement, even if they do not involve people who voice their ideas. For Kahn, the rooms of a single edifice talk to one another, as do the buildings of *The Street*. These permanent records of decorous action remind citizens that they too should value communication and interaction. Within an art gallery, for instance, a visitor converses with the living presence in a painting. In addition, the reader of a book imaginatively engages in discussion with its author. A highly animated interior perspective of the Exeter Library's reading area, drawn by Kahn in 1967, alludes to this and other conversations, where people may interact without talking to one another.

I will begin with the architect's self-contained interiors, and then examine their contribution to his concept of a society of rooms. Conversations take place among varied rooms, which can be within a building or city. The Exeter Library and Salk Institute are critical to my analysis, as intimate rooms in both open onto external spaces, which are like urban streets. The occupants of carrels in the library and studies of the Salk Institute interact with colleagues outside, thereby consolidating the decorum that characterize their institutions.

Rooms within Buildings

While *The Room* is privileged as a setting for just two discussants, Kahn's Gold Medal Acceptance Speech, "The Room, the Street and Human Agreement," explained that many people within a large space could also reach an agreement. *The Room*'s written comment about vectors meeting was first clarified, Kahn arguing that unity arises from a special discussion, where the situation's intimacy is accompanied by the participants' openness to new ideas: "in a small room with just another person, what you say may never have been said before."[3] Yet a conversation can easily lose its inspired character, even in an interior as conducive to interaction as *The Room*.

> It is different when there is more than just another person. Then, in this little room, the singularity of each is so sensitive that the vectors do not resolve. The meeting becomes a performance . . . with everyone saying his lines, saying what has been said many times before.[4]

If several more people are to be accommodated, their interior will expand beyond the size of *The Room*, while the conversations that take place remain untouched by moments of fresh insight. Nonetheless, communication can occur, as Kahn appreciated a coming together of many people, for whom "the event is of commonality."[5] In such a context, "[h]uman agreement is a sense of rapport, of commonness, of all bells ringing in unison."[6]

This argument was formulated while designing his grandest interior, the Assembly Chamber in the National Assembly Building (Sher-e-Bangla Nagar, Dhaka, 1962–83). Referring to the project in 1966, he noted how its future occupants, the politicians, would interact to "touch the spirit of commonness."[7] Kahn stressed that their "assembly is of a transcendent nature."[8] The design was finalized in 1971 when he introduced a vault with concave segments, the same form appearing at this time in *The Room*. The two interiors recall ancient buildings with gored domes or half-domes, such as the Scenic Triclinium at Hadrian's Villa, to enhance the monumentality that is apt for new spaces sheltering conversations leading to agreement. This is attained in *The Room* through the discussants' inspired exchange of ideas, while the Assembly Chamber's politicians share a sense of "commonality." Agreement is therefore pertinent to the making of discrete spaces, whether small or vast.

In Kahn's finest architectural designs, however, *The Room*'s spatial containment and accompanying theme of an inspired conversation had roles in the arrangement of larger settings. While differently scaled rooms were brought together, their relationship was not based on his hierarchical distinction between served and servant spaces. The strategy of consequence involved human inspiration, which has implications for a building's cultural meaning.

This was acknowledged in an idiosyncratic manner, when Kahn delivered his 1971 lecture and referred to the amorphous space around him. It could be transformed, even if only momentarily, to assume a human character:

> This room we are in is big, without distinction. The walls are far away. Yet I know if I were to address myself to a chosen person, the walls of the room would come together and the room would become intimate.[9]

Implications for design were also considered, Kahn referring to an individual who views a work of art and also reads a book. These activities could be valued as inspired discussions among two people, although one of them is not literally present. The argument was informed by the Kimbell Museum and Exeter Library, both then nearing completion.

Within the museum one interacts with a displayed work of art, whose life-like character can be discerned in expressive abstract forms or representations of the human figure.[10] Kahn added to the statement about his own connection as a lecturer with an individual in the audience, by noting that "[i]f this room were the Baptistery of Florence, [an] image would have inspired thoughts in the same way as person to person . . . So sensitive is a room."[11] The interior of the museum accords with this conception of a figure rendered in mosaic that, like a living human being, animates the mind of the beholder, stimulating a conversation.

When moving through the galleries of the Kimbell Museum, the visitor may feel that the overall interior lacks distinction; but once captivated and inspired by an object of art, the intervening space assumes a special identity (Figures 5.4, 5.5). Thus, an emotionally charged domain emerges within the expansive, loft-like interior. Unlike the situation of two people in the lecture hall, however, the affective relationship between viewer and art conforms to the articulation of structure and space. Objects are displayed in different ways, including paintings hung on partition walls that are attached to the beams supporting vaults. Standing beneath one of these vaults, the viewer is in an ideal location to study such a picture. The conversation's intimacy is inseparable from the concrete structure; a notion illustrated by Kahn in a perspective sketch of 1967, where a person in the foreground focuses intently on the abstract painting on the right-hand side of the gallery, while the silver vault rises and falls to create a unifying element (Figure 5.4). It defines a bay that is approximately 20 feet wide.[12] A work of art and its beholder are brought together by a solid but luminous vault, which produces an appropriately scaled, room-like unit of space, and its diffused light.

5.4
Louis Kahn, Kimbell Museum, interior perspective (Architectural Archives, University of Pennsylvania, 217.1.1)

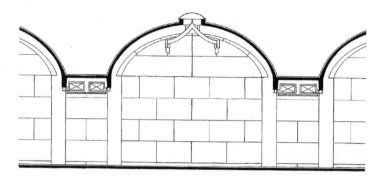

5.5
Louis Kahn,
Kimbell Museum,
section drawing
(Louis Kahn
Collection,
University of
Pennsylvania
and Pennsylvania
Historical and
Museum
Commission,
030.iv.A.730.5.10)

Because the visitor to the Kimbell Museum does not merely gaze upon an inert object of art but engages with its human character, the communication is similar to the exchange and meeting of vectors within *The Room*. In this sketch, the interaction between the discussants is related to the embracing shapes of the window and, on a larger scale, the vault and structural frame of ribs and column at the left. As formulated in Kahn's museum, the paths of the vectors moving back and forth between beholder and work of art are coincident with the profile of a vault and the volume it defines. The space of the museum can therefore be appreciated for its expansive and harboring qualities, the latter inextricable from one's intense involvement with a work of art.

Another meeting of vectors draws the reader and author of a book together, this conversation integral to the institution of a library and building for the Phillips Exeter Academy (Figures 5.6–5.9). In the Gold Medal Acceptance Speech, Kahn immediately followed his account of a painting having a human presence with the comment that "[t]he Book is an offering of the Mind."[13] A reader's thoughts are animated by those of an author. An inspired meeting of minds takes place, particularly if the setting is the intimate and light-filled room of a carrel.

However, reading a book in the Exeter Library is like viewing a painting within the Kimbell Museum, as these conversations are so potent that they resonate throughout entire spatial compositions. Reading is relevant to the library's carrels and other rooms, including the grand central hall where students meet and talk. The individual within a carrel reads a book, reflecting on the ideas of its author and identifying points of disagreement and agreement. Knowledge attained imparts depth to the student's discussions with colleagues in the hall, contributing to the agreement understood as "commonality." For Kahn, reading cultivates one's inner life, which is not alienated from discussions capable of uniting many people. Conversely, debate in the hall has an impact upon a reader, helping to focus his or her responses to an author's ideas. The Exeter Library was founded on a cultural and spiritual ideal, where a person's introverted and extroverted natures are fully realized because they are interdependent. Agreement is therefore an all-pervasive principle: it informs the thoughts and actions of individuals, as well as the composition of their rooms.

Based on varied conversations, the design for the library exemplifies

5.6
Louis Kahn, Phillips Exeter Academy Library, view of exterior (Photo: Peter Kohane)

5.7
Louis Kahn, Phillips Exeter Academy Library, perspective of reading area (Louis Kahn Collection, University of Pennsylvania and Pennsylvania Historical and Museum Commission, 710.140)

Kahn's notion that "a real plan is one in which rooms have talked to each other."[14] While such rooms include the library's brick reading area and book stacks, as well as an unbuilt external court, I have been able to begin an analysis of his comment with just the carrel and hall. The term conversation is applicable to the inspired actions in both interiors, as well as the manner in which they are brought together. Because reading and an actual debate are complementary activities, the carrel and hall balance one another as participants in an architectural conversation.

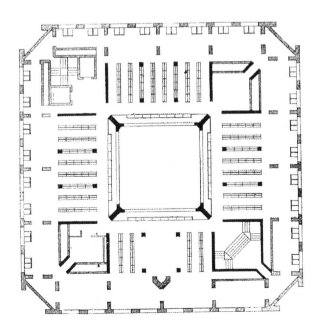

5.8
Louis Kahn, Phillips Exeter Academy Library, plan, third floor (From William Jordy, "Span of Kahn," *Architecture Review* 155, June 1974, 336)

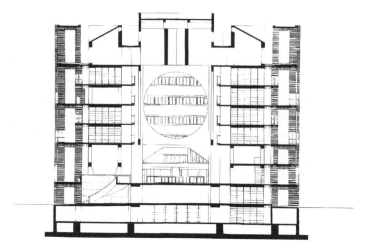

5.9
**Louis Kahn,
Phillips Exeter
Academy Library,
section (Louis
Kahn Collection,
University of
Pennsylvania
and Pennsylvania
Historical and
Museum
Commission)**

This discussion among equals can be contrasted with another kind, where interaction relevant to people and rooms depends on their status as servants and served. Such differentiation is evident in Kahn's National Assembly Building, its outer spaces, primarily offices, not as important as the central Assembly Chamber. An agreement is created, but it is less compelling than that involving the carrels and hall of the Exeter Library.

Dedicated to discussions generating "commonality," the library's hall and National Assembly Building's chamber are impressive in scale and top-lit. Only the Dhaka project includes a surrounding ambulatory; yet the two buildings have comparable peripheral rooms. The arrangement of central and outer spaces in the National Assembly Building is hierarchical: its offices are rooms for every-day activities, while the chamber accords with Kahn's definition of assembly. Agreement involves the mundane servant spaces and a "transcendent" served one. The conversations in an office contribute to those in the chamber, yet the issue of relative importance determines the way that they talk to each other. The Exeter Library is different, as an individual moves between a carrel and the hall, the one including shelves for a personal selection of books, the other looking onto the stacks containing the library's entire collection, which embodies the collective thoughts of the authors. Although different in scale and separated by the ring of stacks, the carrel and hall are profoundly connected: a student in each is surrounded by books, while reading in private stimulates thought, which is expressed verbally, tested when standing to debate with other students. Studying quietly and speaking in public are facets of the one learning process. Unlike the National Assembly Building, agreement in the library depends on peripheral spaces that are at least as significant as the central one.

Thus, when working on the design for the Exeter Library in 1967, Kahn showed his client how students will occupy the building by depicting the reading area, not the central hall (Figure 5.7). The people in his perspective sketch engage in activities and conversations, which have implications for the agreement pertaining to the entire library, as well as its meaning as an institution.

The drawing was enriched by a classical concept in the visual arts, where the importance of an event or topic is communicated to the viewer through the presence of several figures. Each person has an inner life, expressed through gestures and movements that are neither unduly strident nor subdued, but decorous. Actions are dignified and interrelated.[15] This account of human expression was valued by Kahn, who studied its ramifications for a library. His source was an engraving published in 1840 by Letarouilly, in which monks appear in the upper level of Bramante's cloister of Santa Maria della Pace in Rome (Figure 5.10).[16] Two figures converse in the background of the Renaissance cloister, while another pair at the left walk toward the beholder. A solitary reader is immersed in his book in the foreground. Together, these monks represent a worthy topic, namely the pursuit of knowledge.

In Kahn's library perspective, the requisite elevated and decorous mood is established through distinct but interconnected figures, along with the authority bestowed on the setting by the historical references to both Letarouilly's engraving and Bramante's actual cloister. Indebted to the past, Kahn's drawing focuses on the students and their conversations, as well as the articulation of discrete spaces.

He acknowledged a link between a student in a carrel, who is similar to Letarouilly's solitary reader, and colleagues working at the communal table. The latter activity is valued in its own right, the overarching brick frame creating a room-like volume, its light falling from two large windows above the carrels. A brick unit of space therefore accommodates people studying at their table and alone in the smaller rooms of the carrels. Human interaction across these settings informs the agreement

5.10
Paul Letarouilly, engraving of Bramante's cloister of S. Maria della Pace (From P. M. Letaruouilly, *Édifices de Rome Moderne*, 1840)

between spaces, which Kahn addressed in his comment that "[t]he carrel is a room within a room."[17] Additional figures in the sketch appear just beyond those at the tables and in carrels. One person stands and holds a book in the stacks. Others in the background converse and perambulate, following in the footsteps of the monks at the left of the cloister engraving. Strategically located, Kahn's standing, walking and seated students illustrate his statements about a ritual and human agreement.

He invoked a ritual when speaking in 1957 about the origins of a library: "a man with a book goes to the light/ A library begins this way."[18] The ritual for the Exeter Library involves an individual walking across the campus, Kahn arguing that paths should lead to a "court entrance, available to all the students as a place of invitation."[19] Designed but not built, it was to be located in front of the building, serving as an external room for people to meet. Lacking this initial communal setting, one follows paths directly to the library's arcade, then passes through the door, ascending grand curving stairs to the central top-lit hall. The circles cut into the walls frame tiers of books.[20] Stairs in servant spaces give access to the stacks. One of these is at the left of Kahn's perspective drawing, its low height, concrete structure and lack of daylight creating a suitable place for storing books. The continuation of the ritual can be discerned through the figures: a person selects a book in the stacks; then walks with friends; and can sit at a large desk or, having moved closer to the light, in a carrel.

The design for the library, however, was based on this ritual, where students proceed along a single path, as well as the notion of agreement. The latter encompasses varied, or more complex, human relationships and their associated interlocked spaces within the library. I have noted the sketched figures in carrels and at the communal table, the small rooms positioned within their brick-defined one. These several students are not separated from those who perambulate. Kahn's drawing shows how the transverse brick flat arches and their piers divide the reading area into bays. Such structuring of space is informed by human action: figures in the background move along the axis of an internal street; while a student working in a group at a table, or alone in a carrel, values one of the room-like settings. Another kind of agreement is announced by the standing figure in the stacks. As this person could be taking a book to read in a carrel or re-shelving it before walking back to the hall, he or she mediates between the outer and inner rooms; while also alluding to the interdependence of the two conversations, one taking place in the mind of the reader, the other an actual debate. The culminating space of an inspired ritual, the carrel therefore also has a role within Kahn's theory of human agreement. According to this, the rooms of the building contribute to an individual's sense of self and participation in the life of the institution.

Agreement rather than a ritual determined the particular location of a carrel, where the window and its timber wall are aligned with the external face of the library's piers. The peripheral room conforms to the occupant's desire to converse with the author of a book, as well as interact with people outside the building. Such activities are facilitated by the window of a carrel. Visible in the perspective sketch, the opening was also invoked when Kahn explained how "I made the carrel associated with light. It has its own little window so you can regulate privacy and the amount of light you want."[21] The drawing refers to the window by capturing the play of its daylight on a carrel's timber surfaces. An open book would be illuminated, a necessary accompaniment to the reader's inspired conversation with the author. The same window connects one to students outside. The actual view through the carrel opening is not shown in the sketch, but the school buildings that would be seen are framed within an upper window. A relationship between people in the library and campus was addressed when Kahn spoke of regulating privacy; and then argued more forcefully that "[t]he carrel belongs to the world outside. Occasional distraction is as important as concentration."[22] A student therefore engages with the author of a book and people in the campus. The meaning of the window is keyed to these different but related conversations.

Kahn associated the reader's distraction from a book with belonging to a community, one that includes students in the Exeter Academy campus. This situation will be incorporated within my interpretation of agreement and decorum in the following section, which considers the interplay between architectural and urban rooms.

"The Street is a Room"

The individuals within a building have a place in Kahn's understanding of a civic-scaled space. While concern for human activities outside a building is not immediately apparent in *The Room*, where the two figures are united by their intersecting thoughts and conversation, the visitor to the City/2 exhibition recognizes that the human-scaled window of the interior could belong to a building in *The Street*. Such a link between internal and external contexts had been explored in Kahn's recent designs. The carrel of the Exeter Library, for example, is similar to *The Room*, because the feelings or actions of a person in each space are expressed in the configuration of the window, which imparts a human order to an architectural wall. With the library perspective related to *The Room* and *The Street*, the occupants of a building can be shown to enhance the decorum of urban settings.

Kahn's text on *The Street* comprises three key statements, which provide the structure for my analysis of decorum. The drawing's long title is addressed first, as it introduces the general notion that "The Street is a Room by Agreement." Traditional civic places in Italian towns and Philadelphia were studied, their decorum influencing his architectural designs. In exploring this, I will view the Exeter Library in conjunction with Kahn's comment that "from the street must have come the Meeting House." The concept of an urban space preceding the construction of a building for meeting is informed by the design of the library, where the internal thoroughfare or street, namely the brick reading area, is critical to the formation of the central communal hall. The reading area and its carrels are pertinent to *The Street*'s third distinctive comment, in which the walls of a building "belong to donors." By transposing the civic qualities represented in Kahn's urban street to the Exeter Library's campus, as well as the Salk Institute's court, we note how students in carrels and scientists in their studies contribute as donors to decorum.

At the City/2 exhibition, the agreement invoked in *The Street*'s full title was also endorsed by *The City*'s text. The latter, which is set out below the sketch of the walled town, focused on citizens whose "desire for new Agreement" stimulates a culture, while ensuring that "[t]he city from a simple settlement became the place of the assembled Institutions." Agreement underlies both the creation of a single institution and the manner in which it takes its place among others. Over time, a well-ordered town emerges, bounded and decorous.

By emphasizing the principle of agreement, *The City* and Kahn's other City/2 drawings contributed to a theoretical tradition, where a critique of utilitarian values is accompanied by a re-evaluation of urban decorum. A passionate protagonist for this was the nineteenth-century architect, A. W. N. Pugin. His second edition of *Contrasts; or a Parallel between the Noble Edifices of the Fourteenth Century and Fifteenth Century, and Similar Edifices of the Present Day* (1841) includes a well-known image, which combines two illustrations of the same city: one describes the form it took in the English Middle Ages; the other, its current deplorable condition, where the once decorous urban structure has disintegrated in the wake of an emerging industrial civilization.[23] In Pugin's medieval Catholic town, the walls are part of a closely-knit organization of streets, houses, parish churches and central cathedral. For him, this ensemble could only be recreated in the nineteenth century following a revival of the religious life that prevailed before the Reformation. Although later theorists, including Camillo Sitte and Kahn, did not endorse such a categorical rejection of the present in favor of a more religious age, they nonetheless drew inspiration from medieval towns, valued for their interconnected buildings and spaces.[24] Kahn's sympathy with the anti-utilitarian urban tradition can be discerned at the City/2 exhibition, most obviously in *The City*'s textual reference to agreement and the sketched medieval walls.

The buildings in this drawing, however, are too isolated from one another to illustrate the written account of agreement. The problem for Kahn is that a room does not appear as the basic spatial setting for urban dwellers. Bounded spaces of streets and squares, for instance, are occluded by *The City*'s walls. Nonetheless, the statement on the drawing about assembled institutions is relevant to *The Street*. The decorum of Pugin's drawing can be identified in Kahn's delimited civic space, clearly a "Room by Agreement."

With buildings articulating an urban precinct, Kahn's sketch referred to room-like streets and piazzas in Italy. He studied these during a trip in the late 1920s; and then in the winter of 1950–51, when based in Rome as a Fellow at the American Academy.[25]

The earlier journey included a visit to the town of Positano, where the rising and stepped streets were rendered by Kahn as thoroughly contained volumes.[26] He was also impressed by Assisi. In one sketch, the linked masses of the Duomo, campanile and lesser structures add to the spatial identity and decorum of Piazza San Rufino.[27] Another drawing of the town focused on several buildings, which frame a "T"-shaped urban volume. Architecture resists the expansion of space in a manner that was redeployed in *The Street*.[28]

Additional investigations of Italy's bounded civic spaces were carried out by Kahn in 1950. He sketched the renowned medieval squares of Venice, Florence and Siena, attending to unique architectural qualities as well as the underlying spatial type of a room.[29]

11
ouis Kahn,
rawing of Piazza
el Campo, No. 1,
iena, Italy, 1951
astel on paper,
ollection of Sue
nn Kahn)

Two pastel drawings of Siena's Piazza del Campo are extraordinary, as ideas of the poet Wallace Stevens and historian Frank Brown contributed to the rendering of animated built forms. These mould urban space (Figure 5.11).[30] Stevens' theory of the sun's energy and light residing within building materials influenced Kahn's use of yellows, oranges and reds, to capture the luminosity and human-like warmth of the piazza's sloping paved ground and curved or straight walls of buildings. The Siena sketches also ensure that façades along streets leading out from the piazza block one's view, so that the integrity of the overall delimited setting remains intact. A vessel is illustrated. The concave forms of buildings and the ground impart their life to space. By exploring the relationship between a container and shaped volume, Kahn's representation of Piazza del Campo conforms to his and Brown's concurrent studies of the palpable spaces in ancient buildings, such as the Scenic Triclinium.[31] Kahn seems to have discerned a similarity between the piazza's ground plane and the Scenic Triclinium's vault: the radiating segments of both help articulate and enliven space. Italy's medieval civic rooms and ancient interiors were brought together as sources for the Siena drawings; and subsequently remembered at the City/2 exhibition, where *The Room* has a Roman vault and *The Street* is defined by interconnected buildings.[32]

Kahn's defence of an urban room and agreement also drew on streets in Philadelphia, particularly those near his architectural office. While they include the block of Walnut Street in which he lived, the finest examples are to the south of Rittenhouse Square. These run east–west yet are not continuous as they jog slightly. Each block of Delancey Street, for example, is articulated by buildings on four sides to create an urban room. Such a setting has become wider in *The Street* and no longer contains cars. Kahn's sketch and companion one of *The City* can be related to Philadelphia, its urban form admired and studied in his civic-scaled designs.

Although motorcars do not appear in *The Street* and *The City*, both are connected to projects for the movement of traffic around and within Philadelphia. *The City* recalls Kahn's 1962 scheme for a viaduct structure, encircling the center of his city to carry vehicles.[33] He envisaged modern walls to enclose space, an approach that accords with medieval towns, including examples in Italy and Carcassonne, as well as the theory of architects like Pugin.[34] The viaduct scheme also builds on Kahn's Philadelphia traffic studies from late 1951 to mid-1953, where streets dedicated to different purposes are organized to create an urban order. Speeding traffic circumvents the city, while slower vehicles within this boundary use narrower roads. Linear movement is checked in these through intersecting streets and their traffic lights. Kahn valued the resulting spatial containment.[35] To follow his reasoning at the exhibition, *The City*'s walls can be linked to the viaduct structure, the latter surrounding an urban core that includes traditional streets near Rittenhouse Square. These became the precinct without cars of *The Street*. The drawing concluded Kahn's investigations from the early 1950s of Philadelphia's urban form, by arguing that a street is a civic room: it is a place for people to interact and reach an agreement.[36]

The buildings of *The Street* include a tall Gothic structure that resembles several nineteenth-century churches in Philadelphia, although it is intended to be a "Meeting House." This important edifice is drawn in an ambiguous manner. It can be seen to have an entrance court; an appropriate urban gesture and also a pleasant one, given the presence of a splendid billowing tree.[37] On the other hand, the narrow but decorous strip of space disappears, so that the building now fronts the street and takes possession of the tree as a poetic image within its interior. The foliage has a flame-like outline, to establish a connection with the fire in the hearth of *The Room*, which brings the two people together and inspires their conversation. While figures are not shown within the Gothic edifice, human agreement is symbolized by Kahn's tree that is also a fire.

In *The Street*, the Gothic building is accentuated by its more mundane neighbors; the one to the right being low and unadorned, the other having a degree of ornamentation, its entrance grand in scale, while windows are enriched by flat arches. By describing the urban street as a room by agreement, Kahn recognized that each building has an appropriate character. It speaks to others, thereby assuming an active role within the ensemble. In producing the urban whole, defined as a "community room," edifices also serve as models for citizens who learn by imitation to act well, that is, contribute to society. Buildings engender agreement by conversing with one another and members of the public. Illustrating an assembly of institutions that was only discussed in *The City*, the individual structures of *The Street* are linked according to the principle of decorum: they create an urban room and its sense of community. Good social action, which is viewed in terms of speech and agreement, has been clothed in built form.[38]

The decorum of a city is relevant to the interiors of a building. Drawing on the traditional analogy between speech and architecture, an urban precinct is defined by Kahn as a discussion among several buildings, each of which has a plan composed of interconnected rooms. They talk to one another. Such a formulation was enriched in his design work by the belief that a thoroughfare in the city is a room; while, conversely, an interior can have a street-like character.

An obvious connection between a city's street and building occurs when the latter has only a single large space, which is the case for Kahn's fourth exhibited drawing, a project showing how citizens in Philadelphia might celebrate the 1976 Bicentennial of the Declaration of Independence. His scheme, "The American Annonymous [sic] Building," was to occupy a site by the Delaware River, at the edge of Philadelphia's grid.[39] Without a client to present and defend specific requirements, the design was not subjected to the constraints and dialogue that produce his finest outcomes. Kahn's undistinguished project was intended to enclose a vast thoroughfare, the drawing's text referring to this as "a place of the inspired addenda coming from children and adults." The social life enjoyed in the external but bounded spaces of a city is to be sheltered within "an enclosed street several thousand feet long."

While the design contributed directly to the City/2 exhibition, the theme for both being Philadelphia's urban future, it also complemented Kahn's other displayed drawings. More reflective, they comment on his defence of bounded space. The scheme for the Bicentennial is a useful starting point for examining relationships between *The Room* and *The Street*, which were informed by the arrangement of spaces within the Exeter Library.

By viewing Kahn's City/2 drawings as a group, one notes how the interior of the Bicentennial project is organized around a longitudinal axis, while a vertical one is emphasized in *The Room*. These two distinct types of room are present in *The Street*, as is acknowledged in the drawing and its statement that "from the street must have come the Meeting House [,] also a place by agreement." The Meeting House is the Gothic building. Because the flame-like tree is related to the fire within *The Room*, the visitor to the exhibition assumes that people in the Meeting House will also face one another when interacting. The prominent symbolic elements in these two spaces suggest they belong to the same type. In his drawing, Kahn explained how this differs from the type relevant to the urban street, which is a thoroughfare and therefore associated with the long interior of the Bicentennial project. *The Street* also introduced the dimension of time: a thoroughfare is constructed first, then the Meeting House.

Due to an interweaving of urban and architectural themes, Kahn's City/2 drawings illuminate the role of a thoroughfare in a building with several volumes, rather than a single one. These talk to each other in forming a society of rooms. A space for circulation in such a scheme need not be just a corridor, but can expand to accord with communal activities, like those occurring in the public realm. The elevation in status of what otherwise would remain a servant space was addressed in the Gold Medal Acceptance Speech, where Kahn argued that a "lightless corridor . . . aspires to the hall overlooking the court-garden."[40] The hall is an internal thoroughfare yet comparable with a corridor's urban counterpart, a street. An architectural design with such a space would conform to the text on *The Street*, in which the urban thoroughfare is established prior to its Meeting House. A building's internal street, the hall, for instance, therefore accommodates the vital social life necessary for the subsequent formation of other meeting spaces, even one in a more important location and grander in size.

These notions from *The Street* and lecture were outlined when Kahn was overseeing the completion of the Exeter Library. He alluded to the way that the building's top-lit concrete interior and sketched Meeting House are related to their respective thoroughfares, namely the reading area and urban street. Kahn invoked the brick interior when speaking of a corridor's transformation into a hall overlooking its garden. Both the constructed and described spaces are generous in scale, suffused with daylight and connected to cultivated external surroundings. These qualities are appropriate for the reading area that, as Kahn's 1967 perspective shows, harbors activities as varied as those animating a city street. Students engage in conversations, like the one binding the individual in a carrel to the author of a book, which have a bearing on debate in the more public central volume. Such a connection between the brick and concrete spaces for human interaction was endorsed by Kahn, when writing on his didactic drawing about two places of agreement: a street and its Meeting House.

The ideal of agreement also had implications for his re-orientation of a cloister within the Exeter Library. He was well acquainted with the historical setting, having studied actual buildings, as well as books referring to monasteries, including Letarouilly's publication with the cloister at Santa Maria della Pace. Yet when a cloister walk was incorporated within the library, the reader in the carrel views the campus instead of a central space. The inward-facing traditional cloister walk was altered, so that one engages with students outside as well as inside the library. The scope for agreement was broadened.

This expanded field for interaction is implicit in Kahn's statement on *The Street*, where the urban precinct is defined as a "community room [,] the walls of which belong to the donors [,] its ceiling is the sky." The civic place has the vault of the firmament above rather than its representation, as occurs in *The Room* and Assembly Chamber at Dhaka. However, he was primarily concerned with an analogy between the human being and architectural walls. By definition, a donor acts with decorum, to enrich the lives of others. This person is obviously a client or patron, who finances the construction of a building that satisfies individual or familial needs, but also serves as a gift to the city.[41] Decorum in *The Street* is therefore a characteristic of a donor and the exterior of his or her building.

Kahn's emphasis on the walls of buildings delimiting urban space stimulates an additional interpretation of donors, which does not prioritize benevolent patrons but respects the contributions of all citizens to the culture of a city. These people maintain a civic tradition by interacting within an urban setting. *The Street*'s text alludes to such an unusual role for donors, by suggesting that the architectural walls belong to them in the manner of a surrounding protective garment. Kahn's shift in attention – from the owners of buildings to urban dwellers – conforms to his long-standing commitment to the ideal of an egalitarian society.[42]

In a further reassessment of traditional patronage, a donor is within a building's interior rather than the urban room outside. Addressing such a situation in the Gold Medal Acceptance Speech, Kahn spoke about the creation of a room's opening:

> The wall enclosed us for a long time until the man behind it, feeling a new freedom, wanted to look out. He hammered away to make an opening. The wall cried, "I have protected you." And the man said, "I appreciate your faithfulness but I feel time has brought change."

> The wall was sad; the man realized something good. He visualized the opening as gracefully arched, glorifying the wall. The wall was pleased with its arch and carefully made jamb. The opening became part of the order of the wall.[43]

The story is germane to *The Room*, where the emotions and gestures of the two figures are expressed in a window with deep jambs and sill, as well as an anthropomorphized outline. According to the lecture and sketch, the original and momentous act of cutting out an opening underlies the adornment and human order of a fully architectural wall. While this order is generated from within a building, it may be discerned from outside. Both viewpoints are considered in the City/2 exhibition, where the human character of the window in *The Room* is evident in the openings of *The Street*'s buildings. Doors and windows are essential to the making of an urban ensemble. The traditional classical body analogy was therefore endorsed by Kahn, with openings replacing columns as elements imparting human proportion, variety in unity, as well as decorum to the architecture of a street. For him, architectural and urban design strategies cannot be separated, as they refer to the same irreducible type of the human being within an internal room. The window facilitates a person's connection with citizens outside. This can be appreciated by consulting the 1971 lecture and *The Street*'s text, to see how the occupant of a room is a donor. Surrounded by well-composed doors and windows, he or she adds to the life within a civic precinct.

Kahn's statements about donors, personified architectural walls and the formation of a community drew on his designs for the Exeter Library's reading area and, before this, the Salk Institute's study towers.[44] The two buildings are dissimilar in obvious ways, yet a carrel of the library and study within the scientific Institute are both peripheral rooms, in which the occupant works quietly while remaining in contact with colleagues outside. These settings were enriched by historical cloisters and civic spaces, the latter's role in Kahn's two projects remarkable given their non-urban sites and, in the case of the Institute, design of a court that is virtually uninhabitable. Nonetheless, the openings of the Exeter Library and the Salk Institute's towers were configured as though they would address a traditional street.

The library's reading area can be viewed as an internal street that runs beside an imagined urban one. With the text on *The Street* in mind, these two spaces are brought together through donors and their life-like walls. An individual may pass through the library's several rooms, to read in a carrel and become a donor by interacting with people outside. A student in the campus appreciates the reading area's tapered brick piers and flat arches, along with the timber carrels and windows, as frames around the readers.[45] Kahn's account of donors in *The Street* therefore conforms to his transformation of a cloister walk, so that the occupants of carrels in the library's reading area are seated at the outer edge of the building. The walls of the library embrace and consequently belong to readers, who have a place as donors in a broad community.[46]

With the commission in 1959 for the Salk Institute, Kahn and his client, Jonas Salk, discussed the relevance of a traditional cloister to their project (Figures 5.12–5.15). Salk admired the example in the convent of St Francis at Assisi. Kahn knew the building, having sketched it in 1929.[47] He subsequently demonstrated knowledge of the activities accommodated within the historical type: not long before meeting Salk, his unsuccessful competition entry of 1956 for the Washington University Library prompted the writing of a candid essay, in which its flaws were addressed through comparison with a medieval cloister walk. A monk in this moves to an intimate place beside the court, where he can sit and read.[48] The cloister walk contributed to the reading area of the Exeter Library and study towers flanking the Salk Institute's court.

Unlike the central space of a cloister, however, only the long sides of the Institute's court have bounding forms, which are four-storeyed study towers. These stand in front of laboratories. The historical source can be identified at the level of the court, where the concrete structure of the towers delineates units of shaded space, aligned to create a human-scaled thoroughfare, a colonnade. This horizontal composition co-exists with the rise of a tower, which has an open room at the first and third levels, the latter consequently a loggia. Slate blackboards are attached to

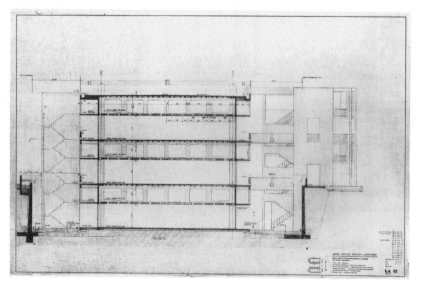

5.12
Louis Kahn, Salk Institute for Biological Studies, cross-section through laboratory, 1963 (Louis Kahn Collection, University of Pennsylvania and Pennsylvania Historical and Museum Commission, 540 O.D.I.A. 12.)

13
uis Kahn, Salk
stitute for
ological Studies,
ew of approach
the court
hoto: Peter
phane)

14
ouis Kahn,
alk Institute for
iological Studies,
iew across the
ourt (Photo: Peter
ohane)

its walls, so researchers can illustrate ideas as well as discuss them.[49] An individual also occupies a study; a pair of these spaces comprise a tower's second and fourth levels.[50] Thus, the court is defined on two sides by series of towers, within which a person can either meet colleagues in an open room or benefit from the relative isolation of a study. Kahn's understanding of one's arrival in the private space was founded on the historical situation, in which a monk walks to a seat beside the central court of his cloister.

5.15
**Louis Kahn, Salk
Institute for
Biological Studies,
view through a
window in a study
(Photo: Peter
Kohane)**

For Salk and Kahn, scientific work is not confined to an efficient, open-planned laboratory where on-going experiments are carried out. A researcher in the Institute can walk between this space and the smaller ones of the study towers.[51] From a laboratory, a short bridge leads to an open room of a tower. Alternatively, one walks up or down a flight of stairs to enter a study.

In Salk's estimation, a scientist who is alone in a quiet study has an opportunity to formulate new insights.[52] These are essential to science; perhaps even more so than the experiments completed in the laboratory, where the individual is absorbed within a group of researchers. Kahn distinguished between the settings for the two activities. While the space of a laboratory is expansive and flexible, its modernity reinforced by sleek stainless steel tables and equipment, the study is an intimate teak room that nestles into the concrete structure of a tower. It has a warm ambience, enhanced by furnishings such as rugs.[53] Salk's views on an individual's thoughts and inspiration influenced Kahn's design for the study, as well as similar but later spaces, like the carrel in the Exeter Library. This building was nearing completion when he made the City/2 drawings. *The Room* acknowledged his debt to Salk, through the statement that an intimate interior is a "place of the mind."

A study in the institute was created for a person whose thoughts are stimulated by external surroundings, which are framed by two large windows. The design was implicated in a discussion from 1964, where Kahn addressed the topic of a room's original opening by emphasizing the occupant's desire to "see wonderful things."[54] When sitting near the window within the triangular bay of a Salk Institute study, the scientist may look into the court below and beyond to the Pacific Ocean.[55] Nature inspires ideas, as does the sense of belonging to a society of researchers. The additional window is therefore equally significant, as it opens directly onto the towers on the opposite side of the court, bringing one into contact with people in the colonnaded spaces, loggias and other studies.

The exterior of a tower has a distinctive character, which can be traced to Kahn's regard for the scientist within a study, particularly the role that he or she has in generating the windows. Like this individual's eyes, each architectural opening looks into the world. A window directs vision from within and, when seen by a person outside, adds to the expressive physiognomy of a tower.

When approaching the Salk Institute from the main road, however, the animated forms of the towers are not visible. They will be revealed in stages. Walking through a grove of trees in front of the raised court, one sees the severe backs of the towers, a formal gesture that would be indecorous had the succession of their diagonal wall planes not dramatically framed the ocean (Figure 5.13). By proceeding, this person arrives at the court and walks in one of its colonnades. The hitherto concealed studies and open rooms of the towers on the opposite side of the central space come into view. Reaching the end of the platform, the scientist can pause and look back, to fully appreciate the human-like presence of the towers. They seem to step out in front of the laboratories and turn towards the water. For Kahn, the beholder empathizes with the stocky concrete structure and is impressed by the vital order of the fenestrated studies.

One discerns subtle differences in the windows of a tower. The concrete frame articulates the open rooms, and holds aloft the studies, each containing the two principal windows and three narrow ones. These openings are repeated, with variations keyed to Kahn's design of four unique spaces. From the end of the court one sees how a diagonal concrete wall shapes an interior, so that the occupant may look through the window facing the water. The scientists in the fourth level studies are privileged, due to their rooms and windows being taller than those below. Another distinction applies to the two adjacent studies on a single floor, which respond to the site with particular plans: the room to the west has a better view; yet the person in the other one is not disadvantaged, as the angled wall extends outwards, adding to the width of the window. Complementing the interplay between the openings to the ocean, both studies on a single level have the important window overlooking the court, but its location in the timber wall shifts. Thus, the eight large windows of the four studies are distinguished by slight changes of proportion or position. The arrangement is enriched through a rhythm generated by vertical slot openings. While such animation invested in different but repeated windows has a musical quality, it is founded on the individual scientists and their role in a community. Because each large window of a study is related to the eyes of the occupants, a tower's exterior has an array of openings characterized by variety in unity, like that underlying the composition of the human face.[56] The analogy, which is not literal but abstract, enhances the beholder's perception of a human character in built forms. A tower has a striking anthropomorphism, as the powerful structural frame supports studies with physiognomic windows.

Although flanked on two sides by towers, whose studies and open rooms were shaped around their occupants, the Salk Institute's travertine court was not built as a place for people to meet. Kahn removed shade-giving poplar trees from the initial design schemes, so that the platform would primarily reveal the brilliance of the Southern Californian sunlight.[57] He seized the opportunity for dedicating the court to the purity of light, in a manner that recalled Wallace Stevens' esoteric writings. The poet had influenced Kahn's travel sketches from 1950–51, where light is a source of life within several monuments. An illustration of the Temple of Apollo in Corinth, for instance, has columns that are solid yet also made of light.[58] A similar transformation of matter is represented at the urban scale of Siena's Piazza del Campo, its paved ground and buildings filled with the energy of the sun. Thus, while Stevens is esteemed as a "Great American Poet" in *The Room*'s text, his ideas were relevant to external settings, whether a sketch of the famous Italian piazza or design for the court at the Salk Institute. In specific terms, the poet's striking images, such as "The sun is seeking something bright to shine on," contributed to Kahn's discussion with Luis Barragan in 1966, when they stood on the site of the unbuilt court and agreed that it should become "a façade to the sky."[59] Kahn conjured a sense of the sublime: as constructed, the platform's canal of water draws attention to the ocean's endless movement and calming effect of the horizon, while the paved travertine surface responds in an unmediated way to the blinding intensity of the sun's light.

Yet the inhospitable court is defined by towers containing the shaded thoroughfare on the first level, along with the loggias and studies above. As a result, the towers have human-scaled openings that, like those of buildings fronting the traditional urban room of a street, belong to donors. A cultural space is fashioned at the Salk Institute, where individuals in the open rooms and studies of the towers can both see and be seen by their fellow researchers.[60] When leaving a laboratory, scientists may participate in another kind of community, one that welcomes their contribution as donors to conversations nourishing the institution.

Kahn recalled his designs for the Salk Institute and Exeter Library at the City/2 exhibition, where the two most important didactic drawings highlight the art of speaking well. The figures in *The Room* sit and talk beside the window; while *The Street* suggests that people in a building can engage with citizens outside, thereby assuming the role of donors. These sketches acknowledge the influence of decorum on his architectural work.

Bringing People Together: The Arts of Oratory and Architecture

The word decorum does not appear in the texts on Kahn's City/2 drawings, as he would likely associate it with a restrictive code of conduct, one that is imposed on individuals. Viewed in such a manner, decorum is incompatible with his statements about an institution and its inspired beginnings. Agreement is emphasized instead.

Yet this is attained in *The Room* because the two figures speak and listen, tempering their behavior, acting decorously. The human situation is relevant to *The Street*, where Kahn implicated the civic-minded gestures of donors in the making of an ordered and decorous urban space. Buildings converse with one another and the public at large. In addition, *The Street* is enriched by the architecture and spaces of Italian towns and Philadelphia; and thereby conforms to his mature design projects, which also engage with exemplary past works. In this kind of architectural conversation, communication with citizens is effective because it occurs within a shared and illustrious tradition. A decorous building takes its place among others in urban and historical contexts. Voicing ideas that are comprehended by the beholder, architecture performs the ethical task of building the social body.

Kahn's City/2 drawings add to a tradition in architectural theory, which includes Pugin's cultural critique of industrial civilization, but has its source in ancient writings about temperance, decorum and oratory. According to authors like Cicero, an orator will take into consideration the topic of a speech and interests of his audience.[61] Reflecting on a wide range of human experiences, he determines the content of the talk and its appropriate language, while also introducing commonly understood historical tropes. Decorum is a characteristic of the speaker and speech, as well as the response of the individual listeners. These people are not passive, as the orator interacts with them, animating their own discussions that lead to an agreement.

Renaissance and later classical theorists studied treatises on oratory in conjunction with Vitruvius' *Ten Books on Architecture*, to argue that a building must be well proportioned and act in a decorous manner.[62] The ancient architect's six fundamental design principles include proportion and symmetry, both closely related to the concept of agreement, discussed by Kahn in the City/2 drawings and the Gold Medal Acceptance Speech. He was aware that proportion, symmetry and agreement all refer to a compositional ideal, in which parts are connected to each other and the whole. This is an attribute of the human being and buildings. Kahn's account of a conversation involving a meeting of vectors or sense of commonality, however, reveals a subtle but significant theoretical shift, where the appropriate term is not agreement but decorum. This is another one of Vitruvius' principles. Like agreement, decorum is a human and architectural characteristic; but it is particularly concerned with action, like an orator's speech or the ensuing conversation among his listeners.

The distinction between agreement and the more active decorum adds to our appreciation of *The Room* and *The Street*. Agreement in both sketches informs the fitting together of architectural parts, to make a well-composed domestic or urban room. According to Kahn, these built forms speak to the people they surround. Decorum underlies such a conception of rooms, which provide the setting for conversations and generate them as well. *The Street* therefore represents interrelated buildings, while the text explains that their walls belong to donors. Like an orator, a donor exercises temperance and decorum when interacting with an audience. Because donors and their personified buildings promote discussions among people, the urban space is valued as a community room.

Unfortunately, Kahn's theory is not fully developed in *The Street*, which convincingly illustrates the interaction among buildings but not citizens. Nonetheless, the visitor to the City/2 exhibition can study *The Street* and *The Room* together, noting how the latter draws attention to the decisive connection between architecture and people.

Decorum is respected because the power of speech, invested in *The Street*'s individual buildings, is distilled in *The Room*'s window, vault and structural frame. The profile of the window explicitly addresses the two discussants, who respond by facing one another. The niche-like segment of the vault directly above the opening also embraces the figures, as does the frame of ribs and the column. While the different forms work together in making the overall interior, the logic for the composition is not structural. Even the ideal of agreement cannot fully explain the drawing. With the formal elements impacting upon the two discussants, Kahn stressed that the art of oratory and principle of decorum are relevant to the formation of a room.

Like a traditional architect influenced by an orator, he recalled the past to establish a foundation for communication with an audience. Historical and present contexts were mediated in the design of rooms, which harbor memories capable of uniting people. With this conciliatory approach, decorum counters the dogmatism that Kahn could identify in the architecture of the International Style, where history is rejected; and, on the other hand, early twentieth-century Gothic and classical revival buildings, in which the imitation of the past was too explicit. At the Philadelphia Museum of Art exhibition, *The City*'s text endorsed the innovation of the modernists, Kahn noting how new modes of agreement ensure the viability of an institution. The unique problems of the changing present, however, prompt an inquiry into earlier activities and spaces. Conversations occur across time. Historical achievements are constantly re-evaluated, often critically, to invigorate an institution. When alluding to this in *The Room*, one of its inspired discussants says something that had not been said before; while the medieval structure refers to spaces like a monastery's chapter house, along with the conversations among its occupants. Another dimension to the argument about history can be discerned in the perspective sketch of the Exeter Library's reading area. The ritual and agreement were conceived with reference to current students, as well as monks in a traditional cloister walk. The new and old spaces are not the same, as Kahn's re-use of the cloister responded to prevailing concerns about an individual's place in a modern democratic society. The dynamic relationship between contemporary and historical situations is a facet of, rather than antithetical to, the principle of decorum.

In this chapter, Kahn's three finest buildings reveal his respect for decorum. It began with the Kimbell Museum, focusing on a vaulted room-like gallery within the overall interior. The principle of decorum informs the profile of the vault, which was calibrated to heighten a discussion between the visitor and a human presence within a painting. The Salk Institute also accords with the theme of conversation. The building was considered last, as Kahn built up the design around the external court. Scientists in the studies and open rooms of the towers face one another across the open space, their interaction adding to social cohesion and decorum. The studies set into their concrete structure were re-configured as the carrels of the Exeter Library, these small timber rooms once more linking the individual occupants to a community. The library was the central example, because the carrels are connected to external and internal spaces. Located at the very edge of the building, a carrel contains a window to the campus, yet is within a room-like bay of the brick reading area and related to its grand public counterpart, the top-lit concrete space. Decorum underpins an ensemble of rooms. These speak to each other in a way that is appropriate for a library, given that one learns by conversing with an author and fellow students.

Our appreciation of topophilia is enriched by analysis of these projects, along with Kahn's City/2 drawings and Gold Medal Acceptance Speech. For him, a building is admired because its rooms harbor their occupants and, more importantly, bring them together. This is defined in terms of a conversation, where the participants act decorously to reach an agreement.

Acknowledgments

Research for this essay was funded by an Australia Research Council Discovery Grant. I would like to thank Michael Hill and Steven Fleming for their assistance.

Notes

1 This comment was included in the text on Kahn's 1971 drawing entitled *The Room*.

2 The exhibition has not been considered in scholarship on Kahn. It is noted by Mark Vincent, "Bicentennial Exposition," in David B. Brownlee and David G. De Long (eds), *Louis I. Kahn: In the Realm of Architecture*, New York: Rizzoli, 1991, p. 414. The lecture was delivered in 1971, when the exhibition was still open. It was published as Louis I. Kahn, "The Room, the Street and Human Agreement. A.I.A. Gold Medal Acceptance Speech, Detroit, June 24, 1971," in *A. I. A. Journal* 56(3), September 1971, 33–34. The text is re-published in Louis I. Kahn, *Louis I. Kahn: Writings, Lectures, Interviews*, intro. and ed. by Alessandra Latour, New York: Rizzoli, 1991, pp. 263–269.

3 See Kahn, *Writings*, p. 264.

4 Ibid. Kahn had explored related ideas in his significant essay, "Form and Design," which he presented at the 1959 CIAM Conference and published during the early 1960s in various books and journals. His text notes that "A teacher or a student is not the same when he is with a few in an intimate room with a fireplace as in a large high room with many others." Ibid., p. 114.

5 Ibid., p. 264.

6 Ibid., p. 266.

7 Quoted in Sarah Williams Goldhagen, *Louis Kahn's Situated Modernism*, New Haven, CT: Yale University Press, 2001, p. 168. The source is Kahn's first draft of statements for the publication of his drawings for the Capital Complex, "North Carolina," Box 56, Kahn Collection.

8 Quoted in Goldhagen, *Kahn's Situated Modernism*, p. 168.

9   Kahn, *Writings*, p. 264.

10 For Kahn and many artists of his generation, a person can perceive a life within the forms and colors of an abstract painting. These constitute its spiritual aura.

11 Kahn, *Writings*, p. 264.

12 The dimensions of the vault changed during the design process. In the 1967 scheme, it is 20 feet wide and 150 feet long. The constructed version is 23 × 100 feet. See Patricia Loud, "Kimbell Art Museum," in Brownlee and De Long, *Louis I. Kahn*, pp. 397–398.

13 Kahn, *Writings*, p. 265.

14 Kahn's comment derives from a lecture titled "I Love Beginnings," which he presented in 1972 at the International Design Conference in Aspen, Colorado. See ibid., p. 291.

15 Kahn's library drawing endorsed traditional ideas regarding an elevated mood in art, established through historical allusion, as well as human actions that can be construed in terms of a conversation. On this topic, see Leon Battista Alberti, *On Painting* (1435), trans. by Cecil Grayson, intro. by Martin Kemp, Harmondsworth: Penguin, 1991, 2.40, pp. 75–76.

16 Letarouilly's drawing is discussed in Peter Kohane, "Louis I. Kahn and the Library: Genesis and Expression of 'Form'," *Via* 10, 1990, 114–115.

17 Quoted in Richard Saul Wurman and Eugene Feldman, *The Notebooks and Drawings of Louis I. Kahn*, Cambridge, MA: MIT Press, 1962, p. 179.

18 See Louis I. Kahn, "Spaces, Order and Architecture," *The Royal Architectural Institute of Canada Journal* 34(10) October 1957, 375–377. Reprinted in Kahn, *Writings*, p. 76.

19 See Louis I. Kahn, "Room, Window and Sun," *Canadian Architect* 18, June 1973, 53. The court is discussed in Kohane, "Louis I. Kahn and the Library," p. 109.

20 Kahn's account of books as the ornament for the central space was based on Etienne-Louis Boullée's drawing of the interior for the proposed New Hall of Exposition of the National Library, ca. 1788. See Kohane, "Louis Kahn and the Library," pp. 111–112.

21 See Wurman and Feldman, *The Notebooks*, p. 179.

22 Louis Kahn, quoted in William Jordy, "Criticism," *Architectural Review* 155, June 1974, 333–334.

23 For a discussion of Pugin and his context, see Françoise Choay, *The Modern City; Planning in the 19th Century*, trans. by Marguerite Hugo and George R. Collins, New York: G. Braziller, 1970, pp. 102–108; and Pheobe Stanton, "The Sources of Pugin's *Contrasts*," in John Summerson (ed.), *Concerning Architecture: Essays on Architectural Writers and Writing Presented to Nikolaus Pevsner*, London: Allen Lane, 1968, pp. 120–139.

24 For Sitte, see George R. Collins and Christiane C. Collins, *Camillo Sitte: The Birth of Modern Planning, with a Translation of City Planning According to Artistic Principles*, New York: Rizzoli, 1986. The Austrian edition of Sitte's book, *City Planning According to Artistic Principles*, was published in 1889.

25 For the earlier journey, which took place in 1928 and 1929, see Jan Hochstim, *The Paintings and Sketches of Louis I. Kahn*, New York: Rizzoli, 1991, pp. 49–112; and Eugene J. Johnson and Michael J. Lewis, *Drawn from the Source: The Travel Sketches of Louis I. Kahn*, Cambridge, MA: MIT Press, 1996, pp. 34–66.

26 Hochstim, *The Paintings and Sketches of Louis Kahn*, p. 76, figs 56, 57; and Johnson and Lewis, *Drawn from the Source*, p. 59, figs 49, 50.

27 Hochstim, *The Paintings and Sketches of Louis Kahn*, p. 85, fig. 69; and Johnson and Lewis, *Drawn from the Source*, p. 44, fig. 28.

28 Hochstim, *The Paintings and Sketches of Louis Kahn*, p. 84, fig. 68.

29 Ibid., pp. 240, 248–251 and pp. 252–255, figs 338, 339, 341–346, 349–352.

30 Ibid., p. 240, figs 338, 339. The influence of Stevens on Kahn's work is noted in Daniel Friedman, "The Sun on Trial: Kahn's Gnostic Garden at Salk," PhD dissertation, University of Pennsylvania, 1999, p. 77.

31 For Kahn and Frank Brown, see Vincent Scully, "Louis I. Kahn and the Ruins of Rome," in his

Modern Architecture and Other Essays, Princeton, NJ: Princeton University Press, 2003, pp. 310–312.

32 Kahn and several of his contemporaries in Philadelphia valued medieval urban spaces. For instance, Edmund Bacon emphasized the definition of space in the piazzas of Italian cities. Examples within Todi and Venice were discussed in the section entitled "The Structure of the Square" from his *Design of Cities*, London: Thames and Hudson, 1976 (first pub. 1967), pp. 95–99. Both Bacon and the Dean of the Graduate School of the Fine Arts, G. Holmes Perkins, introduced their students at the University of Pennsylvania to exemplary historical settings, in which space is contained. For Bacon's ideas and Perkins's role as Dean, see Ann Louise Strong and George Thomas, *The Book of the School: One Hundred Years*, Philadelphia: Graduate School of the Fine Arts, 1990, pp. 126–149.

33 The nature of viaduct architecture was explored by Kahn between 1959 and 1962. See Peter Reed, "Philadelphia Urban Design," in Brownlee and De Long, *Louis I. Kahn*, pp. 310–311.

34 Kahn wrote about Carcassonne's walls in his 1953 essay, "Towards a Plan for Midtown Philadelphia," *Perspecta* 2, 1953, 23. He visited the town in 1959.

35 For such ideas about traffic, see ibid. His schemes are discussed and illustrated in Brownlee and De Long, *Louis I. Kahn*, p. 65 and figs 64, 65. See also Reed, "Philadelphia Urban Design," pp. 304–308.

36 The Philadelphia Museum of Art was an ideal venue for Kahn to reconsider agreement, decorum and the nature of a room, as his ideas on these were shaped by the buildings of Philadelphia. For instance, one of the city's finest interiors, the choir-like reading room within the University of Pennsylvania Library, contributed to *The Room*'s exploration of human action and delimited space.

37 Kahn may have referred to nineteenth-century buildings in Philadelphia, including John Notman's Saint Mark's Church (1847–51). Located on Locust Street, near Kahn's office, this building has a grass area between the footpath and the exterior of the nave. For the building, see Edward Teitelman and Richard W. Longstreth, *Architecture in Philadelphia: A Guide*, Cambridge, MA: MIT Press, 1981, p. 92.

38 For a discussion of decorum in architectural theory, see Peter Kohane and Michael Hill, "The Eclipse of a Commonplace Idea: Decorum in Architectural Theory," *Architectural Research Quarterly* 5(1), 2001, 63–77.

39 See Mark Vincent, "Bicentennial Exposition," in Brownlee and De Long, *Louis I. Kahn*, pp. 414–417.

40 Kahn, *Writings,* p. 265.

41 On one of his sketches for the Mellon Center for British Art, Kahn added his title of the "Palazzo Melloni." He associated his client Paul Mellon with Italian Renaissance patrons, who recognized the ethical foundations for the building of their palaces. Kahn's sketch is published in Brownlee and De Long, *Louis I. Kahn*, p. 134, fig. 229.

42 For a discussion of Kahn's interests in a modern community, see Goldhagen, *Kahn's Situated Modernism*, pp. 11–40.

43 Kahn, *Writings*, p. 267. Kahn attributed feelings to windows in earlier lectures and discussions. In a talk with students at Rice University from 1964, he explained how

> The wall did well for man./ In its thickness and its strength/ it protected him against destruction./ But soon, the will to look out/ made the man make a hole in the wall,/ and the wall was very pained, and said, "*What are you doing to me?*"/ And the man said, "*But I will look out!/ I see wonderful things,/ And I want to look out.*"/ And the wall was very sad. Later, man didn't just hack a hole through the wall,/ but made a discerning opening, one trimmed with fine stone,/ and he put a lintel over the opening./ And, soon the wall felt pretty well.

See Kahn, "Talks with Students," in *Writings*, p. 157. Kahn contributed to a twentieth-century debate about the appropriate form of a window. This is considered with reference to the work of

Le Corbusier in Bruno Reichlin, "Stories of Windows," in Vittorio Magnago Lampugnani (ed.), *The Architecture of the Window*, Tokyo: YKK Architecture Products, 1995.

44 The building was completed in 1965, the year that Kahn obtained the commission for the library. I am indebted to Maryam Gusheh's comments on the connection between the Salk Institute and the Exeter Library.

45 The response to the exterior is further enriched by the manner in which the building's corners are cut away. The viewer is able to gauge the depth of the reading area, sensing the life within the brick and timber room-like spaces.

46 Because students and their internal spaces contribute to the articulation of an architectural exterior, Kahn offered an alternative to the emerging interest in the façade as a thin surface with attached symbols. He was aware of Robert Venturi's pioneering views on this design topic, which were explored in the 1960s and published in book form with *Complexity and Contradiction in Architecture*, New York: The Museum of Modern Art, 1966.

47 See Daniel Friedman, "Salk Institute for Biological Studies," in Brownlee and De Long, *Louis I. Kahn*, pp. 330–331.

48 See Kohane, "Louis Kahn and the Library," 104–105.

49 These informal meeting places are considered by Friedman, in Brownlee and De Long, *Louis I. Kahn*, p. 333.

50 The two towers at the entrance end of the court are different, as their width is determined by a single study, rather than a pair of them.

51 This formulation involves a critique of the Alfred Newton Richards Medical Research Building (Philadelphia, 1957–65) on the grounds that the primary determinant of its design was the laboratory. Salk viewed the building when he visited Philadelphia in 1959 and discussed his own project with Kahn. See Friedman, "The Sun on Trial: Kahn's Gnostic Garden at Salk," p. 233.

52 The importance for Salk of isolating a study is noted by Friedman in Brownlee and De Long, *Louis I. Kahn*, p. 333.

53 A distinction was created between the stainless steel realm of the laboratories and the "oak and rug" character of the studies. See Friedman, in Brownlee and De Long, *Louis I. Kahn*, p. 333.

54 This statement from the talk is in the quote included above, in fn. 43.

55 Some studies have ocean-facing windows that do not offer a view of the court. These are in the two towers closest to the water.

56 In classical architectural theory it was common to liken the door to the mouth and the windows to eyes: for example, see Vincenzo Scamozzi, *L'idea dell'architettura universale*, Venice, 1615, part 1, book 3, pp. 318–319.

57 The decision to remove the trees from the court was influenced by Luis Barragan's visit to the site in 1966. This is discussed by Friedman, in Brownlee and De Long, *Louis I. Kahn*, pp. 333–334. Trees were included in several representations of the project, including a 1962 model and sketch from December 1965. See Brownlee and De Long, *Louis I. Kahn*, p. 98, fig. 158; and p. 99, fig. 160.

58 The drawing is illustrated in Hochstim, *The Paintings and Sketches of Louis Kahn*, p. 280, pl. 382.

59 The poem is called "Like Decorations in a Nigger Cemetery." It was published in *Ideas of Order*, 1937. See Wallace Stevens, *The Collected Poems of Wallace Stevens*, London: Faber and Faber, 1955, p. 157. The 1966 meeting with Barragan was recalled by Kahn in a text that he published in 1968. See Louis I. Kahn, "Silence," *Via* 1, 1968, 89; quoted in Brownlee and De Long, *Louis I. Kahn*, p. 100. Also see Friedman, in Brownlee and De Long, *Louis I. Kahn*, p. 334.

60 In early designs for the study towers, Kahn emphasized the interaction across the court by sketching human figures within the study towers. For an important sketch in this regard, see Heinz Ronner and Sharad Jhaveri (eds), *Louis I. Kahn: Complete Work, 1935–1974*, 2nd edn, Basel and Boston: Birkhaüser, 1987, p. 140, fig. SRI, 51.

61 Cicero defined decorum as a characteristic of temperance, which is one of the four moral principles,

the others being wisdom, justice and fortitude. See his *De Officiis* (55 BC), 1.28.100. He applied decorum to a theory of oratory in *Orator*, pp. 21–29 and *De Oratore*, Book 3.

62   Decorum was one of Vitruvius' six principles. However, as his comments were brief, theorists from the Renaissance looked to ancient texts on oratory for guidance. The principle of decorum became central to the classical tradition. See Kohane and Hill, "The Eclipse of a Commonplace Idea."

The Character of a Building

Paul Cret's Human Analogy, Louis Kahn and Yang Tingbao

Xing Ruan

Human Character

In 1962, a young Chinese architect went on a pilgrimage to the office of the famed Louis Kahn in Philadelphia. Instead of preaching to the young man, Kahn was apparently very curious to find out the well-being of his Chinese classmate T. P. Yang (the name Yang Tingbao was known by in the West) at the University of Pennsylvania (hereafter abbreviated as Penn), whom Kahn allegedly called "a genius architect" in front of the young admirer. Surprised, and perhaps a little bewildered by Kahn's interest in Yang, the Chinese architect told Kahn that he had in fact been taught by Yang in China.[1]

Although still little known to the world outside China, Yang is regarded as one of the most instrumental architects in twentieth-century China and a guru in architectural education. In 1983, a monograph of Yang's architectural works and projects was published by the China Architecture and Building Press, the first of such publication on an individual architect in the history of China.[2] Yang, unfortunately, did not see his own monograph; he died just a few days before it was printed. But like Kahn, Yang lived long enough to witness the recognition of his achievements as an architect, at least within China. Endless books and articles have been published on Kahn in the West, and an increasing number of publications on Yang in China after his death. Neither Kahn nor Yang, though, would have contemplated any scholarly scrutiny of their works on a par many years after their deaths.[3]

From 1921 to 1925 Yang studied architecture at Penn and gained a Bachelor of Architecture and a Master of Architecture. Kahn, who happened to be born in 1901,[4] the same year as Yang, also started his architectural education at Penn in 1921, but only completed his Bachelor of Architecture in 1924 without pursuing the Master of Architecture. They both studied under John Harbeson in their junior years, and under Paul Philippe Cret in their senior years of architectural design studio. Harbeson was then a respectable assistant professor, who, in 1927, published *The Study of Architectural Design*, a guide book on the Beaux-Arts teaching and learning of architectural design, which became influential and widely used around the world.[5] Cret, who was recruited to Penn in 1903 as a young and distinguished Ecole des Beaux-Arts graduate, had already established himself as an authority of Beaux-Arts teaching in America during the 1920s.

Yang was a star pupil and a protégé of both Harbeson and Cret.[6] In Harbeson's *The Study of Architectural Design*, two of Yang's student projects, to which I will return later, were included as exemplary works. Yang's achievement as a student is also evidenced in a story published in a Philadelphia newspaper, *The Evening Bulletin*, on 2 September 1925. The newspaper clip of this story is still kept in the Penn archive. The article, entitled "Chinese Student Gets High Honor," quoted the architectural Dean Warren Laird: "Yang is one of the most brilliant students there . . . He has won more individual prizes for his drawings than any other student in many years."[7] Although evidently not as shining a student as Yang, Kahn, contrary to his frequent assertion that he was a very poor student and naturally bashful, in fact did well and even won some design medals and mentions under Cret.[8] At Yang's graduation ceremony in 1925, Cret asked Yang to stay and work for him. Yang happily accepted the offer but only spent a year in his Philadelphia office. En route to China, Yang briefly completed the expected "Grand Tour" for a young architect throughout Europe.

Between 1944 and 1945, Yang visited Kahn's office in Philadelphia. This was Yang's second, and also his last, visit to the United States. In his various recorded memoirs, Yang only made a light mention of his visit to Kahn's office,[9] but recalled in some detail a meeting with Frank Lloyd Wright and his stay at Taliesin, Spring Green, in Wisconsin.[10] But Kahn must have remembered Yang and his jovial character. In the same news story in *The Evening Bulletin*, Yang was described as "by no means a 'grind'," and "his joviality and his readiness to help underclassmen with their work have made him popular on the campus. His attainments have not turned his head in the least."[11] In an anecdotal manner, Yang, in his final years in China, recalled Kahn as a talented young pianist who diligently juggled his architectural studies with playing piano for silent movies. In retrospect, it was not coincidental that Yang did not speak much about Kahn's architecture.[12]

In the 1924 Penn yearbook, we see the usual pose of graduating young architects. Kahn, looking serious and a little clumsily bashful (in his own words), seemed to have a mission ahead of him, whilst Yang, in the same photo, posed with his typical cheerful smile, as if nothing would come unexpected in his future career (Figure 6.1).[13] This chapter, starting with a speculative portrait of the two architects, will trace an analogy between that of human character and that of a building's "character" back to Cret's Beaux-Arts teaching.

6.1
Graduation photo in the 1924 Penn yearbook. Louis Kahn (second back row, third from the left), Yang Tingbao (second back row, third from the right) (The University of Pennsylvania Yearbook, 1924)

None of the characters, therefore, is about a magnified alter ego of the architect represented via their buildings.[14] To paraphrase the theme of the book, this chapter is an attempt to reconcile *topophilia* and *topophobia*, which, in Kahn's case, is between the individual and the larger world (in a cosmic sense that is beyond historical and cultural bounds); and in Yang's case, between the building and its inhabitants. One important form of topophilia lies in familiarity and attachment, which may range from a pair of old slippers, clothing, to a home, or a neighbourhood.[15] A building, like clothing, is the second skin for the occupier that not only sheathes the body, but also may help to give an identity to the occupier, often when there is a match between the character of the inhabitant, or the nature of inhabitation, and that of the building. Though this is the legacy of French Beaux-Arts teaching, and seems self-evident, too often the character of a building is desired in vain in modern times, for the separation of inhabitants and the making of a building is the hallmark of modern production. When "clothing" is stripped away, the threat to one's identity and to his or her position in the world poses not familiarity and attachment, but a lost sense of security. *Topos* thus becomes the larger world beyond the warmth of familiar places; it may be a threat to some but appealing to others. Tuan's important reminder that place is security, space is freedom is the starting point, but it is the second half of his reminder – we are attached to the one and long for the other[16] – that begs the question of the interchangeable paradox of topophilia and topophobia, which is brought to a head through a comparison of Kahn and Yang's architecture. Topophobia as a threat to one's sense of place is a necessary condition for topophilia, which is the very meaning of a building that must provide protection as well as a state of mental stability against the changing outside world.[17] Architecture, if we return to the "beginnings" as Kahn would have requested, is an enclosure to address our topophilia. But Kahn must have also declared: topophilia is only the need! "Need is so many bananas. Need is a ham sandwich," which Kahn actually said in a public lecture.[18]

The story in this chapter tells of the struggles of two architects: while one made architecture a "hearth," the other extended the limit of architecture to that of the "cosmos."[19] The essential task of Kahn and Yang, however, was to position the human figure in the center of an architectural enclosure, which transcends the opposition between topophilia and topophobia. The key to achieve such transcendence, I shall argue, is the use of a human analogy – that of the character, which enabled the two architects to derive their architecture out of basic and yet profound human conditions, which too often are common sense. Everything else, Kahn would say, is circumstantial. The most difficult thing for an architect to overcome doubtlessly is the historical and cultural bounds solidified as architectural styles. As the story goes, Kahn's buildings not only look but also are primordial and eternal, for he saw modernism merely as "a circumscribed style, like Gothic or baroque;"[20] Yang's buildings look eclectic, for he was unconcerned with the historical and cultural differences of architectural styles.

The Character of a Building

In 1908, Cret published an article in *Architectural Record* to defend Beaux-Arts teaching in the American context. The article, entitled "The École des Beaux Arts: What Its Architectural Teaching Means," urged American architects and students not to see Beaux-Arts as a stylistic doctrine, but rather consider it to be a "complete liberalism."[21] Cret reminded readers that, in the middle of the nineteenth century, Ecole students had rebelled against Viollet Le Duc's examination in aesthetics. Since this "revolution," with the exception of scientific and technical studies, every course in architectural education was optional. The Ecole, therefore, produced no advertisements and made no promises. Every architect had the right to teach as long as one could attract a sufficient number of followers; every pupil hence had the right to choose a theory or an artistic taste. Cret believed that, like any school, what the Ecole could give was "a method of work," rather than a defense or promulgation of any special theory.

Curiously, other than telling the reader that the discussion of method was an endless task, and quoting hurriedly a few of Guadet's principles of design at the end of the article, Cret made little effort to elucidate his method. Instead, he discussed at length the slow cultivation of human character. At the beginning of the article, Cret painted this idealistic picture of the Ecole in Paris:

> Amid these almost cloistral surroundings the students go to spend a few years of a new life, laugh, become enthusiastic and start in every direction to try in many different countries to put into lasting form their aspirations and personal qualities – high, it may be, or vulgar, ingenious or commonplace.[22]

This romantic tone was resumed in the middle of the article with a tulip blossom analogy. Being a poor gardener, Cret told the reader a mistake that he had made: instead of letting tulip buds stay in the shade to delay their blossom, he exposed them to the first March sun. While the green stems came up and reached their full development, the buds never opened, because the roots did not have enough time to build strength underground. While Cret was talking about the amount of time it takes to accomplish the importation of a foreign architecture, it would be appropriate to relate these analogies of human cultivation to architectural design. Without much further elaboration, Cret at this point in the article made a swift connection: "The Ecole develops in an admirable way the study of design, respect for the program and the research of a special *character* (emphasis by the author) proper for each kind of building."[23]

It was Harbeson who carefully transformed this human analogy into tangible measures in architectural design. *The Study of Architectural Design* by Harbeson was a comprehensive elaboration of the American version of Ecole des Beaux-Arts teaching, and, in this context, it can be seen to have been influenced by the teaching of Cret.[24] In this book Harbeson devoted two specific sections to the matter of "character." Although these sections did not constitute a substantial portion of the book, the implication of the issue was woven into the flow of arguments throughout the entire book. In addition to the expected discussion of character in style and period, of which Harbeson made a sweeping mention, as well as the character of a building's use, Harbeson, above all, began by looking at the atmosphere of a building: for a church – reverence; for a domestic building – intimacy; and for a fortress – strength, etc.[25] But Harbeson had more to say on the complex relations between the use of a building and its psychological feel. A bank, for example, needed to have an appearance of solidity and strength in order to guard its content from outside assaults, but, on the other hand, needed to disguise this character to be inviting enough to draw in customers.[26] This, inevitably, led Harbeson to the most fundamental method of design: "If it is 'A Bank,' ask you yourself, 'What is a bank'?"[27] Here one cannot help recalling Kahn's gnomic utterance: What does a building want to be? Existential it may sound, but it may simply be repeating the Beaux-Arts' question of character.

The complexity of character could not be achieved via façade only, warned Harbeson. He even speculated on John Ruskin's complaint about his teaching being overdrawn: Ruskin actually meant, according to Harbeson, his own teaching of the character in a façade.[28] What was not always clearly understood, Harbeson argued, was the character in *plan*; by this he meant the walls and supports and the arrangement, size, shape and treatment of rooms, courts and open spaces. The essential role of the Beaux-Arts *poché*, which renders the building as an inhabitable container by blackening the solids in plan, was to do precisely that, rather than merely relying on the "decorative" *mosaics*, which indicated surface textures and furniture.[29] A more potent and yet complimentary Beaux-Arts notion in portraying the pattern of a plan, or its essence rather than the actual shapes and dimensions, is the *parti* diagram, which, according to Harbeson, was analogous to the meaning of "party line," hence a choice. The emphasis on the *parti* diagram can be seen as a conscious acknowledgement of the instrumental power of an architectural plan.[30] But Harbeson's example of the contradictory character of a bank foreshadowed an unresolved relationship between his "character in design" and "character in plan," or between what might be called the "figurative character" and the "instrumental character" of a building. The following, through a rereading of a few selected architectural works of Kahn and Yang, will reveal the successions of struggles and choices the two architects made in the constitution of different characters in architecture, and their relationships to the building and the larger world.

Fit or Unfit

The earliest evidence of Yang's architectural design can be found in the two student projects included in Harbeson's *The Study of Architectural Design*. Of these, one was awarded the First Prize and First Medal Class A Problem from the Beaux-Arts Institute of Design in New York, the other was a pencil study for a Class A Project. The merits of winning the design award and being chosen for inclusion by Harbeson were achieved due to a skillful and proper *fit* between the character of the building and its use, which was the program. The award-winning project, "A Municipal Market," was remarked by Harbeson that, in both plan and elevation, the restaurant and the market were "unmistakably expressed" (Figure 6.2).[31] The symmetrical axial plan was

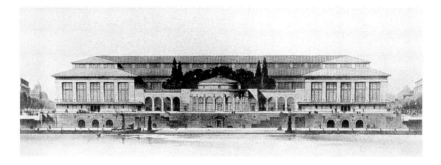

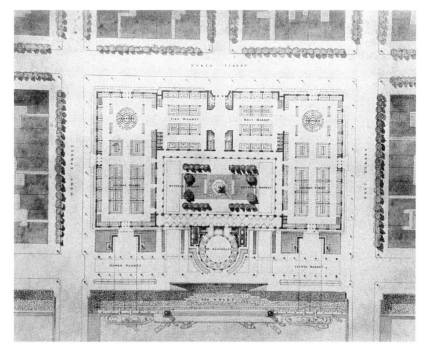

6.2
Yang Tingbao, a municipal market, Class A Problem, University of Pennsylvania (Elevation and plan from John Harbeson, *The Study of Architectural Design*, New York: Pencil Points Press, 1927, p. 180)

convenient to achieve clarity and legibility in the arrangement of the program, which incorporated several indoor markets (meat, fish, vegetables and groceries), an outdoor flower market and a restaurant. The façade was eclectic, but made sense in the context of the program and its spatial character. The restaurant's Spanish-style roof cleverly corresponded with the double-eave roof of the market, which, in the meantime, allowed extra skylights between the two eaves to illuminate the deep and high indoor market.[32]

The other project of Yang's included in Harbeson's book, "Pencil Study for a Crematory," was used to discuss the necessity of revision in architectural design; it in fact explicitly illustrated how the character of a building (in façade in this case) should be made more appropriate to its program. Harbeson commented that a few columns in the existing elevation were changed from Ionic to Doric to significantly improve the aspect. Harbeson did not elaborate on what the "aspect" was, but he probably meant that the Doric order was more suitable for the character of a crematorium.[33] One of Kahn's Class A projects in 1924 showed a similar attempt to create a character in plan, in this case a mighty form for barracks and battalions. The overall plan for "An Army Post" was asymmetrical, but each individual building was symmetrical and axial.[34] Not as refined as Yang's "A Municipal Market," Kahn's *poché* and *parti* had a somewhat clumsy crudeness in planning, which would become more evident in the differences in how Kahn and Yang wrestled with the problem of human characters in their buildings, which inevitably, though subconsciously, reflect that of their own personal characters.

Yang was an early bloomer. By 1935, when Kahn had established his own practice and begun to work on his first independent project, the Ahavath Israel Congregation, Yang had already restored some major historical monuments in Beijing, including the famous Temple of Heaven, and had completed over thirty large-scale public buildings, including banks, universities, hospitals and railway stations. Yang's first project, after he returned to China in 1927, was a major railway station of about 7,000 square meters for Shenyang City in northern China. Though the typical Beaux-Arts "stripped classicism" and symmetrical axial planning may seem unsurprising, it was Yang's first successful attempt at achieving a building character proper to both its context of the time and the building's content (program). This railway station, like many of his other buildings, has worked for more than half a century.

Yang initially proposed a building with a European modernist appearance, but the railway officials, as well as Yang's architectural colleagues, all argued for a Western classical design that would recall an old neoclassical railway station in Beijing, which was the supposedly familiar image of a railway station in China. Yang's design in the end had a touch of Western ornamentation while maintaining a clean-cut simplicity (Figure 6.3). Without using classical orders and colonnades, the concourse space was grand, well lit, and, most importantly of all, open due to its steel-arch structure. The ticket windows, waiting rooms, and other facilities were housed in three-storey flat-roofed buildings that were tied together by the ground-level verandas, and these in turn surrounded the concourse symmetrically. The flat-roofed components were dressed with simplified eave details and gables, and the large-span roof structure of the concourse was fittingly built into the overall

.3
ang Tingbao,
Shenyang railway
tation, Shenyang,
927, exterior
iew (From *Yang
Tingbao jianzhu
heji zouping ji*,
Beijing: China
Architecture and
Building Press,
1983, p. 11)

massing, as if the arched space grew out of the flat podiums. This visual feature was further enhanced by a vertical compositional theme. At the age of 26, the integrity in this building indicated Yang's extraordinary confidence as an architect. But above all, and in addition to the workings of its plan, the skillful fit of the railway station into its socio-cultural context and content evoked a character that, rather than being regional, catered to China's voracious appetite for things Western in the early twentieth century.

If Yang's early Beaux-Arts practice indicated a search for the character of a building that would fit its context and content, Kahn's early public institutional buildings showed, as it appears, the opposite approach. It was more than twenty years after Yang's railway station in China that Kahn began to receive major commissions for public institutional projects. Immediately after his first well-known building, the Yale University Art Gallery (1951–54), Kahn produced his less well-known AFL Medical Services in Philadelphia (1954–57), which becomes more meaningful when it is read against Yang's railway station.

The program of AFL was to provide free medical care for the 70,000 members of one of the largest labour unions in the country. The site was on Vine Street at the edge of the city center. The *poché*, not unlike the Yale University Art Gallery, was an austere box with carefully controlled fenestration. Also like the Yale University gallery, AFL had the three-dimensional "space frame" ceiling, though in the latter it was slightly finer, deeper and more usable. While still a lattice-like grid, this time it was the Vierendeel truss rather than the tetrahedral ceiling used at Yale. But the building's *parti* (different to that of the Yale University Art Gallery despite the similarities of their *poché*) had little to do with this techno "space frame;" it was about the character that Kahn wanted to give to the building – that of a "palace."

Kahn said because his clients were working people, he had to make the building as close as possible to a palace. The building, therefore, had to impart nobility

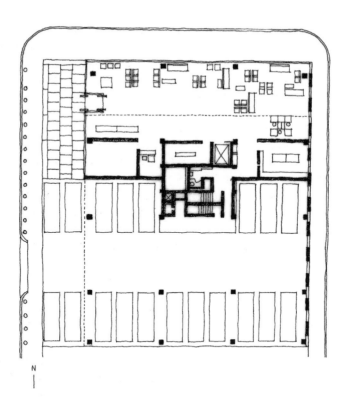

6.4
Louis Kahn, AFL Medical Services, 1954–57, ground floor plan (Redrawn by Xing Ruan)

N

and express their faith.[35] To achieve this noble character, Kahn alternated polished granite with glass panels across the building's surface and elongated the ground level entry hall to create an imagined grand procession along the axis, which is the essence of the building's *parti* (Figure 6.4). Kahn's AFL Medical Services, with a character, literally, unfit for its inhabitants, was to harbor the hopes of the working people for what they did not have – creating, we may say, an imagined *fit*. Whether it was Yang's discerning fit or Kahn's romanticized fit, to give life to a building by creating a character evinced a deep concern for the centrality of a human person in his or her place – topophilia on the one hand with familiarity and attachment (a known railway station), but seemingly topophobia (an imagined palace for the working people) on the other, which has been used, honorably, to provoke topophilia. Kahn had hoped that the dignity and spirit of his working people would soar with his "architecture of palace."

In the late 1940s and early 1950s, Kahn's architecture was devoid of historical references. Kahn no doubt was interested in Anne Tyng's ingenious geometry and the notion of the "space frame,"[36] but he was torn between Buckminster Fuller's techno organism and his own desire to test the capacity of the space frame in order to readdress the centrality of the human character in his or her world. Kahn's triangle concrete lattice-grid for the Yale University Art Gallery was, structurally, much heavier than it needed to be, and was by no means a Tyng and Fuller kind of structural space frame. The heavy concrete grid was not unlike Le Corbusier's *brise-soleil*, but was used horizontally to form a ceiling with spatial depth. This gave Kahn the opportunity to create a human scale and hence address the human figure underneath the deep ceilings[37] – a centrality lost under Mies van der Rohe's flat ceiling. But Kahn's use of concrete coffer might have come from his "*rupture*" experience in Rome when the Yale Art Gallery was conceived.[38] As for human centrality in a truly internalized world, that is, an architectural enclosure, no experience can be more compellingly real than that of under the coffer dome of the Pantheon. Kahn might have liked the fact that concrete coffering was a Roman invention; hence it possesses a kind of "zero ground" primordial beginning. Arthur Danto has suggested that the soaring coffers under the Pantheon dome, which gradually grow smaller as they ascend toward the oculus, are "like a chorus of angels."[39] Kahn, on the contrary, used the concrete coffer ceiling to press down, so it is perhaps not far-fetched to imagine that he symbolically created a sense of topophilia in these buildings. Kahn renamed the space frame "hollow stone," not only for the poetics but also for its connotation of nature, which can be readily linked to order, cosmos and the universe. Kahn probably hoped that the "scientific" property of the name (space frame) would afford him an abstract language to achieve human centrality without relying on historical precedents, which incidentally were not in vogue at the time. To prove this, consider Kahn's later monastic obsession in the design of various public institutional buildings, ranging from a colleague student dormitory, a library to a science laboratory, two of which will be discussed later. It misses the point to perceive Kahn as a modernist architect if the monastic austerity in his buildings is associated with a minimalism of aesthetic taste. Kahn's love of monasteries, I should like to think, is beyond the matter of taste: it is the appeal of a scientific truth, like that of a mathematic formula, and the consequential austerity and splendour that Kahn found in monastery architecture. But Kahn was never subordinate to the techno regime. In 1972, two years before he died, Kahn inscribed a portrait he did for Tyng in 1946. While showing affection and acknowledgement on the one hand, he had this to say on the other: "[Anne Tyng] was the geometry conceiver of the Philadelphia Tower. Well that is not exactly so because I thought of the essence but she knew its geometry."[40]

Whose Character?

Kahn reached his architectural maturity in the 1960s; Yang had produced his last significant project in the early 1950s. This was the Beijing Peace Hotel, the only building in his œuvre with a modernist look. However, rather than any modernist doctrine, a careful scrutiny of the hotel's *parti*, and its *fit* into its context and content, reveals Yang's skillful Beaux-Arts methods in creating a character that reflected the building's inhabitants and was legible to them.

To address the specific site, the asymmetrical and diagonal composition of the Beijing Peace Hotel was determined by three existing trees and an ancient well (Figure 6.5). A portion of an old courtyard house and a new wall were used to form an enclosed open space in front of the hotel, which was intended to echo Beijing's urban pattern of courtyard houses. The plan, although asymmetrical, was clearly worked out according to a number of axes. Yang believed that axial planning had the potential to create what he called an "interest center," which was the

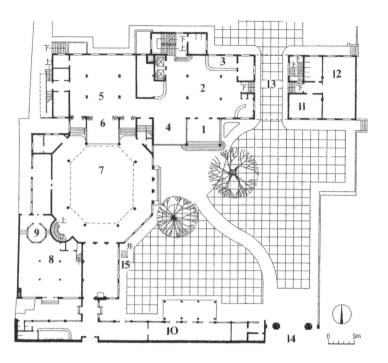

6.5
Yang Tingbao,
Beijing Peace
Hotel, 1951–53,
ground floor plan.
Key: 1. Entry;
2. Lobby;
3. Reception;
4. Sitting area;
5. Dining; 6. Stage
7. Banqueting hall,
8, Kitchen; 9. Light
well; 10. Existing
teahouse;
11. Hairdressers;
12. Club room;
13. Passageway;
14. Compound
entry; 15. Existing
ancient well
(From *Yang
Tingbao jianzhu
sheji zouping ji*,
Beijing: China
Architecture and
Building Press,
1983, p. 182)

invisible soul of the space.[41] Yang's elaboration was, once again, a human analogy. Given that he wrote very little, surprisingly Yang once theorized on the meaning of an axis as both a concept and a method. He went on to give evidence, ranging from bodies and plants to machines and societies, of the axis as both corporeal and conceptual. Yang emphasized, however, that an architectural axis was not only three-dimensional, since it also involved a time factor related to movement. In Yang's conception, an architectural axis generates "memories" and "imaginations" and thus is a "mental axis."[42] In the case of the Beijing Peace Hotel it was a matter of turning and twisting axes, like that in Chinese gardens and temples described by Yang in his theory of the axis.[43] As a result, the ground level of the hotel was a complex combination of axes for each spatial "interest center." The Beaux-Arts *poché* was conveniently used to tuck away "servant spaces" (to use Kahn's notion), and along with the axis, to create, simply, a sense of center in each room.

　　The austere modernist look of the building, devoid of ornamentation, was Yang's strategy to respond to the budget under the then relatively poor economic conditions in China, though the extravagant Chinese classical revival was at its peak (Figure 6.6). Major public and institutional buildings, for example, often were crowned with gigantic Chinese temple roofs of concrete structure. The Beijing Peace Hotel was initially designed as a local hotel; halfway through construction the government decided to use it for the Asia-Pacific Region's Conference on Peace. Yang further simplified the design in order to have the building completed in fifty days; a building stripped of ornamentation made construction easier and faster. Although Yang had great difficulties in getting the approval from the city planning authorities, the building

6
ang Tingbao,
eijing Peace
otel, 1951–53,
erial view of the
verall complex
Redrawn by Xing
uan, based on
ang and Qi (eds),
*ang Tingbao tan
anzhu*, Beijing:
hina Architecture
nd Building
ress, 1991, p. 2)

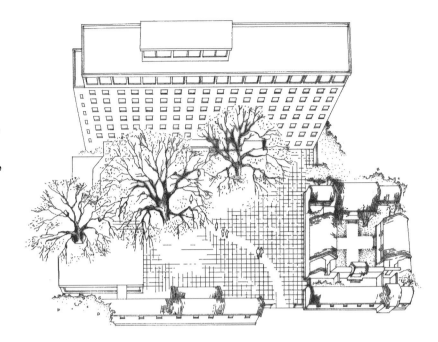

subsequently had an interesting socio-political life. After its completion, the efficient construction process and the modest budget impressed the then Premier Zhou Enlai, who later advocated a government building policy for the next three decades in China, which was to be functional, economical, and aesthetically pleasing whenever possible.

Yang, working with humility, skill and imagination, always managed to find the character proper for a building. This enduring search for character made him obliged to neither historicism nor modernism. The Beaux-Arts design method preached by Cret was imbued into Yang as his professionalism, which was that of a craftsman tailor. The characters that Yang created for his buildings were, naturally, diverse, but none of them reflected his sense of self or his own worldview. In other words, Yang's architecture was not used as a carrier for ideology, and it did not attempt to set the world to rights. The tailor mentality of Yang's methods is that of pacifism rather than didacticism. Like an artisan, Yang refrained from making moral judgements through his "trade" – architecture.

In search of human centrality in architecture, Kahn deployed the same Beaux-Arts methods (axial planning, for example) more strongly in the 1960s, but his *parti* had a different agenda: it must support moral weight. The centrality thus could only be felt when a figure in Kahn's room matched the character of the building. When in the late 1950s Kahn began to resume his interest in historical precedents and his earlier Beaux-Arts education under Cret, he made this famous claim: "The program is nothing!"[44] In fact, Kahn never completely gave up Beaux-Arts axial planning; the imagined procession in the AFL Medical Services was the proof. Along with the axis, Kahn showed great interest in "useless" spaces that were not related to a specific program, such as the garden, the ambulatory and the arcade. Kahn's ideal *parti* for creating a sense of centrality was a concentric "meeting room" with choices and contemplations at the peripheries, be it a chapel, a library or a parliament house. Far from being a genius working in isolation, Kahn was gregarious, and was always surrounded by people.[45] This ideal *parti*, therefore, was Kahn's remedy for balancing the individual and the larger world of collective life, which he phrased as learning and meeting. Kahn once described this *parti* by using a chapel analogy:

> So, what is a chapel really? A chapel, to me, is a space that one can be in, but must have excess of space around it, so that you don't have to go in. That means, it must have an ambulatory, so that you don't have to go into the chapel; and the ambulatory must have an arcade outside, so that you don't have to go into the ambulatory; and the object outside is a garden, so that you don't have to go into the arcade; and the garden has a wall, so that you can be outside of it or inside of it. The essential thing you see, is that the chapel is a personal ritual, and that it is not a set ritual, and it is from this that you get the form.[46]

When Kahn was working on the Adath Jeshurun Synagogue scheme in 1954, his choice of centralized hexagonal and triangle plans and the use of a concrete coffer ceiling for the sanctuary still indicated his interest in abstract geometry. The analogy for the synagogue was somewhat different: a meeting place under a huge tree, with the sanctuary as the hollow tree trunk.[47] During the design process Kahn developed a concentric double-ring plan, which was explained to the building committee as a functional solution – moveable screens would ensure the intimacy of the inner ring during the small weekly congregations, while the outer ring would accommodate large gatherings on the High Holidays. The plan, however, could be seen as the prototype of Kahn's later interest in the ambulatory and arcade outside a concentric meeting room. More significantly, Adath Jeshurun planted the seed for Kahn's future ideal *parti*.

Kahn was not committed to a totally centralized *parti* in the Adath Jeshurun scheme. In the last attempt before he was dismissed by the building committee, Kahn presented a scheme where, on the one hand, the concentric triangular sanctuary was inscribed in a circular embankment (an ambulatory perhaps), and on the other hand, there came off a rectangular school wing (Figure 6.7). It was logical that the noisy school area was separate from the quiet sanctuary.[48] But in Kahn's design for the First Unitarian Congregation (1959–61) Church and School, the total centrality was an unbent rule from the outset. Although the standard Unitarian church layout contained separate school and auditorium wings, Kahn began with the concentric plan. The central square auditorium was surrounded by the school, with a circular corridor and ambulatory in between. Kahn later claimed that the *parti* was inspired by a speech about Unitarianism that the minister had given when the architect first met with the congregation.[49] After a lengthy and painful process of negotiating with the building committee and meeting the budgetary constraints, the executed design was still concentric, but with the square auditorium surrounded asymmetrically by the school. There was a corridor separating the central auditorium

.7
ouis Kahn,
dath Jeshurun
ynagogue, 1954,
ection and plan
ketch in a letter
o Anne Tyng
From The Rome
etters 1953–1954,
Jew York: Rizzoli,
997, p.171)

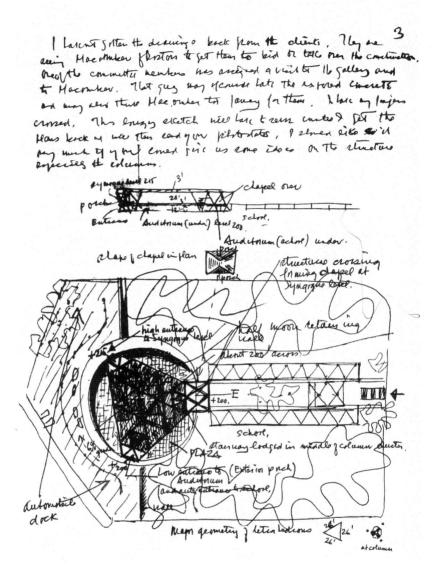

and the school at the periphery, though the initial circular ambulatory was sacrificed. Kahn eventually was satisfied with the design and used the scheme development at various stages to illustrate his famous "Form" and "Design" diagram: practical and budgetary requirements can be resolved by the "Design," but the "Form" must be held, which for Kahn was the universal concentric *parti* (Figure 6.8). In a rather shrewd manner Kahn mythologized the whole design process for the First Unitarian Congregation as a single and intense meeting with the clients.[50]

Kahn's "Form," the ideal *parti*, subsequently proved to be the common ground in his different building programs, so long as he had ideal clients to match it. In the Phillips Exeter Academy Library (1965–72), the building committee gave Kahn

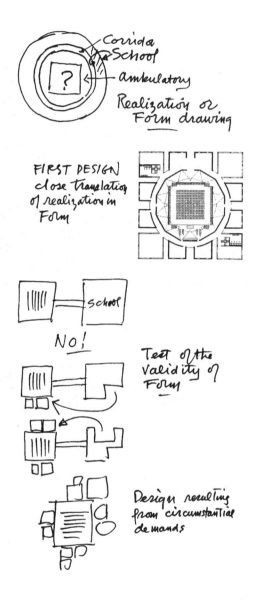

6.8
Louis Kahn, First Unitarian Church and School, Rochester, New York, 1959–69, the various stages of plan development showing Kahn's diagram of "Form and Design"

an auspicious beginning with two major agendas: the symbolic significance of the library and the centrality of the human person. The library committee wanted a quiet retreat not only for study and reading, but also for reflection, and therefore the emphasis of their library "should not be on housing books but housing readers using books."[51] Despite the similarly lengthy and difficult process, in the Exeter Library Kahn achieved a potent and yet legible symbolization: searching for knowledge in the darkness (artificially lit bookshelves) and bringing it to the light (naturally lit reading carrels). Kahn's *parti*, a concentric and multi-layered "doughnut" in this case, was intended to create an experience that was mediated between an individual and the group through a library (Figure 6.9). The central grand hall, a symbolic sanctuary with

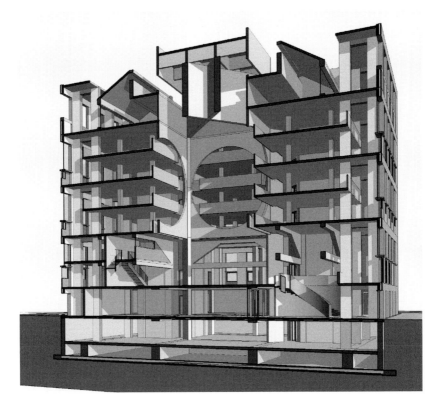

large circular openings on the wall revealing bookshelves, was designed to seduce readers as well as to be used for gathering and reflection (Figure 6.10). Then there are the inner bookshelf layer, the corridor and the outer reading carrels divided into private cloisters (Figure 6.11). There is the arcade on the ground level, which makes it difficult to find the entry; when wandering in the arcade, of course, one has the choice of not going into the library.

In the National Assembly Complex in Dhaka, Kahn, finally, was able to indulge in monumentalizing his obsession with the ambulatory – the multi-layered and multi-storey spaces surrounding the assembly hall. Kahn also duplicated this *parti* in other spaces, the Prayer Hall, for example, at the outer ring with the same concentric *parti*. As to the monumental scale in the assembly complex, Kahn justified it by using the example of the Baths of Caracalla in Rome: he claimed that you could bathe just as well under an 8-foot ceiling, but bathing under a 150-foot ceiling would make a man a different kind of man.[52] It was also during the development of these projects, from the First Unitarian Congregation, to the Exeter Library and the National Assembly Complex in Dhaka, that Kahn indicated his dislike of glare and vulnerable glazing. His preference was for defused natural light from the sky window, which often was uncannily let in and caused shadowless serenity. The mystical quality of the light epitomized the symbolic wisdom of his ideal *parti*, the experience of which he liked to call transcendental.

6.10
Louis Kahn,
Phillips Exeter
Academy Library,
central void. Note
that there are
opened books
displayed on the
desks, as what
Kahn would have
hoped, to seduce
the reader (Photo:
Xing Ruan, 2000)

Kahn was evidently aware of the authoritarian practices of Ayub Khan, his client and the Supreme Commander who took up the reins of government by imposing martial law in East Pakistan.[53] With complete freedom and an unlimited budget, Kahn had faith that his architecture would enshrine democracy. Regardless of the different building programs, the repeated application of the same *parti* reveals

Kahn's greatest concern, that is of common humanity rather than any religious and cultural specificity. Unlike Yang, who was an artisan, Kahn was a missionary who wanted to fabricate a way of life that was universally worth living. In 1968, when Kahn had already reached the culmination of his worldview, as well as the maturity of his architecture, he remarked: "Did Mozart ask society what he should compose? Of course not. He composed, and society became a different thing. The architect makes a work which inspires society to take a different turn."[54]

Characters of the Good and the Real

Cret's Beaux-Arts teaching produced two architects for the twentieth century who shared a fundamental affinity – in creating a character for a building they both sought to locate the human person in the center of his or her place. Their difference, however, lies between a didactic missionary and a modest tailor, each deploying different methods: one was to preach a way of life while the other was to capture it. But neither of them belonged with some of their twentieth-century peers who were mainly concerned with a beauty contest in architecture, which in effect is a nineteenth-century legacy of bow-tied gentleman architects as style traders (despite the fact that Kahn often wore bow ties). Both Kahn and Yang, trained by Cret's Beaux-Arts, had the skill to accommodate the body in scale and proportion, in other words, to make a building work. Cret preached the creation of a character proper to the building; Kahn and Yang elevated the corporeal body to a higher level. Yang's architecture housed vagaries of characters: "qualities high, it may be, or vulgar, ingenious or commonplace," to again paraphrase Cret; whereas in Kahn's architecture only lifted souls were accommodated.

Kahn showed no interest in refinement, in fact, he preferred a somewhat clumsiness; his architecture needed be heavy for it had to carry a worldview that was to be shared. Yang, never concerned with his own artistic identity, searched for appropriateness in architecture through his trade and craft. For Kahn, architecture was a means to achieve the social good; for Yang, architecture was a trade in enchantment.[55] In an uncompromised search for the truth, Kahn created a character of the good;[56] Yang's search for the proper is a compromise, but his character is of the real, the "vagaries of the souls" as Cret would have said.

Kahn contemplated a romantic picture when he designed the Salk Institute (1959–65), a science laboratory for biological studies in La Jolla, California. In the central plaza, which is bound by two rows of concrete buildings and is open to the infinite Pacific Ocean on the cliff site, scientists would walk up and down between the laboratory building and the plaza; they would engage in heated debates about the problems of the world, and would pause to "chalk an equation or draw a diagram" on the slabs of slate that Kahn had placed there for their convenience. But as Danto has observed: "[no]body was ever there . . . nobody but architectural tourists . . . Kahn was almost hopeless in his romanticism, hoped people would rise to the architecture, but they rarely did or do."[57] Yang, on the other hand, made too much compromise, both in life and in architecture, which saved him from being completely purged in the Chinese Cultural Revolution,[58] and which also let him lead the design team to produce Chairman Mao's Mausoleum in 1976 – the last monument for the totalitarian statesman.

Kahn, though a "cosmopolite"[59] who always longed for the enshrinement from the larger world, never wanted to leave his home Philadelphia even when he was invited by the president of Harvard to hold a position there. When declining the offer, Kahn was quoted by saying this sentimental line: "What is a Philadelphian going to do in Cambridge, Massachusetts?"[60] Yang, more drawn to the warmth of "hearth," was on the other hand rarely bothered by cultural differences. The previously mentioned news story, "Chinese Student Gets High Honor" in Philadelphia's *Evening Bulletin*, had this amusing subtitle: "Boy dislikes Rice." Yang was reported to have told the Americans that rice was not his favorite: "The American idea that rice is the chief food of the Chinese is wrong. Many eat it in the districts most visited by American tourists, but in the province of Honan [Henan], where I lived, rice is eaten very little." Yang in fact had chosen to see more common ground than differences when he imported the American version of Beaux-Arts to China with ease.[61] One does not have to identify a clear differentiation between Kahn and Yang, but it is the paradox of their search for the human character in architecture that makes the promise, which is the promise for a human centrality in the familiar world, as well as in the larger world. If we call these worlds *topos*, the role of architecture in a reconciliation of *topophilia* and *topophobia* ought to be an instrumental one.

Notes

1 Pan Guxi (ed.), *Dongnan Daxue jianzhu xi chenli qishi zhounian jinian zhuanji*, (Memorial Symposium for the Seventy Years' Anniversary of the Department of Architecture at Southeast University), Beijing: China Architecture and Building Press, 1997, p. 69.

2 Yang Tingbao, *Yang Tingbao jianzhu sheji zuopingji* (Yang Tingbao, Architectural Works and Projects), Beijing: China Architecture and Building Press, 1983.

3 Lai Delin, "Yang Tingbao yu Luyi Kang" (Yang Tingbao and Louis Khan), in Pang Zuxiao and Yang Yongsheng (eds), *Bijiao yu chaju* (Comparison and Gap), Tianjin: Kexue Jishu Chubanshe, 1997, pp. 258–269.

4   According to Anne Tyng's recollection, Kahn told her that he was actually born in 1902, but the year of his birth was incorrectly documented as 1901 by an immigration officer when he entered the United States. See Anne Tyng (ed.), *Louis Kahn to Anne Tyng: The Rome Letters 1953–1954*, New York: Rizzoli, 1997, p. 8.

5   John Harbeson, *The Study of Architectural Design: With Special Reference to the Program of the Beaux-Arts Institute of Design*, New York: Pencil Points Press, 1927.

6   I have argued elsewhere that Yang's success as a student at Penn may be due to the accidental cultural affinities between China's artisan traditions and the Beaux-Arts methods. See Xing Ruan, "Accidental Affinities: American Beaux-Arts in Twentieth-century Chinese Architectural Education and Practice," *JSAH* 61, March 2002, 30–47. Some of the materials from this essay have been used here, but in a different manner and for different arguments.

7   Yang Tingbao won three major awards from the Beaux-Arts Institute of Design: the Municipal Art Prize, the Emerson Prize and the Warren Prize. He also won the Samuel Huckel Jr. Prize, 1922–23, and the Sigma Xi, honorary fraternity for scientific achievement.

8   See Heinz Ronner and Sharad Jhveri (eds), *Louis I. Kahn: Complete Work, 1935–1974*, Basel and Boston: Birkhäuser, 1987, pp. 9, 11. Also see David B. Brownlee and David G. De Long (eds), *Louis I. Kahn: In the Realm of Architecture*, New York: Rizzoli, 1991, p. 21.

9   Qi Kang (ed.), *Yang Tingbao tan jiangzhu* (Yang Tingbao on Architecture), Beijing: China Architecture and Building Press, 1991, pp. 99–100.

10 Zhang Zugang (ed.), *Yang Tingbao jianzhu yanlun xuanji* (Selected Architectural Writings of Yang Tingbao), Beijing: Xueshu Shukan Chubanshe, 1989, pp. 56–60.

11 Philadelphia newspaper *The Evening Bulletin*, 2 September 1925.

12 This was a widely circulated story in the Department of Architecture at the then Nanjing Institute of Technology, when the author started his first year architectural course in 1982. Also see Note 9.

13 University of Pennsylvania Yearbook 1924.

14 Contrary to his normally regarded sage status, Kahn never took himself too seriously; he could always laugh at himself. "Look at him (pointing at Kahn's photo sitting on the shelf), everyone adored him, men and women. He could make fun of himself; he had charm and vitality." Anne Tyng said this to the author at an interview on 6 October 2003 in Philadelphia. Yang was particularly known for his humility. A widely circulated story in China is that when he was in charge of refurbishing the Temple of Heaven in Beijing, he often took craftsmen and builders to dinners in order to learn from them the construction techniques of the pre-modern Chinese architecture.

15 Yi-Fu Tuan, *Topophilia: A Study of Environmental Perception, Attitudes, and Values*, New York: Columbia University Press, 1990, p. 99.

16 Yi-Fu Tuan, *Space and Place: The Perspective of Experience*, Minneapolis: University of Minnesota Press, 1977.

17 This is the point that Tuan has subtly pointed out in Chapter 2, which is more fully elaborated on in the prologue.

18 Quoted by Arthur Danto, "Louis Kahn as Archai-Tekt" in *Philosophizing Art: Selected Essays*, Berkeley, CA: University of California Press, 1999, p. 189.

19 Beyond physicality, "space and place" are metaphorically represented as "cosmos and hearth", see Yi-Fu Tuan, *Cosmos and Hearth: A Cosmopolite's Viewpoint*, Minneapolis: University of Minnesota Press, 1996.

20 Danto, "Louis Kahn as Archai-Tekt," p. 191.

21 See Paul Cret, "The École des Beaux Arts: What Its Architectural Teaching Means," *Architectural Record* 23, 1908, 367–371.

22 Ibid., 367.

23 Ibid., 369.

24 There should be sufficient reasons to believe so: Harbeson as a student "blossomed under Cret's tutelage." When he taught at Penn as an assistant professor, Cret was Professor of Design, he

learnt the role of authority in the teaching of architectural design. Harbeson also joined Cret's practice in 1910, and later became a partner of the firm. See Ann L. Strong and George E. Thomas (eds), *The Book of the School: 100 Years*, Philadelphia: GSFA, 1990, pp. 76, 72. In *The Study of Architectural Design*, Harbeson included some of Cret's works from his student days at the Ecole, to competition works, built works and even teaching sketches in America.

25 Harbeson, *The Study of Architectural Design*, p. 91.

26 Ibid., p. 94.

27 Ibid., p. 76.

28 Ibid., p. 97.

29 Ibid., pp. 97, 99, 101.

30 See Robin Evans, *The Fabrication of Virtue: English Prison Architecture, 1750–1840*, New York: Cambridge University Press, 1982, and Robin Evans, *Translations from Drawings to Building and Other Essays*, London: Architectural Association Publications, 1997.

31 Harbeson, *The Study of Architectural Design*, p. 179.

32 Lai Delin makes a similar observation in "Yang Tingbao yu Luyi Kang," (Yang Tingbao and Louis Kahn) in *Bijiao yu chaju* (Comparison and Gap), edited by Pang Zuxiao and Yang Yongsheng, Tianjin: Kexue Jishu Chubanshe, 1997, pp. 258–269.

33 Harbeson, *The Study of Architectural Design*, p. 395.

34 Brownlee and De Long, *Louis I. Kahn*, p. 21. Brownlee sees the asymmetrical planning as a sign of Kahn's future creativity, and mentioned Harbeson's specific discussion on "asymmetrical plan" in his *The Study of Architectural Design*. But Harbeson did not have a section of "symmetrical plan" in the same book. The issue, in Cret and Harbeson's Beaux-Arts teaching, was axial planning. See my own discussion on this matter in Ruan, "Accidental Affinities," pp. 30–47.

35 Sarah Williams Goldhagen, *Louis Kahn's Situated Modernism*, New Haven, CT: Yale University Press, 2001, p. 80.

36 Tyng, *Rome Letters*, pp. 38–59.

37 Sarah Goldhagen makes a similar point that the concrete grid ceiling appears lower, hence more scaled to the human body than it is. See Goldhagen, *Situated Modernism*, p. 59.

38 Danto, "Louis Kahn as Archai-Tekt," p. 195.

39 Ibid., p. 198.

40 Tyng, *Rome Letters*, 213. In my interview with Anne Tyng in October 2003, Tyng admitted that Kahn did not really want to acknowledge her contribution to the project.

41 Yang Yongsheng and Qi Kang (eds), *Yang Tingbao tan jianzhu* (Yang Tingbao on Architecture), Beijing: China Architecture and Building Press, 1991, p. 76.

42 Ibid., pp. 75–77.

43 Ibid. Like his elaboration of axial planning, Yang has been remembered by his colleagues and students as a "flexible character" who could be "turned and twisted" to suit a specific situation.

44 Louis Kahn, "New Frontiers in Architecture: CIAM in Otterlo 1959," in Alessandra Latour (ed.), *Louis I. Kahn: Writings, Lectures, Interviews*, New York: Rizzoli, 1991, p. 84.

45 According to Anne Tyng, Kahn almost lived a nomadic life and often stayed in his office until early morning. Although he collected many books, he had no patience to read them. Instead he learnt things from the people around him. Author's interview with Anne Tyng. See note 14.

46 Kahn, "New Frontiers in Architecture," p. 86.

47 Goldhagen, *Situated Modernism*, pp. 92–100.

48 See Goldhagen's explanation, ibid., p. 96.

49 Robin Williams thought this was doubtful because Kahn had met no minister in Rochester, but he did discuss Unitarianism with a minister in Philadelphia prior to meeting his clients. See Brownlee and De Long, *Louis I. Kahn*, p. 340.

50 Ibid., p. 343.

51 Peter Kohane in ibid., p. 390.

52 Goldhagen, *Situated Modernism*, p. 175.

53 Ibid., pp. 163, 166.

54 Ibid., p. 5.

55 Alfred Gell's view of art as a technology of enchantment can be applied here: the trade of architecture, as a series of technical virtuosities and their efficacy, can be enchanted to create magic – that is art. See Alfred Gell, *The Art of Anthropology*, London: Athlone, 1999, pp. 159–186.

56 In the sense of how Iris Murdoch might have put it in *The Sovereignty of the Good*, London and New York: Routledge, 1970.

57 Danto, "Louis Kahn as Archai-Tekt," p. 202.

58 See note 43.

59 Tuan, *Cosmos and Hearth*, p. 16. It is worth noting here that Tuan wrote this book from the view of a "cosmopolite."

60 Joseph Rykwert, "Louis Kahn: An Introduction," in *Louis Kahn: The Construction of the Kimbell Art Museum*, Milan: Skira, 1999, p. 10.

61 For a full discussion on Yang's importation of Beaux-Arts to China, see Ruan, "Accidental Affinities," 30–47. Also refer to note 6.

7

Potential Places, Places of Potentiality

Levitation and Suspension in Modern Italian Architecture

Ross Jenner

Even to speak of the air as a place seems strange, let alone building something there. Yet much of modern architecture attempted to do just that: to free itself from the substance of the earth and build in the air. This propensity is usually attributed to a will to rise above and remake the world in a new mold, to break away from the weight of traditional materials and localities.[1] Hence, to build in the air was tantamount to rejecting earthly materiality, the body, and the past; for the earth shows traces, gets worn, accumulates history. Air does not. A *tabula rasa*, it offers least resistance to being imbued with new projects.[2] The air is the source of change; flowing, and "space prior to all localization,"[3] it is the element of opening itself.

Rather than place, it is more usual to speak here of space. A characteristic conception of space in modernity is that of a universal homogeneous expanse, equivalent in all directions, which issues an ever-increasing challenge. In modernity that challenge was to its complete occupation and possession through colonization, or the forging of extensive lines (maritime, terrestrial, and aerial) of transmission, entailing surveillance and mutual threat between economic and political powers. A universal rationality thus displaced the experience of place.

Modern architecture is identified with materials that appear "dematerialized": glass, reflective surfaces and white walls. It is also identified with the interpenetration of interior and exterior, and with primary geometries and hovering forms, which seem not to belong to the ground. The metaphor of "hovering" stems from several factors: the values of open air; a tendency to conceive geometric bodies as transparent and imagine them as weightless; the drive towards ever greater lightness in technology; and the changed spatiality wrought by aeronautics.[4] Detachment from the ground indicated a tendency, in ascent and revolt, to break free from traditional values of place deemed oppressive.

Such refusal to stand on the ground may be termed a *topophobia*. Here, space stands opposed to place. Applying Yi-Fu Tuan's distinction "[P]lace is security, space is freedom"[5] to modernity in general, the demand for freedom may imply the loss or obliteration of place. Then, the experience accrued within place is overcome by a sense of insecurity and dislocation. But a further distinction has to be made: there is freedom *from*, and freedom *within*. The first leads to an abandonment of the earth and its treatment as *tabula rasa*, to a potentiality in the form of a power through the act of clearing and seizing space, which wants immediately to pass into actuality. The second promises a freedom within the necessities of materiality, the body and the earth, where the potential of the *tabula rasa* is a suspension of actualization, rather than a clearance. To be "in the air" implies something imminent and virtual. It is one thing to treat the world as a continual building site. Another is to design with a programmatic incompletion. A blank, void, or suspension of realization, in making absence present, can draw attention to the unnoticed and unthought. And so they open a space to reflect on architecture in an era of dislocation, where a return to livable and sheltering places seems to have become a nostalgic dream. Works that respond to this condition make a call to understand the very nature both of place and space. In this regard, the ephemeral works by some sidelined architects can offer insights. During the difficult and mired era from Italian Futurism to Rationalism, they realized little, yet had great potential. Their works attest to, and render, an image of a condition of suspension that offers insights, not only into the standard definitions of modernism, but also into present states of dislocation.

The compulsion to escape the earth base was first conspicuously expressed in Futurism. Filippo Tommaso Marinetti's 1909 *Founding Manifesto of Futurism* promoted flight, speed, and the dissolution of matter into energy as means of overcoming gravity and the past. The Futurist project was nothing less than the destruction and remaking of space and time. Marinetti – intent on fleeing, rising above, and overcoming the earth in aerial transcendence – published *Mafarka le Futuriste*. Mafarka-el-Bar, barbaric king, brutal conqueror of Africa and hero of the novel, dies while giving birth. His "son," an Icarus/Superman, an "invincible and giant bird, has great flexible wings made to embrace the stars."[6] Mafarka's technological procreation coincides with the destruction of the past as place through a will to actualize the future in speed and flight. The newborn bird-man-plane kills his father, springs immediately into the air, destroys the earth, and flies off to Mars. Flight escapes all forms of closure and exteriorizes the will, uniting desire with the exterior world of machines, the sky, and the universe.

Umberto Boccioni in his *Pittura e Scultura futuriste* (1914) shared this enthusiasm for verticality and voluntarism: "There is only one necessity, only one will: to ASCEND." Matter must be transformed into more energetic forms by dissolving, fragmenting or multiplying them into fields of energy. Atomization, intensification and dispersion of force flows undo the solidity and values of place. The distance between things turns into "continuities of matter of different intensity."[7]

Movement and light destroy materiality. Matter itself becomes permeable, without fixed surface, and co-extensive with universal space.

Place, then, if it can be called such, is that of the metropolitan periphery and its uncontrollable development – a building site, and hence programmatically incomplete. Boccioni's most famous painting, *The City Rises*, depicts a scene of brutal and frenetic construction in an empty lot filled with light speckles, dust, smoke, molecules. The ground below is itself under construction, articulated in a "tumultuous abyss" of turbines.[8] Above, the city ascends in scaffolding, the very image of an unfinished state. Building as event progresses within a field of interconnected forces. Place, matter, work, action and becoming are conflated. "We must reinvent and rebuild the Futurist city *ex novo* like an immense and tumultuous shipyard, agile mobile and dynamic in every detail," wrote Sant'Elia in 1914.[9] And Boccioni, at the same time: "The future is preparing for us a sky invaded by architectural scaffoldings."[10] This echoes Marinetti's proclamation that "nothing is more beautiful than the scaffolding of a house under construction,"[11] symbolizing "our burning passion for the coming-into-being of things."[12] The site of the future in its actualization is what matters.

For Gaston Bachelard, the blue sky is itself a form of *tabula rasa* and, for Aristotle, the cleaned writing tablet the very condition of potentiality of thought suspended from actuality.[13] In the "endless emptiness" of cosmic space one can, as Malevich states, "sense . . . the creative points of the universe."[14] The potentiality of Futurism, however, promises not only an overcoming of our terrestrial state but also mastery of the earth which itself becomes a *tabula rasa* and hence susceptible to effacement and destruction.

Later, Hans Sedlmayr's notion of "loss of centre" expresses concerns about an invalidation of all stable co-ordinates of world order: gravity and the relation between heaven and earth. It directly confronts the simile of levitation:

> Above all, the revulsion from the earth has . . . become incomparably stronger. It is as though the art of flying, long dreamed of and now at last realized, were drawing the very art of building itself away from the earth.[15]

The threat of losing all security through a dissolution of place similarly underlies Carl Schmitt's writing. From 1940, he used the term "spatial revolution" (*Raumrevolution*) to denote how the conceptual structure of space is everywhere altered. Empty, void space becomes available as "the field of human energy, activity and achievement."[16] Space becomes homogenous as its traditional structures, derived from the division of land and sea, collapse. The disintegration of spatial relationships culminates in aerial warfare where the "absolute dissolution of locality and, therewith, the pure destructive character of modern air war" is demonstrated.[17]

Massimo Cacciari will later draw the inevitable conclusion from this process. Space, deprived of place, is now completely available for conquest. The mobilizing and uprooting universalism of the world market reduces the entire planet to "free space."[18] The metamorphosis is completed when, in the form of "panoptical pre-potency,"[19] the sky dominates:

No place resists, just as no time is lived; places and times get uprooted, *pulled up there* in the unity of the gaze that dominates everything from on high. "Up there" stands to indicate not another, new place, but, on the contrary, the overcoming of every earthly and earth-time determination. Perfect *Auf-hebung*: place is really re-posed "on high," it is overcome, that is, posed above, conceived in the superior unity of its *idea*, that is, perfectly seen.[20]

Already in post-WWI Futurist "Aeroarchitecture," flight took on a sinister aspect in the project of beautifying and remaking Italy – as seen from the air – to advance colonial expansion of Mussolini's Regime – from the Alps to the "free space" of Mogadishu.[21] Marinetti's "ideal hypersensitive hanging observatory" of airplanes prefigured today's satellites.[22] The air becomes the predominant point of surveillance, providing "exactness," "normality" and a novel gaze over the earth: of surveillance and inspection.

With this alienation, the earth that is *here*, under the feet, is acrobatically stunted – spied upon and alienated, it becomes a *there*.[23] In this move, the distance gained in displacement results in estrangement. In Futurism, the impulse to an exultant ascension, to upward projection, comes in Fillia's paintings to an end, arrested in an alien space of the Absolute.

Rationalism founded and legitimized itself in the echo of its absolute antiquity in ancient *ratio*, removed from historical contingencies. "Mediterraneanness" was an expression of a timelessness, as were Franco Ciliberti's "primordial values." Thus, in the Roman projects of Giuseppe Terragni, who is hailed as Rationalism's leading exponent, levitation is carefully contextualized in relation to the ancient aura of their sites (Figure 7.1). In *Scheme A* for the *Palazzo Littorio* competition, hanging over the *Via del Impero*, the *Duce* was to be heroically elevated on a cantilevered podium, cutting through a gigantic curved wall of red porphyry 80 meters long held together by bands of steel that crinkle it according to the isostatic lines of its suspension. *Scheme B* floats in gigantic cantilevers. The transcendent element is disclosed above all in the *Danteum* project (all in the proportions of the Golden Section) with its ascent to the crystal columns and sky of *Paradiso*. Under the Regime, the role and expression of the means of production in architecture were obscured. Construction, divorced from moral and social values, was, particularly in the period of economic self-sufficiency (*autarchia*), reduced to a primordial act. The space of freedom was imagined not in terms of social freedom, but as the reconstitution of lost ancient harmonies and the spiritual rediscovery of the Subject in its encounter with the Absolute.[24]

Alberto Sartoris' Rationalism is similarly oriented towards transcendence in geometry and number (Figure 7.2). In his drawings in parallel projection, buildings are lifted to the sky or descend from the white page, out of which they emerge, already materialized in the mind's eye. As both an anticipation of the real appearance of the constructed object and as dream-like, suspended images, they raise the viewer from the tangible to the abstract, from the physical nature of things to the mental processes which govern the creation of architecture. Space is a game for the mind rather than the body.[25]

7.1
Terragni et al., project for Scheme A for the first phase of the Palazzo Littorio competition, 1934 (Courtesy of the Centro Studi Giuseppe Terragni, Como)

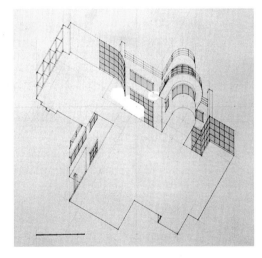

7.2
Alberto Sartoris, building for artisan community, Parco Valentino, Turin, 1927–28. Sviluppo delle volumetrie della prima soluzione, January 1928. Pencil, brown ink, sepia wash on paper, 62 × 47 cm (Courtesy of the Fonds Alberto Sartoris, Archives de la Construction moderne, École polytechnique fédérale de Lausanne)

Sartoris, unconcerned with the particular, obtained surreal effects by severing his buildings from their context to the point of lifting them into the air in his drawings. In contrast, Edoardo Persico in journalism and in his very brief design career aspired to reframe the social, aesthetic and industrial context of everyday Italy. Like his younger contemporary Franco Albini, however, he fits less neatly within this idealistic strain.

Given the political circumstance of the fascist regime, design opportunities for young Rationalists such as Persico and Albini were limited throughout 1930s. In the limbo of *allestimento*,[26] they designed exhibition pavilions, stands, installations, furnishings, and furniture to create a potential architecture. Being sidelined from major commissions became productive: their work made an image of their condition of suspense as a withholding, as well as of freedom and release. Exposition provided Milanese modernism with one of its most effective vehicles for the diffusion of knowledge. It also opened a parallel world from which to suspend place and gravity, a place apart from the heavy monumentality of the predominant *Novecento* style. *Allestimento* became a typically Italian phenomenon, concerned with the preparation for an event, an ephemeral construction not destined to survive it – but proper to it.[27] Lightness, associated with exhibition spaces since the Crystal Palace, in Guiseppe Pagano's account of exhibition design, takes on new connotations:

> Perhaps in no other field have modern architecture and the most con-temporary sense of interior design tried to fight such a harsh battle against the laws of statics and the conventional to obtain surreal effects, to reach a new equilibrium, to dissociate space in lyric images.[28]

In the two Milan Parker pen shops Persico designed in 1934–35, optically vibrating lines rhythmically interplay with their background. "A picture plane," wrote Malevich, "suspended over the abyss of the white canvas, gives to consciousness a sensation of immediate space, and the strongest."[29] The background in these shops is no longer an inert substratum; "the white is transformed from a negative and static element into a concrete and active one," as in contemporary graphics.[30] Space is the ground.

Here, whiteness is like Aristotle's metaphor of the writing tablet, on which nothing is actually written – whose blankness expresses a way in which the pure potentiality of thought exists.[31] It is not a form of erasure, repression or essentialism. Elsewhere, Aristotle observes that "What is potential is capable of not being in actuality. What is potential can both be and not be, for the same is potential both to be and not be."[32] Developing Aristotle's idea, Giorgio Agamben notes: "all potential to be or do something is . . . always also potential not to be or not to do"; otherwise potentiality would always already have passed into actuality and would be indis-tinguishable from it.[33]

The Parker pen shops (Figure 7.3) prize open a reserve of possibility that exists in non-actualization, in not fully being. They intimate a suspension conserving and exercising, in the realized work, a potential not actualized. Raffaello Giolli noted: "everything is reduced to purpose. But in undressing architecture thus to the point of making it only a vibration of lines, Persico went beyond that point."[34] It is here that an event of materialization might occur, manifest as a *typos*, a trace, through the stroke of the pen. Keeping actuality in suspension reveals the traces of a process of thought that does not quite touch its other.

Persico worked often within fraught circumstances, for example, in the contexts of the 1934 advertising installation in the *Galleria Vittorio Emmanuele*, with its scaffolding in the shape of a distorted airplane and the 1936 *Salone d'onore*, which he did not live to complete. At the 1934 *Exhibition of Italian Aeronautics* at the Milan Palazzo dell'Arte, the *Sala delle Medaglie d'Oro* was widely regarded as the foremost exhibit and celebrated as Persico's finest architectural work (Figure 7.4). It was, as Vittorio Gregotti put it, "one of the most rigorously poetic experiences of the whole of Italian Rationalism."[35] The hall commemorated the exploits of Italian aviators in

7.3
Persico and
Nizzoli, Parker
shop, Largo Santa
Margherita, Milan
1934, interior
(From Eduardo
Persico, *Scritti
d'architettura*
(1927/1935), ed.
Giulia Veronesi,
Florence: Vallechi,
1968, vol. 2
unpaginated)

7.4
Persico, Nizzoli
and Fontana,
Hall of the Gold
Medals, Exhibition
of Italian
Aeronautics,
Milan, Palazzo
dell'Arte, 1934
(From Eduardo
Persico, *Scritti
d'architettura
(1927/1935)*, ed.
Giulia Veronesi,
Florence: Vallechi,
1968, vol. 2
unpaginated)

the First World War. According to the catalogue, "the immensity of space where the heroes experienced the war" detached them "from every earthly thing."[36]

The lightness of the supports of the apparently floating objects produced an impression of suspension and displacement: *of* the frame as much as *within* the frame. To place something within a frame, or grid, is to suspend it by graphing it in an abstract space, releasing it from the shackles of gravity and reality and objectifying it in a parallel world. The work is like a page layout in three dimensions. The whole exhibit was illuminated solely by concealed, diffused and reflected light. Above head-height, a frame ran lengthwise through the hall, like a fuselage in translucent scrim, carrying the floating relics of heroic death. The uprights were laid out in strict files implying indefinite extension: horizontally, into the illuminated walls and, vertically, into the darkened ceiling and the floor, appearing to pass right through the confines of the room. This was nothing like Marinetti's eulogy of flight as willed ascent and mastery; by contrast, ascent became loss of ground and consciousness, on the verge of vanishing. The void of the sky and the void of the ground were the same. The exhibits remained suspended between and at the threshold between oblivion and consciousness. What was evoked in the glowing shadowless space between two planes of darkness in the *Room of the Gold Medals* was still aerial: the sky itself figured in black and white.

In his Hall of Honor at the 1938 Triennale, the pursuit of abstraction is taken to the limit beyond which architecture would be an imaginary exercise. A series of off-set panels create a sustained experience of being at the brink, it is all threshold. Persico's initial sketch, defined by the vertical lines of a *peripteron* and the wing-like arms of the figure, summarizes the whole spatial dynamic: space flutters (Figure 7.5). Gio Ponti wrote of "the apparition of a thought become reality."[37] The work is a pure appearing, a ghost of thought suspended in a realm of possibility. One experiences an event without actualization: only a presage "Potentiality," argues Agamben, "is not simply non-Being, simple privation, but rather the existence of non-Being, the presence of an absence"[38] (Figure 7.6).

7.5
Eduardo Persico,
sketch for the
Salone d'Onore
From Eduardo
Persico, *Scritti
d'architettura
(1927/1935)*, ed.
Giulia Veronesi,
Florence: Vallechi,
1968, vol. 2
unpaginated)

7.6
**Persico, Nizzoli
and Fontana,
Salone d'Onore,
Milan Triennale,
1936 (From
Eduardo
Persico, *Scritti
d'architettura
(1927/1935)*, ed.
Giulia Veronesi,
Florence: Vallechi,
1968, vol. 2
unpaginated)**

A recurring strategy of using light elements to achieve a sense of sudden displacement also surfaces in several of Albini's projects. Immateriality cuts away the solidity of the regime's rhetoric, or simply the solidity of quotidian expectations, by opening onto other cultural frameworks, to nature, or the cosmos. Irony and paradox often accompany these de-grounding effects, which, a far cry from the Futurist and Rationalist abandonment and transcendence of the earth, present another lightness, a return to earthly being cast in a fresh mode.

Suspended as many of Albini's works are, they do not, by that fact, attempt to free themselves from matter (though they toy with its absence). They stem, rather, from empirical testing, traditional craftsmanship, and trade practice. Albini reasoned with his hands and his bodily weight. In a "horizontal" process of reasoning, he avoided the vertical leap to transcendent reason. The final result is solid while preserving possibilities not being fully actualized. He frequently circumscribes what is absent and makes it appear – ceilings, walls, and even floors, are defined but "missing." They show that emptiness can be just as real as solid bodies. Logic is suspended in paradox. Reality and imagination change places. The outside is inside, lead floats, and a bookshelf is an engineering problem that looks all the more fantastic for being completely logical.[39] Lightness is not simply an absence of materiality nor simply opposed to the weight and fixity of the earth.

After the Futurist ascent, lightness comes back to the ground: the earth is made light. Another relation to ground emerges: not as permanent base, but as a site of equilibrium which allows events to reframe the boundaries of fixed conceptions. In "On the Spirit of Gravity," Nietzsche wrote: "who will teach men to fly one day will have moved all boundary stones; to him all boundary stones in themselves will fly into the air, he will baptize the earth anew – as 'the Light One'."[40] In this conception of lightness, freedom is no longer seen as an escape *from* materiality to a higher world but as a release of other, freer spaces *within* this one.

In a neglected book, *L'elemento "verde" e l'abitazione*, the Rationalist Luigi Figini posed a diagram of the relationship between dwelling and nature as two separate circles in different stages of overlapping that would in an edenic state perfectly overlap. But consciousness itself precludes such a point.[41] Any image of complete interpenetration implies a strong metaphysical note of dreamlike unreality. The last pages of the book illustrate Albini's *Stanza di soggiorno in una villa*, for the 7th *Triennale*, 1940. Albini's installation opens, past birds perched behind a net, onto a void without horizon or surroundings (Figure 7.7). It manages to evoke a note of unreality resulting from an inversion, or interfolding, of "exterior" and "interior." A dream-like space is formed through splitting, splicing and eliding. The meadow, blooming with flowers of the field, passes under the glazing at ground level invading half the space. The other half, a rustic floor of split stone, brings the paving inside from the outdoor terrace. A tree from the meadow carries blossoming branches to the upper level and the birds, with their own diminutive tree in their cage, entwine the space with a natural world "outside." Everything pulsates in a binary rhythm by splits, slats and stripes. The daisies sprout thickly, the tree blossoms. It is spring (Figure 7.8).

A temporary work in the twilight of an epoch on the eve of war, but also an oneiric vision in the bright blue of day, it caught in suspension what is most fleeting – like the original meaning of *soggiorno*, the quiet flutter of the ephemeral in the temporality of a sojourn: staying for a day. Carla Zanini saw, in "this plunging of man into nature," the awareness of a moral value: the "desire not to contain oneself egoistically but to remain open and tied to the living elements of the world."[42] This moral value might be figured, to return to Figini's initial postulate, by the interpenetrating circles, the immediacy of whose unity is the paradox of being outside while inside. It would express a condition of equivalence between exterior world and the "house of man," which is the "theoretical limit to which we tend, unreachable after the sin of the first man,"[43] a state of grace (Figure 7.9).

A decade later, with the *Museum of the Treasury of San Lorenzo* (1952– 56), Albini set out in quest of the grail – another quest for a center of gravity, where

7.7
**Franco Albini,
Living Room in
a Villa, Milan
Triennale, 1940
(Courtesy of
Marco Albini)**

what seems out of this world is really in this world. Though it is underground, the Museum still retains the element of suspension. It also is the building most directly related to Albini's *allestimenti*,[44] and is itself an *allestimento* in the form of a building (Figure 7.10).[45]

Set partially under the cathedral of Genoa, it is hidden in a limbo cleared from the everyday of the city to leave a space of surprising silence, an intense mysterious void (Figure 7.11). It has no relation with the dense urban fabric above and no status as an object. It is composed of four cylindrical *tholloi*, like small sacristies, which increase in size as one progresses. The smallest, containing the *Sacro Catino*, once thought to be the Grail, appears at the threshold from a disjointed passage, by

.8
ranco Albini,
iving Room in
Villa, Milan
riennale, 1940
Courtesy of
Marco Albini)

.9
ranco Albini,
.iving Room in
Villa, Milan
riennale, 1940,
letail of glass
loor and lawn
Courtesy of
Marco Albini)

way of a narrow stair from the cathedral. This pivotal work is therefore the first treasure seen on entry and the last before leaving. Franca Helg noted of Albini: "how much he enjoyed it that a small object could be heavy and a large one very light" – it was his way of "searching for a preciousness through an unexpected sensation."[46]

The Museum is a wholly interior world, without horizon or vanishing point, "a perfect and precious artificial universe."[47] But it wavers between the inwardness

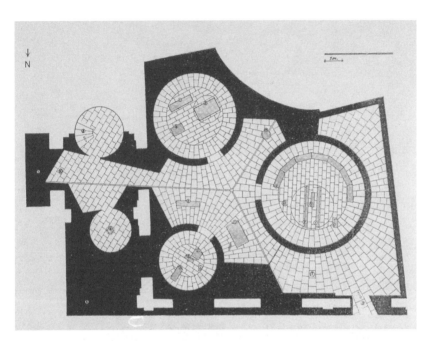

7.10
**Albini and Helg,
Treasury of San
Lorenzo, Genoa,
1952–56, plan
(Courtesy of
Marco Albini)**

7.11
**Albini and Helg,
Montecatini
Stand, display
of Rhodiatoce
products at Milan
Trade Fair, 1954
(Courtesy of
Marco Albini)**

of the earth, as an embedded body, and the evocation of the forces of the universe itself. The tension between the poles of gravitational attraction around which the museum is structured, suggests the suspension of stellar bodies or iron filings in a magnetic field. The interior is an exterior. It is underground but with intimations of the extraterrestrial.

Given the subterranean location, the mass of local Promontorio stone and the absence of any tectonic suspension save in the expository devices, it may seem perverse to exemplify the Museum as light. It might be presumed that Albini shifted course after the war, away from his distinctive trait of suspension towards an exploration of the weight of materials, or that the new attention to place and local materials, widespread after the war, seeks to reveal some genius loci. Buried or subterranean buildings, however, are not by that fact heavy, being tectonically unrelated to the horizon and surface of the earth, they may appear to float underground.[48]

The central void seems broken up haphazardly but proves to be in the form of a hexagon into whose alternate vertices are inserted three larger *tholloi*. The hexagon just happens to coincide with the geometry of the guiding element: the *Sacro Catino*. This void is generated by the three surrounding *tholloi*. The center is an excluded space, a space outside. To be there is to be closed outside a castle, closed within ramparts without a keep, or closed in a castle which has been turned inside out. Subtly converging and diverging lines of vision offer varying lateral, oblique, and transverse views from this space, but access to the center is frustrated, as if ideally they would be impenetrable ramparts or monads (Figure 7.12).

7.12
Albini and Helg,
Museum of the
Treasury of San
Lorenzo, cases
for vestments
(Courtesy of
Marco Albini)

This zone is the space of a quest. On descending, the visitor turns a corner, steps through an iron gate, and into an anteroom, and past the *thollos* of the *Sacro Catino*. Albini encloses the emerald-colored basin in a glass case, cylindrical like the cell in which it is isolated, and mounts it on a pole, magnifying its modest artistic value by association with the Holy Grail of the Knights of the Round Table. Then, in the detail of the metal mounting, he re-figures the basin as a radar dish, as if the receptacle were itself searching the depths of space (Figure 7.13). It is set into red velvet split in a triangle and prefigures the central space, where the tips of the

7.13
Albini and Helg, Museum of the Treasury of San Lorenzo, statue of San Lorenzo with Sacro Catino in case beyond (Courtesy of Marco Albini)

stellar beams do not quite manage to meet, leaving a tense split which quietly rends the central void. If "things themselves are places,"[49] then this thing becomes a place. Turning to the right, the space narrows again in a short tunnel, then suddenly opens into the void. In one sense, the visitor ventures on an allegorical path into darkness, in search of the treasure, gains knowledge of art and history, and re-ascends. But the return to earth base also brings with it the experience of exteriority. The center's exclusion points to the perennial quest of place in the drama of existence. Albini sublimates all these esoteric referents, abstracting them in suspended images of the numinous, dreamlike atmosphere of the Grail Castle, floating in the earth, under the stars, in space.

The museum is the culmination of a path to an immanent lightness – elegant, and unreal – that is conceived as a freedom *within* the earth and materiality, rather than as a freedom *from* them, and as a condition of potentiality rather than potency. One cannot actually build in the air, but instead of the illusion of hovering without support, Albini provided "assisted suspension," achieving an element of grace which provided an entry into freedom: to do something within necessity by fulfilling but suspending it. This happens in the moment of becoming, where the necessary turns into possibility. Between image and function, a work arises from grace, in a return to the contingency of things, rather than what seems their sheer nature. When design or art is rooted in an event which ordains its chance between taking place and non-place, the infinite emerges as latent in the finitude of the material. Albini's style of reasoning with hands and body was, perhaps, like that of a dancer, not a "thinking caught in a body but as body which is thought."[50]

The provisional and ephemeral, the fragile and the unstable occasioned in *allestimenti* anticipate a strand of thinking today, which relates building less to sites, conceived as permanent, than as a taking place, as the vibration of an event. These airy works reveal place in modernity as a liminal condition: they "discover the limit not as a defensive barrier but as an intermediate space," as Franco Rella writes, which "allows the gathering of the thing itself as a tension, as a constellation of events and possibilities."[51] Of course, the very idea of a project is unthinkable without the category of possibility.[52] Designing is itself this condition, it "means constructing the place of difference since what is only possible might become real."[53] But it also means that place must reveal something potential, preserving itself in and yet surviving actuality. Without this, place becomes all too fully actualized as the banal "non-places" that are all too familiar, even when designed with place in mind.

Not surprisingly, perhaps, most modernist architects, despite their theoretical disillusionment with the notion of rooted place, were nevertheless embroiled in the politics of place. Their buildings were always local for some, and permanent – despite or because of their intentions. At the same time, permanence and local references were compromised by a will to deny place. And this is what these *allestimenti* point to: the taken-for-granted tendency in modernist architectural practice, ruled as it was by a rhetoric of space, nevertheless to regard buildings as real, actualized and permanent places. This compulsion has barred, for a long time, the recognition of an alternative to the conceptual opposition of space and place. Place, after modernity, is but a potential.

In these *allestimenti*, an aerial suspension with its grids, frames and blanks provided some of the clearest images of hovering on the edge between being and non-being in brushes with consciousness that touched on the luminousness of the possible. The propensity to levitation in modern architecture indicated a potentiality to master space and a potentiality to suspend that mastery. Now, when all the blanks on the maps have been filled and spatial extension rebounds on itself, the challenge is to rethink both the difference between these two potentialities and those inherent in our current dis-placement.

Acknowledgments

My thanks to Tina Engels-Schwarzpaul for her invaluable editorial support.

Notes

1   See Adolf Max Vogt, "Das Schwebe-Syndrom in der Architektur der zwanziger Jahre," in *Das architektonische Urteil. Annäherungen und Interpretationen von Architektur und Kunst*, Basel: Birkhäuser, 1989, pp. 201–233, and John Rajchman, "Lightness," in *Constructions*, Cambridge, MA: MIT Press, 1994, pp. 37–53.

2   See Alberto Boatto, *Della guerra e dell'aria*, Genoa: Costa e Nolan, 1992, p. 14.

3   Luce Irigaray, *The Forgetting of Air in Martin Heidegger*, trans. Mary Beth Mader, Austin, TX: University of Texas, 1999, p. 8.

4   See Felix Philipp Ingold, *Literatur und Aviatik: europäische Flugdichtung 1909–1927: mit einem Exkurs über die Flugidee in der modernen Malerei und Architektur*, ed. by Jean-François Bergier et al., Basel: Birkhäuser, 1978; Robert Wohl, *A Passion for Wings Aviation and the Western Imagination 1908–1918*, New Haven, CT: Yale University Press, 1994, and Christoph Asendorf, *Super Constellation. Flugzeug und Raumrevolution*, Vienna: Springer Verlag, 1997.

5   Yi-Fu Tuan, *Space and Place: The Perspective of Experience*, London: Edward Arnold, 1977, p. 3.

6   Filippo Tommaso Marinetti, *Mafarka le Futuriste: Roman Africain*, Paris: Sansot, 1909, p. 211.

7   "Fondamento plastico della scultura e pittura futurista," 1913, in Umberto Boccioni, *Altri inediti e apparati critici*, ed. by Zeno Birolli, Milan: Feltrinelli, 1972.

8   Marianne W. Martin, *Futurist Art and Theory*, Oxford: Clarendon Press, 1968, pp. 86–87.

9   Antonio Sant'Elia, *Futurist Architecture: Manifesto* (1914) in Enrico Crispolti (ed.), *Attraverso l'architettura futurista*, Modena: Fonte d'Abisso, 1984, p. 95.

10   Boccioni, "Architettura Futurista. Manifesto," in Crispolti, *Attraverso l'architettura futurista*, p. 93.

11   Filippo Tommaso Marinetti, *Le futurisme*, Paris, 1911, p. 16.

12   *Birth of a Futurist Aesthetic* (1910).

13   See "The Blue Sky," in Gaston Bachelard, *Air and Dreams: An Essay on the Imagination of Movement*, Dallas, TX: Dallas Institute of Humanities and Culture, 1988, pp. 161–174.

14   Quoted in Charlotte Douglas, *Swans of Other Worlds: Kazimir Malevich and the Origins of Abstraction in Russia*, Ann Arbor, MI: UMI Research Press, 1980, p. 53.

15   Hans Sedlmayr, *Art in Crisis: The Lost Centre*, trans. O. Muller Brian Battershaw (trans. of *Verlust der Mitte; die bildende Kunst des 19. und 20. Jahrhunderts als Symptom und Symbol der Zeit*, Salzburg, 1948), Chicago: Henry Regnery Company, 1958, p. 106.

16   Carl Schmitt, *Land and Sea*, Washington, DC: Plutarch Press, 1997, p. 58.

17   Carl Schmitt, *The Nomos of the Earth in the International Law of Jus Publicum Europaeum*, New York: Telos Press, 2003, p. 320 (trans. modified).

18   Massimo Cacciari, "Adolf Loos e il suo Angelo," in *Adolf Loos: Das Andere*, edited by Carlo Pirovano, Milan: Electa, 1981. This had a tradition: under the international doctrine of *terra nullius*, a nation could gain title to any uninhabited land which it "discovered" and occupied.

19   Massimo Cacciari, *Geo-filosofia dell'Europa*, Milan: Adelphi, 1994, p. 63.

20 Ibid., p. 69.

21 Filippo Tommaso Marinetti, A. Mazzoni and M. Somenzi, "Manifesto Futurista della Architettura Aerea," in Ezio Godoli, *Il Futurismo*, Rome-Bari: Laterza, 1997, p. 195.

22 Filippo Tommaso Marinetti *et al.*, *F. T. Marinetti futurista*, Naples: Guida, 1977, pp. 56–57.

23 Boatto, *Della guerra e dell'aria*, p. 84.

24 See Vittorio Gregotti, "La mimesi della ragione," *Rassegna* 31, September 1987, 5.

25 Sartoris notes,

> The proper character of this modern phenomenon is the complete absorption of the finite in the infinite. This phenomenon could thus be identified in a sort of pantheism. Its distinctive trait is elevation, and it could not have two contradictory essences. It borders on, by this fact, the great conceptions of metaphysics, fundamental conditions of the human spirit. The modern phenomenon of architecture is not circumscribed within the limits of a determined expanse, because it is this incorruptible tide of artistic and constructive creation which is found in the region of eternal truths. It yields not a step to matter, but follows the traces of sublime notions. By it, the idea of infinity and the incommensurable penetrates to the heart of darkness.
>
> (*Encyclopédie de l'architecture nouvelle*, Milan: Hoepli, 1948, p. 123)

26 There is no precise English equivalent for the word or practice of *allestimento*, a sphere of activity covering the design of exhibitions, stands, installations, displays, shop-fronts and interiors.

27 Not dependent on full embodiment, *allestimento* is, in Sergio Polano's words, "suspended between construction and representation" in "the conjunction of the heavy tectonic of construction and the lightness of chance, consistent instead with exhibiting." Sergio Polano, *Mostrare: L'allestimento in Italia dagli anni Venti agli anni Ottanta*, Milan: Lybra Immagine, 1988, p. 40.

28 Giuseppe Pagano, "Parliamo un po' d'esposizioni," *Costruzioni-Casabella* 159–60, March–April 1941.

29 Malevich, quoted in Massimo Cacciari, *Icone della legge*, Milan: Adelphi, 1985, p. 209.

30 Guido Modiano, "Tipografie di Edoardo Persico," in *Campo Graphico*, monographic edition dedicated to Persico, nos 11–12, November–December 1935, quoted in D'Auria, "Persico architetto e grafico," in Cesare de Seta (ed.), *Edoardo Persico*, Naples: Electa, 1987, p. 134.

31 Aristotle, *De Anima*, 430 a 1.

32 Aristotle, *Metaphysics*, 1060b 10.

33 Giorgio Agamben, *Potentialities: Collected Essays in Philosophy*, ed. Daniel Heller-Roazen, Stanford, CA: Stanford University Press, 1999, p. 215.

34 Raffaello Giolli, "Negozi a Milano," *Casabella* 109, January 1937.

35 Vittorio Gregotti, "Milano e la cultura architettonica tra le due guerre," in *Edoardo Persico*, p. 21.

36 Antonio Monti in *Esposizione dell' aeronautica italiana, giugno–ottobre 1934, XII Catalogo ufficiale*, Milan: Edizioni d'arte Emilio Bestetti, p. 91.

37 Gio Ponti, "La Sala della Vittoria," *Domus* 103, July 1936, 6.

38 Agamben, *Potentialities*, p. 179.

39 See Albini's Lead and Zinc Pavilion for Montecatini, Mostra Autarchica del Minerale Italiano, Rome, 1938 and his "Sailing-ship" bookcase, 1938–40.

40 Friedrich Nietzsche, *Thus Spoke Zarathustra*, Harmondsworth: Penguin, 1968, p. 238.

41 Luigi Figini, *L'elemento "verde" e l'abitazione*, Milan: Domus, 1950, p. 27. Figini exemplifies this by two paintings of De Chirico. "*Interno*", 1926, portraying a forest and surf *inside* a room, and "*Interno in una valle*", 1927, items of a living room *outside* in a valley and notes: "the same phase can also express the theoretical limit to which we tend, unreachable after the sin of the first man."

42 Carla Zanini, "A proposito di un arredamento esposto alla VII Triennale," *Costruzioni-Casabella* 157, January 1941, 38.

43 Figini, *L'elemento "verde" e l'abitazione*, p. 27.

44 In fact, in the same year, he uses the model of bent stellar rays in the Palazzo Grassi in Venice with the Miracle of Science and in the tent of threads for the exhibition Genoese Fabrics of the XVI Century. The ethereal environment of the Rhodiatoce room at the Milan Fair (1953–54) develops the basic schema of the Museum: cells within a geometric container, combining it with the arrangement of sixteenth-century copes hanging like glow worms.

45 See Pier Federico Caliari, *La forma dell'effimero: Tra allestimento e architettura: compresenza di codici e sovrapposizime di tessitura*, Milan: Lybra Immagine, 2000, p. 43.

46 Franca Helg, in Livia Carloni, Enrico Valeriani and Benedetta Montevecchi, *Franco Albini architettura per un museo*, Rome: De Luca Editore, 1980, p. 7.

47 Cesare De Seta, "Franco Albini architetto, tra razionalismo e technologia," in De Seta (ed.), *Franco Albini, Architettura e design 1930–1970*, New York: Rizzoli, 1981, p. 23.

48 See Greg Lynn, "Differential Gravities," *Architecture New York*, March–April 1994, p. 20.

49 Martin Heidegger, *Die Kunst und der Raum*, St. Gallen: Erker Verlag, 1969, p. 11.

50 Alain Badiou, "La danse comme métaphore de la pensée," in *Petit manuel d'inesthétique*, Paris: Seuil, 1998, p. 110.

51 Franco Rella, *Limina: Il pensiero e le cose*, Milan: Feltrinelli, 1987, p. 18.

52 A project is

> an anticipation of the coming-to-be of something that, with respect to the future, could be qualified as possible. It is evident that the idea of project is quite extraneous to a rigorously deterministic conception of the real. The necessary and the impossible, in fact, radically contradict the ability of something to be conceived of as project.
>
> (Francesco Calvo, "Progetto," in *Enciclopedia Einaudi*, Turin: Einaudi, 1980, p. 127)

53 Rella, *Limina*, p. 18.

8

Transparency in the Contemporary Australian House

Harry Margalit

> To ward off anguish by understanding and absorbing its causes would seem to be one of the principal ethical exigencies of bourgeois art. It matters little if the conflicts, contradictions, and lacerations that generate this anguish are temporarily reconciled by means of a complex mechanism, or if, through contemplative sublimation, catharsis is achieved.[1]

The opening line of Tafuri's *Architecture and Utopia* lays out a dynamic that, although unfashionable in its embrace of the terminology of classical ideology, nonetheless presents an intriguing line of interrogation for architecture. This is particularly so for Australian architecture, and its ongoing fascination with the detached house as an object of architectural experimentation. The award of the Pritzker Prize in 2002 to Glenn Murcutt, largely on the basis of his houses, underlines this tendency and its projection abroad.[2] The jury citation for the prize noted Murcutt's Miesian beginnings, and it also stressed that his "is an architecture of place, architecture that responds to landscape and to the climate."[3]

Murcutt's work has also been perceived as quintessentially Australian, an interpretation the architect has attempted to counter by writing about his work in rational or pragmatic terms.[4] He is at pains to demonstrate how much of his work emanates from catalogue items and practical considerations. However, much of the primary appeal of his work lies in its openness, and a commitment to the modernist principle of a reconciliation between interior and an idealized external "nature" (Figure 8.1).

Murcutt is not alone in designing houses along these principles. The glazed pavilion has been emulated by a number of architects a generation younger than him. In the Sydney region Peter Stutchbury has produced a distinctive body of work that relies on a similar dissolution between interior and exterior, and a

8.1
Glenn Murcutt, Fletcher-Page House, Kangaroo Valley, NSW (Photo: Anthony Browell)

corresponding sensitivity to materials and building techniques (Figures 8.2, 8.3). This regional architecture has also been taken as representative of Australian architecture as a whole, as it projects specific notions of the architectural potential inherent in the local climate, topography and vegetation.[5]

8.2
Stutchbury & Pape, interior, Bangalay, Kangaroo Valley, NSW (Photo: Michael Nicholson)

3
tutchbury &
ape, interior,
pringwater,
eaforth, NSW
Photo: Michael
icholson)

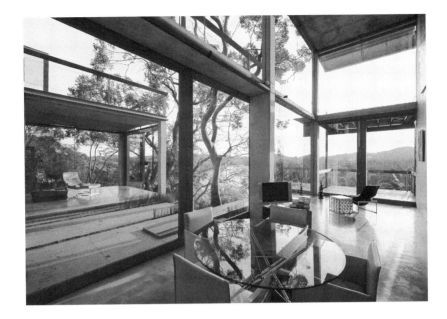

The reception of Murcutt's work has generally been in terms of these polarities – the universal opposed to the local, the practical as against the transcendental, and how his work can be placed on the ensuing spectra. However, following on from Tafuri's statement, how might Murcutt and other exponents of the reconciliation of interior and exterior through transparency be regarded if we introduce the notion of "anguish," and its reconciliation, into their work?

The genesis of the "open" house, with its large expanses of glass and operable walls, can be traced back to the strong post-war modernist movement which popularized modernist planning and architecture in Australia. The orthodoxy of post-war modernism found expression in the work of architects such as Neil Clerehan in Melbourne, with his designs for commissioned houses as well as his work for the Small Homes Service sponsored by the Royal Victorian Institute of Architects and *The Age* newspaper that were intended to popularize modernist principles in modest houses. In these designs the rationalization of daily life supersedes any specific notion of Australian-ness. Their planning dissects the operations of the nuclear family, and considerable ingenuity is brought to bear on the problem of cheaply housing the complex "living patterns," in Clerehan's words, that underlay domestic life.[6]

The influence of these early modernist houses can be seen in much contemporary Australian domestic planning. Murcutt, for one, inherited the linear plan and his architecture is inconceivable without it.[7] The sequence is evident when we look at Clerehan's house T372 of 1957, with its revealed circulation passing through each room and exposing the functions to the front of the house (Figure 8.4). Murcutt's Fletcher-Page House uses a similar device, and a number of his other houses use the linear circulation and the crosswall room divider.

The advantages of this system are easy to discern. In the Australian climate, they offer easy cross-ventilation by presenting a plan that is one room deep. They also

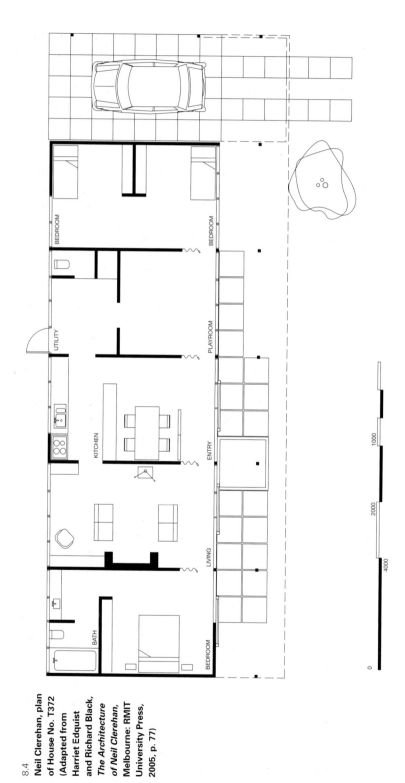

8.4
Neil Clerehan, plan of House No. T372 (Adapted from **Harriet Edquist and Richard Black,** *The Architecture of Neil Clerehan,* Melbourne: RMIT University Press, 2005, p. 77)

BEDROOM

BEDROOM

UTILITY

KITCHEN

PLAYROOM

ENTRY

BATH

LIVING

BEDROOM

0   4000   2000   1000

allow each room to be exposed to the view, with fully glazed window/walls. The image of transparency thus engendered is an alluring and persistent one. The wide appeal of the Case Study houses emanating from John Entenza's publication *Arts and Architecture* no doubt also added to the ideal of the transparent house. Both Clerehan and Murcutt met with designers of Case Study houses: Clerehan visited Charles and Ray Eames in 1952, and Murcutt met Craig Ellwood some years later in 1973.

The linear, heavily glazed house can be explained in rational terms as a suitable response to the Australian climate. The cross-ventilation is direct and effective, and the climate allows the house to be opened up throughout the year for longer or shorter periods. Yet the Brutalist era reminds us that other compelling arguments have been put forward in the past half-century for other very different manifestations of the Australian house, many of which performed particularly well in the lower Australian latitudes. Harry Sowden's photographic volume *Towards an Australian Architecture* of 1968, for instance, presents a range of buildings steeped in Brutalism and early Stirling, and a taste for deep shading. Sowden was documenting the proliferation of Brutalism in all building types across Australia in the 1960s, and the style continued with some vigour into the 1970s, especially in new educational buildings.[8]

The argument over what form a rational Australian house should take could be resolved through empirical measurement of performance, but this would be beside the point. The issue was never definitively resolved in the 1980s, when the linear plan reasserted itself with its attendant transparency. Thus the change can be attributed as much to intention as to empirical conviction, in particular an intention grounded in a certain psychological interpretation of the Australian house as a fit for the living patterns of Clerehan, or what might coldly be called the site for the production and reproduction of the nuclear family dynamic.

The specific question that can be posed, then, is why has the transparent pavilion become a dominant architectural type in a climate where its opposite has, at times, been the domestic norm? And, as an extension to this, what is the significance of the shift in the conception of "interior" that this entails?

The modernist tendency to expose the interior by rendering it transparent cannot be explained purely as a liberating move without considering what it is that it is attempting to banish. The vigour of this spatial transformation can be traced through some key texts. The Sydney architect Walter Bunning's vision of the post-war Australian house and its surrounds was set out in his 1945 polemic *Homes in the Sun*, wherein he made an argument for a rational approach to planning based on solar access and an appreciation of the emerging cultural dimension of the Australian climate as it came to be expressed in the later term "lifestyle." Bunning's arguments have their origins in the ideas he imbibed as a travelling scholar to England from 1936 to 1939, especially his ideas about the relevant housing form for the various stages of domestic life: elevator apartments for single individuals and childless couples, row houses for couples with young children etc., all representing an orderly unfolding of structured, modern life.[9]

Many of Bunning's ideals must be read against the acute housing shortage experienced in Australia through the 1940s. Yet even accounting for this austerity, a term the Australian historian Max Freeland used to characterize the period, there remains a formal ideal made explicit by Bunning and reiterated by Freeland. In an early review of the seminal Melbourne *Glenunga Flats* designed in the early 1940s by the Swiss immigrant Frederick Romberg, Bunning notes the large glazed walls to the living rooms. He writes: "From the interior this window helps to achieve a fusion of interior and exterior, which is one of the main aims of contemporary architectural design."[10]

The point is taken up some years later by Freeland in a manner which reveals the hold this move exerted on the Australian architectural imagination. Freeland, whose eye for hypocrisy owed much to a dislike of the blatantly commercial in architecture, seems to falter in providing a clear explanation for the trend to merge the interior with the exterior. It was a move too deeply rooted in the circumstances of his own intellectual formation, and the buildings which embodied it remained touchstones, for Freeland, of an intellectual purity. His description of the tendencies of early Sydney and Melbourne modernists deserves extensive quoting:

> Most of them were young Turks and most of them were idealists convinced of the rightness of directness and the importance of climate and the environment . . . One and all they were sensible and logical. For the first time they gave greater weight to aspect and prospect than to public effect . . . They rediscovered that the Australian climate is conducive to outdoor living and built cantilevered balconies or paved terraces covered by shadow-casting pergolas or verandahs outside the living room. They almost dissolved the wall between the two by means of a transparent net consisting of a series of glazed doors placed next to each other. The linking of the outside with the inside was part of the overall approach to the controlling of space. Internal doors between dining room, living room and entrance became broad openings across which folding glass doors could be drawn if needed but which visually linked each area with the next. While each area was confined and contained, it was no longer a self-contained or isolated box but part of a larger pattern in which the parts were related to and dependent upon each other.[11]

This passage is significant for its comprehensive description of the emerging ideals in domestic architecture of the period, but there is also a sense of the elusiveness of the intent behind these moves to the author. Clearly Freeland is basing many of his judgments on correcting the deficiencies represented by the "straw man" of the Victorian or Federation house, with its arrangement of rooms dictated by the orientation to the street, and the ensuing plan dictated by a formal sequence of reception rooms rather than solar orientation and "paramount consideration to the convenience and pleasure of the occupants," as Freeland put it.[12] This same argument is followed by Bunning, who includes in *Homes in the Sun* an illustration of this generic Victorian house against which he defines his proposals.

What is particularly interesting in Freeland's description is the sentence where he describes this new planning as being part of the overall approach to the *controlling of space*. The qualification which follows conveys an image of space which might be closed off, but which retained a contiguous visual connection that destroyed the isolation of the individual room in favor of a pattern of room planning that stressed the proximity of spaces and their visual, if not actual, continuity. Freeland's description is made with an implied recognition of the rightness of this approach, in his terms. The passage is without irony or the judgmental distance that he brings to bear on so many other architectural examples in his *Architecture in Australia*.

If, for Freeland, the veracity of this emerging trend was beyond question, then it is to other observers we must turn in order to historicize this shift. The major correspondent from the past, as it were, who articulated this shift in acutely observed social terms is the post-war Melbourne architect and commentator Robin Boyd. Boyd's purview was smaller than Freeland's, and consequently considerably more fine-grained. Instead of relying on the oversimplified distinction between the Victorian/ Federation house and its proto-modernist successor, Boyd overlays a satiric sensibility that undermines the neatness of Freeland's periodization.

For Boyd, the persistence of the ill-fitting Victorian or Federation house was a result, in part, of the slow adaptation of colonial Australia to the reality of its relocation. He writes:

> From the earliest days and throughout the nineteenth century the unquestioned aim of every house had been to fight the un-English qualities of Australian climate. The sun was shunned. The north side was occupied by servants' quarters and service rooms. Dark louvred shutters, closed for most of the year, and verandahs, window-hoods and heavily lined curtains, put up a formidable barrier to bright light.[13]

This explanation echoes Bunning and Freeland, but despite his thesis that design became more responsive to sun and light from the 1930s on, for Boyd the discomfort of houses in Australia derived as much from the deformed aspirations they housed as from the climatic anxieties of an earlier age. Writing in 1952, he declared:

> Whenever an Australian boy spoke to an Australian girl of marriage, he meant, and she understood him to mean, a life in a five-roomed home. He had never questioned its desirability . . . Not until he had won his home, had lived in it for some fifty years, did he begin to doubt. Then . . . he turned on the unhappy thing he had reared. Yet this clean and tidy house could hardly be blamed. It had not been built for happiness . . . Even such an elementary pleasure as a chair in the afternoon sun with a french-window open to a lawn was banned; grass would be carried indoors and trodden into the carpet.[14]

Boyd's extended consideration of Australian domesticity was first published in 1952 as *Australia's Home: Why Australians Built the Way They Did*. It is an interweaving of sentiment, pragmatic decisions and a portrayal of a stultifying mid-twentieth-century culture that drove culturally curious Australians abroad. Indeed, there is an element of caricature about it, a discomfort with so many aspects of Australian life, expressed in Boyd's sharply observed detail such as his drawing *Part of a Living-room, c. 1950* (Figure 8.5). His accompanying text has an almost Auden-like desperation:

8.5
Robin Boyd, *Part of a Living-room, c. 1950* (Robin Boyd, *Australia's Home*, 2nd edn, Ringwood, Vic. Penguin, 1978, p.130. Permission courtesy of the Boyd family.)

Part of a Living-room, c. 1950

> The gross armchair (part of a suite of two chairs and a sofa) had a core of roughest boxwood; it was cheaper to make than a smaller chair which exposed its wooden frame. Light-coloured fabric sometimes covered the sides and back, but patterned Genoa velvet disguised dirt marks on all wearing surfaces. Similarly the pattern of the Axminster carpet and the shadow tissue curtain disguised dirty footprints and fingerprints respectively. The cocktail cabinet was walnut, the radio plastic, the ornament glazed coloured china, the lampstand chromium and cream plastic, the picture a print of a fox-hunt scene, the colour accents usually cream and burgundy.[15]

Boyd closes the nexus between habitation and form in a way that Freeland cannot. Boyd's social anxiety, or at least his snobbishness, allow him to describe distinctions in architectural taste as representative of broader questions of taste bound up in historical rectitude, consumption and, in his eyes, the numbing effects of class conformity.

One cannot but be struck by the pessimistic tone of much of Boyd's description of domestic life. Consider this passage:

> Family life had become, for the female, an endless sequence of cooking and restorative work behind the activities of the male and the infant. For the male, it was a fruitless search for quietness and peace in a jungle of kitchen and cleaning equipment and dissatisfied children. For the children it was a constant conflict against restrictions. All parties sought enjoyment in various forms away from home.

The most obvious escape for the adult was in alcohol. Although Australians drank and were noted for drinking as much as any other people in the world, they consumed all but a small proportion away from home and away from members of the opposite sex. The male killed two birds with one stone when he drank. He escaped from the dull prison of the home he had built and from the atmosphere of women, with whom he associated the restrictions of home life.[16]

Two points should be made here about *Australia's Home*. The first is that it attempts to deal with both popular and high taste in domestic design, and in this sense it is egalitarian, if only grudgingly so. The second is that it does not reinforce a simple distinction, based on a modernist teleology, between the follies of pre-modernist design and the virtues of modernism. Boyd has his exemplars of good designers, but they are the distinctly early twentieth-century Melbourne ones of Robert Haddon, Desbrowe Annear, Burley Griffin, the mid-century Mewton and Grounds, and the post-war pairing of Peter and Dione McIntyre. Yet his pessimism is persistent. In the epilogue to the 1968 edition of *Australia's Home*, sixteen years after its initial publication, Boyd noted of the 1960s that "[w]ith stolid fortitude Australia's home was still overcoming most attempts to make it better."[17]

The sentiment that seeps through Boyd's writings presents a problem only partly architectural. Architecture seems to play out a dynamic that is rooted in the continuing reproduction of an emotionally stunted existence. The key is the way in which Boyd moves easily from the problem of the popular house to that of the architect-designed one, which always represented a tiny proportion of Australian detached houses. The subtext, for Boyd, is a culturally pervasive inability of Australians to live well in their environment.

This point of view has sustained other critiques of Australian architecture, although not perhaps with the sense of tragedy that Boyd imparts. Freeland, for example, states that in the 1950s "[m]uch of the architect's trouble was psychological. In 1951 they were shaken to be shown that the sort of architecture that was happening in America and which they thought local conditions withheld from them could be produced in Australia."[18] He is referring to the Rose Seidler House, a widely publicized modernist icon from 1949 built by Harry Seidler for his mother on Sydney's northern outskirts, but the implication is that the barrier to producing suitable houses lay in a limited outlook rather than in other objective conditions.

The issue which arises here – how changing notions of the good life were expressed in domestic architecture – is illuminating for the type of Australian house which emerged in the 1980s. Any reading of the form of these houses takes place against an evolving attitude to the dynamics of domesticity itself.

Tafuri's statement leaves the mechanism of warding off "anguish" open, but the intimate connection between what might be called the psychic dimension of domesticity (in the Freudian sense) and the ideal type of domestic house has been partially explored in a number of contexts in recent years. Sylvia Lavin's 2004 *Form Follows Libido* traces the influence of psychoanalysis on the work of Richard Neutra. Lavin's analysis works through specific case studies, and concerns itself with Neutra's architectural response to specific psychoanalytic concepts such as *empathy*, as well as his relationships with his clients. Regarding transparency, for instance, Lavin writes:

> The most noted feature of Neutra's work during the 1950s was an intense concentration on dismantling conventional barriers between inside and out. The glass house type, with its apparently easy access to the outside world, seems to be an obvious response to the birth trauma.[19]

In a more general sense, the Freudian concept of the uncanny has been taken up by Anthony Vidler as a fertile category mediating between modernity and architecture. In a chapter on transparency, Vidler elucidates what he sees as the irony of transparency. He quotes early observers of the connection between modernity and transparency, including Walter Benjamin who remarked:

> To live in a glass house is a revolutionary virtue par excellence. It is also an intoxication, a moral exhibitionism that we badly need. Discretion concerning one's own existence, once an aristocratic virtue, has become more and more an affair of petit-bourgeois parvenus.[20]

Both these interpretations of the significance of transparency in transforming the domestic interior have their historic dimensions. Lavin is acutely aware of this – she stresses the diffusion of psychoanalytic concepts into everyday American life.[21] Vidler offers a number of readings of transparency, including highly culturally specific ones:

> In France at least, the spirit of the age is still haunted by the ghosts of technocratic "rational" architecture from Durans and Viollet-le-Duc to Pierre Chareau, continued in the sixties with the technological expressionism of the Centre Pompidou, and, more recently, Norman Foster's Town Hall for Nîmes, next door to the Maison Carré.[22]

If we accept historical specificity in the reading of transparency, what particular interpretations could be attached to it in recent Australian domestic architecture, particularly if we acknowledge Boyd's work in sketching out the negatives of domesticity?

The literature which deals with the failings of Australian life in the postwar years – the crucible of the fecund anti-colonial phase of Australian culture that flourished in the 1970s and 1980s – is limited but sharp. Its popular arm comes from the host of Australians who left for Europe and America in the 1960s and have become a curious mirror for assessing cultural progress. Most notable among these are Germaine Greer and Clive James, but many who returned after short or long stays tried to articulate a similar cultural disquiet to that felt by Boyd. The extent of this can be gauged from Clive James' description of leaving Sydney on his first voyage to England on New Year's Eve 1961: "From the stern I watched the lake of light divide into two pools, one of them going with me and the other staying. Passing between the Heads was like being born again."[23]

Neither Lavin's interpretation of the psychodynamics involved in the design of an individual house, nor Vidler's leaning towards a culturally institutionalized dialectic of the uncanny and transparency, seem to resonate with the Australian experience. There is, for instance, the perceived Australian antipathy towards intro-spection. Citing the social commentator Donald Horne on this issue, the historian of psychology Joy Damousi notes that "Horne was echoing the sentiments of many of his generation who believed that during the 1950s and 1960s Australia was a vast suburban expanse which bred indifference, mediocrity and hedonism, rather than reflection and self-analysis."[24] Yet she notes that theirs was a palpable disquiet with the culture of the time:

> It is indeed a paradox that while writers, artists and performers left Australia in the 1950s because they identified a conformity and indiffer-ence which stifled creativity, others such as [painter John] Brack and writer Patrick White agreed, but at the same time drew their very inspi-ration from it. In Brack's work, the suburbs were a repository of anxieties, repressions and fears, of various neuroses and sinister possibilities. In White's portrayals of rural and suburban life, the psychological was ever-present: gloomy, menacing and unpredictable.[25]

If in painting and in literature this particular manifestation of the Australian uncanny could be explored with some latitude, in architecture the sentiment is more difficult to pin down. In painting, for example, Brack occasionally invokes a satiric vein that found its most public expression in the Barry Humphries character of Dame Edna Everidge, the subject of a Brack portrait. Architecture can be conscious of satirizing suburbia, yet it cannot comfortably sustain a cynicism towards its client.

One Brack image entitled *The Car* both incorporates the uncanny and also provides a clue as to how the contemporary Australian house deals with some of the tensions inherent in both its program and its cultural identity (Figure 8.6). The painting shows a family of four in their car, and has a cartoon-like technique. The father is a surly cut-out figure at the wheel, the children in the rear seem trapped and expres-sionless in their compliance. Only the mother is rendered with any expression as the face of familial decorum, her expression one of a fixed grin verging on the obsequious. What is particularly striking in the construction of the painting is the transparency of the car, with a stylized view of the Australian landscape beyond. It is as if the

8.6
John Brack,
Australia 1920–99,
The Car 1955,
oil on canvas,
41.0 × 102.2 cm
Purchased 1956,
National Gallery
of Victoria,
Melbourne)

transparency throws the relations within the car into sharp relief, a precondition for recognition.

From these few examples we can infer that the object of disquiet in the Australian context is too persistent to conform to the notion of the uncanny as the Freudian propensity (in Vidler's terms) "of the familiar to turn on its owners, suddenly to become defamiliarized, derealized, as if in a dream."[26] It bears more resemblance to the formulation offered later by Vidler where he quotes Freud:

> This uncanny is in reality nothing new or alien, but something which is familiar and old-established in the mind and which has become alienated from it only through the process of repression . . . The uncanny [is] some-thing which ought to have remained hidden but has come to light.[27]

The shapes of the Australian disquiet as expressed through its literature have been vigorously fleshed out by Bob Hodge and Vijay Mishra in their *Dark Side of the Dream*. Subtitled *Australian Literature and the Postcolonial Mind*, the authors attempt to pin down some of the dynamics that have inversely shaped the national character as portrayed in Australian literature. Their thesis is that a great deal of Australian culture needs to be read in the negative, that is it needs to be examined for inconsistencies and undercurrents that intimate what is being avoided or suppressed. Analysing key Australian texts, Hodge and Mishra argue that in establishing a culture at once compliant and oppositional, Australian identity became locked in a "doubled form of consciousness," with schizoid results.[28] This is the only way, they argue, we can understand the clearly atypical Australian of nationalist literature: "If he is read for his surface value . . . he is an incomprehensible carrier of Australian identity. He only makes sense when he is read with the schizoid consciousness that is in practice the primary marker of Australianness."[29]

If this observation is transposed onto architecture, it allows a reading which is predicated on repression as much as on active response to circumstances. Instead of seeing transparency in domestic architecture as a singular attempt to achieve some sense of reconciliation between the inhabitant and place, understood as a unique configuration of the natural environment, it can also be read as a denatur-ing of the interior. The interior, in this view, can be seen as the historically constituted realm for the production and reproduction of family relations with its complex, but distinctive, issues of gender and identity that Boyd so poignantly outlined in *Australia's Home*.

One of the characteristics of domestic architecture is that it cannot sustain a critique of home life with the wide compass of a literary work. Few architects can maintain the critical stance, or indeed the cynicism, necessary to both accommodate and, at the same time, undermine the dynamics and living patterns of a client family. Yet any architect properly briefed is privy to these dynamics as both specific to their clients and representative of a broader socialization. A house, in these cases, can be seen as a therapeutic entity which presents a specific form of accommodation between family members. As such, transparency can be interpreted as a refusal to provide space for the playing out of hidden family relations which undermine the ideal. The large glazing of individual rooms is not conceived in isolation: it seeks to provide individual family members with a connection back to nature as a means of correcting and loosening the negative ties of domestic life. Neutra may have adopted design as individual therapy, but in contemporary Australia architecture as therapy follows categories rather than individuals, and attacks common conceptions of repression.

Nature, here, becomes a psychic balm. The projection outward that transparency encourages displaces the anxiety associated with the interior with a view of nature, a constant referent of normality because it is invested with an equilibrium borne of a millennial time scale. Thus nature soothes because it offers a complexity that is nonetheless in balance, and it offers a neutral alternative to the judgments inherent in social interaction. Unable to contemplate itself, domesticity looks outward.

The aestheticization of the Australian domestic experience, the imaginative merging of circumstance with ideology, has been problematic throughout the twentieth century. The gender awkwardness that is part of this issue was outlined by the feminist historian Miriam Dixson as early as 1976, when she noted that "human beings may be physically close to each other, perhaps even sharing the same house, but far apart 'relationally' . . . In Australia, I suspect the relational distances between the sexes is, by and large, stretched thinner than in comparable communities."[30]

Transparency, then, is a response to the family dynamic or the gender relations embedded in it. It is an acknowledgment of their intransigence through the utilization of a technique, the transparent, which allows these issues no purchase on the interior. But it also harbors a therapeutic intent. The therapeutic challenge posed by transparency is whether one can endure the scrutiny of an imagined "other" in all aspects of one's domestic existence. Failure here can be interpreted as falling short of the contained identity necessary to expose oneself to the exterior, an identity that mimics a primitive state of grace.

The reductiveness of transparency thus emerges. As an element in the construction of the identity of the contemporary Australian house it delineates the underside of architectural idealism through its role as a dissolver of interiority, where the dynamic of the private realm plays itself out. The fear of the interior is a strong theme in early modernist critiques of pre-modernist Australian architecture, serving as a cipher for an enduring unease with the memory of what it contained. Yet modernism too has to shoulder its portion of blame here. Much of the aesthetic dimension of the modernist interior derived from a narcissistic viewpoint, which was predicated on a monadic self-fulfillment.[31] This was prefigured by Corbusier's apartment at 24 rue Nungesser et Coli in Paris, with its introspective collection of artistic endeavours. The aesthetic identity of the family has proven highly elusive within modernist iconography generally, even as an ideal. Privilege has occasionally served as a model to fill this void, but its use is limited to the collective privilege of space, privacy, amenities such as swimming or sports facilities, or the suspension of the everyday that the holiday house represents.[32]

The issue of aesthetic transformation is a key one. Whatever the portrayal of gender or familial relations may be in Australian literature, the order of everyday life and the enormous achievements of the public realm continue to shape the

Australian experience. The problem is not that everyday life is harsh – it is that it often defies imaginative transformation. Hence the tendency of so much Australian culture to coalesce around the sensual, with its immediate aesthetic presence.

The idealization of domestic life, such as that undertaken under John Entenza's direction in the Case Study House program (1945–66) in California, have been largely displaced in Australia by tensions emanating from the specifics of its history. Hodge and Mishra's sweeping outline of these remains pertinent. They write:

> [Australia] is a lapsed colonial power locked in an unresolved and undeclared struggle with the original possessors for legitimacy and land, producing a neo-colonial form of literature from a neo-colonial mentality that is still obsessed with the exploited Other. Into this complex is embedded a flourishing oppositional postcolonial development in politics, culture and literature.[33]

The tension between the neo-colonial and the post-colonial in architecture can be seen in the valorization of corrugated iron in recent years as a desirable building material. Its association with colonial buildings is strengthened by its lightness and impermanence, which lightens the responsibility of the architect for the displacement of nature that building entails. The naturalism which drives much of Australian contemporary architecture – its form responding to climatic performance, prevailing winds, outlook, etc. – is a form of intellectual transparency, skirting difficult, perhaps intractable, architectural challenges. The largest have been posed by mass immigration, perhaps the most significant achievement of the post-war Australian state. Immigration has proven particularly problematic for Australian culture insofar as it reinforces the brittle stereotypes of Australian identity at the same time as it parodies them. It has also brought waves of immigrant architects who have not subscribed to the neo- and post-colonial tensions of Australian architecture, and as such have carved parallel identities around different concerns. The problem, at least in architecture, can be highlighted by the fact that if architects were asked to describe a meaningful architecture for immigrant Australians, the exercise would soon become absurd.

We seem, then, to be confronted by a strange time lag. The most lauded attributes of Australian architectural culture, embodied in the works of Glenn Murcutt and widely emulated, are responses to an historical identity whose contours were traced, with increasing complexity, in the second half of the twentieth century. Murcutt himself is aware of this, and has been cited as regarding the quest for national identity as "a great mistake."[34] But the choice may not be his to make. Warding off anguish, or charting a course through the disquiet of an Australia still defined by a neo-colonial complex and its evolving family and gender dynamics, remain shapers of contemporary architecture if only by the evasive tactics adopted.

This brings us full circle, as it were, to the conclusion that these houses do indeed represent a distinctive Australian identity. However, this takes place not through their careful siting or immaculate execution, but rather through the experiences that these attributes ward off. Here we come close to an understanding of architecture as ideology in the Lacanian sense promulgated by Žižek, when he writes that:

Ideology is not a dreamlike illusion that we build to escape unsupportable reality; in its basic dimension it is a fantasy-construction which serves as a support for our "reality" itself: an "illusion" which structures our effective, real social relations and thereby masks some unsupportable, real, impossible kernel (conceptualised by Ernesto Laclau and Chantal Mouffe as "antagonism": a traumatic social division which cannot be symbolized).[35]

But we can demystify this formulation in the Australian context by substituting discrete historical phenomena for the "kernel." Thus the houses of Murcutt or Stutchbury, whose Arcadian overtones determine their warm reception in architectural circles, describe their identity as much by what they attempt to exorcise.

This is not necessarily a negative attribute. The polarization this engenders has produced work of great sophistication in its own terms, which will continue to be part of how Australia projects itself and, in turn, is viewed. But in the Australian context it will always have a limited cultural dimension, a playing out of the Anglo-Celtic identity as articulated in Miriam Dixson's *The Imaginary Australian.*[36] As such, it retains a privileged place in the practice of architecture, with a history tightly bound to the legal and economic origins of contemporary Australia. The issue, though, is whether in its absorption with a specific identity it may be bypassed. Much of Australia is yet to find a similar voice, not in terms of what it emulates but in terms of how it uses its specific anxieties to articulate different aesthetic regimes. This process seems integral to how architecture functions presently in its capacity as an ideological vehicle, and it seems naïve to imagine it can be transcended.

If transparency is a symptom of domestic life poorly imagined, then moving beyond transparency is dependent on a richer conception, even in an idealistic sense, of the relational possibilities of domesticity. It is difficult to imagine these would emerge from architecture, which occupies a small part of the cultural realm: rather, they would emerge from within popular culture, which can deal with them in more complex and subtle ways. Architecture needs to look for signs of this redefinition. It may not recognize them immediately, being unsure of what to look for, but an appreciation of the ideological operations at work at least opens the door to those possibilities.

Notes

1 Manfredo Tafuri, *Architecture and Utopia: Design and Capitalist Development*, Cambridge, MA: MIT Press, 1976, p. 1.

2 http://www.pritzkerprize.com/full_new_site/81/pdf/murcuttbw.pdf#page=1, accessed 20 February 2007.

3 Ibid.

4 Regarding perceptions of Murcutt's work, see Haig Beck and Jackie Cooper, "Ideology, theory, tactics," in H. Beck and J. Cooper, *Glenn Murcutt: A Singular Architectural Practice*, Melbourne: Images Publishing Group, 2002, p. 9. See also Glenn Murcutt, "Basic lessons of the utilitarian" in the same volume.

5 Commenting on Sydney (domestic) post-war architectural culture, Philip Goad states:

It is a specifically local culture which (rightly or wrongly) has come to symbolise for many international commentators that which constitutes (or should constitute) an Australian architecture . . . Peter Stutchbury can be regarded as the natural heir to this externally constructed lineage.

    See Philip Goad, "In the company of people and places," in Philip Drew, *Peter Stutchbury*, Sydney: Pesaro, 2000, p. 14.

6 Cited in Philip Goad, "Foreword," in Harriet Edquist and Richard Black, *The Architecture of Neil Clerehan*, Melbourne: RMIT University Press, 2005, p. 9.

7 See Beck and Cooper, *Glenn Murcutt*, pp. 22–23.

8 Harry Sowden, *Towards an Australian Architecture*, Sydney: Ure Smith, 1968.

9 Walter Bunning, *Homes in the Sun: The Past, Present and Future of Australian Housing*, Sydney: W. J. Nesbit, 1945.

10 Walter Bunning, "Flats in Melbourne," *The Home*, 1 May 1942, 28.

11 J. M. Freeland, *Architecture in Australia: A History,* Ringwood, Vic.: Penguin, 1985, pp. 260, 263.

12 Ibid., p. 263.

13 Robin Boyd, *Australia's Home: Why Australians Built the Way They Did*, Ringwood, Vic.: Penguin, 1978, p. 105.

14 Ibid., p. 281.

15 Ibid., p. 130.

16 Ibid., pp. 281–282.

17 Ibid., p. 304.

18 Freeland, *Architecture in Australia*, p. 273.

19 Sylvia Lavin, *Form Follows Libido: Architecture and Richard Neutra in a Psychoanalytic Culture*, Cambridge, MA: MIT Press, 2004, p. 58.

20 Anthony Vidler, *The Architectural Uncanny: Essays in the Modern Unhomely*, Cambridge, MA: MIT Press, 1992, p. 218.

21 Lavin, *Form Follows Libido*, pp. 30–31.

22 Vidler, *The Architectural Uncanny*, p. 220.

23 Clive James, *Always Unreliable: The Memoirs*, London: Picador, 2001, p. 161.

24 Joy Damousi, *Freud in the Antipodes: A Cultural History of Psychoanalysis in Australia*, Sydney: UNSW Press, 2005, p. 231. See also Donald Horne, *The Lucky Country: Australia in the Sixties*, Ringwood, Vic.: Penguin, 1966. Horne intended the title to be an indictment of Australian lassitude, enabled by a country whose abundance allowed the second-rate to flourish.

25 Damousi, *Freud in the Antipodes*, pp. 231–232.

26 Vidler, *The Architectural Uncanny*, p. 7.

27 Ibid., p. 14.

28 Bob Hodge and Vijay Mishra, *Dark Side of the Dream: Australian Literature and the Postcolonial Mind*, Sydney: Allen & Unwin, 1991, p. xiv.

29 Ibid., p. xvi.

30 Miriam Dixson, *The Real Matilda: Woman and Identity in Australia 1788 to the Present*, Sydney: UNSW Press, 1999, pp. 62–63.

31 In this vein, see Christopher Lasch, *The Culture of Narcissism: American Life in an Age of Diminishing Expectations*, New York: W. W. Norton, 1978.

32 As Robert Bruegmann states: "One of the major reasons the suburban house has been so successful is that it has been a way to obtain many of the advantages of privacy enjoyed by the millionaire on Fifth Avenue at much less cost." Robert Bruegmann, *Sprawl: A Compact History*, Chicago: University of Chicago Press, 2005, p. 110.

33 Hodge and Mishra, *Dark Side of the Dream*, p. xiv.

34 Beck and Cooper, *Glenn Murcutt*, p. 9.

35 Slavoj Žižek, *The Sublime Object of Ideology*, London: Verso, 1989, p. 45.

36 Miriam Dixson, *The Imaginary Australian*, Sydney: UNSW Press, 1999. Dixson argues for the

acknowledgment of the central role this identity has played in shaping Australian society and its continued relevance as a cultural armature, despite some of the deep deficiencies she identified in her earlier work *The Real Matilda.*

9

The Voyage and the House

Bernard Rudofsky's Search for Place

Alessandra Como

[W]hen I woke thus, my mind restlessly attempting, though successfully, to discover where I was, everything revolved around me in the darkness, things, countries, years. My body, too benumbed to move, would try to locate, according to the form of its fatigue, the position of its limbs in order to deduce from this the direction of the wall, the location of the furniture, in order to reconstruct and name the dwelling in which it found itself.

(Marcel Proust, *Swann's Way*, Paris, 1913)

To cover the world, to cross it in every direction, will only ever be to know a few square meters of it, a few acres, tiny incursions into disembodied vestiges, small, incidental excitements, improbable quests congealed in a mawkish haze a few details of which will remain in our memory: out beyond the railway stations and the roads, and the gleaming runways of airports, and the narrow strips of land illuminated for a brief moment by an overnight express, out beyond the panoramas too long anticipated and discovered too late, and the accumulations of stones and the accumulations of works of art, it will be three children perhaps running along a bright white road, or else a small house on the way out of Avignon, with a wooden lattice door once painted green, the silhouetted outline of trees on top of a hill near Saarbrücken, four uproarious fat men on the terrace of a café in the outskirts of Naples, the main street of Brionne, in the Eure, two days before Christmas, around six in the evening, the coolness of a covered gallery in the souk at Sfax, a tiny dam across a Scottish loch, the hairpin bends of a road near Corvol-l'Orgueilleux. And with these, the sense of the world's concreteness, irreducible, immediate, tangible, of something clear and closer to us: of the world, no longer as a journey having constantly to be remade, not as a race without an end, a challenge having constantly to be met, not as the one pretext for a despairing acquisitiveness, nor as the illusion of a conquest, but as a rediscovery of a meaning, the perceiving that the earth is a form of writing, a *geography* of which we had forgotten that we ourselves are the authors.

(Georges Perec, "The World," in *Species of Spaces*, Paris, 1973–74)

Bernard Rudofsky (1905–88) devoted his entire life to travel. His experiences and journeys molded and influenced his writings, the exhibitions he organized, as well as his design work (mainly houses) in Italy, Spain, Brazil and the United States. The connection between Rudofsky's work and his travels is the subject of this chapter which considers the œuvre of the Austrian architect, generally known above all as the author of *Architecture without Architects* (1964), a text which made his reputation as a student of vernacular architecture.

Rudofsky used travel as his first source of knowledge from his earliest studies when he left Vienna – where he was studying architecture – for Asia Minor to discover situations which were completely different from his origins. Subsequent journeys were to take him to various destinations in Europe – but the places that most fascinated him, which became his main points of reference, were countries in the Mediterranean, in particular, Italy and Greece where, on the island of Santorini, he worked in 1929 on his doctoral thesis which concerned "primitive" building techniques using concrete employed in the Cyclades.

From the beginning, Rudofsky regarded his travel experiences as a personal apprenticeship and architectural investigation, which stemmed from his fascination with vernacular architecture. He brought back photographs, travel notes, as well as watercolors, which he exhibited in Berlin and Vienna. The pattern of creating exhibitions after periods of travel became a standard practice which Rudofsky maintained in subsequent years, for his numerous post-war exhibitions, mainly at the Museum of Modern Art in New York.

Following these initial journeys, which had a formative influence on his work, Rudofsky returned repeatedly to areas of the Mediterranean, also visiting the United States in 1941, Mexico in 1951–52, Japan in the latter half of the 1950s, and India in 1985. Travel became a constant feature of Rudofsky's life, involving his energies and resources, and became the thread which linked his various activities and interests. This is how Rudofsky commented on his voyages:

> I learned a great deal by travel . . . The acquaintance with foreign countries; with foreign towns, dead and alive, early became a habit with me. Every year, at the end of June I would depart for points south, and not return before the last days of October.[1]

Dis-placements

Rudofsky's knowledge of "foreign" lands was not only acquired through his travels but also from direct observation, since he lived in the places he studied. Rudofsky would continually change his residence, and a transitory existence became his situation in life. After spending his childhood and his studies in Vienna, he went to work in Berlin, before moving to Capri in 1932, the island where he remained for over two years. From there he went to live in Naples in 1934, Procida in 1935, in New York for nine months, returning to Europe in 1936, specifically to Vienna and Italy again – Naples, Positano and Milan. Since he was Jewish, to avoid the racist laws of Nazism and fascism, Rudofsky left Europe for Argentina, moving then to Brazil, where he lived for six months. In 1941, he returned to New York, where he remained for the rest of his life. Together with other places of constant reference in Europe, New York became his chosen home and the base for new journeys.

Rudofsky's permanent condition as an exile and foreigner – partly a question of choice and partly imposed by political events – was therefore to represent an essential characteristic of his life, a life made up of hotel rooms and fragmentary points of reference in various parts of the world; transitory places were to become his home, hotel rooms his domestic spaces, illustrated in his watercolors with his things, suitcases and other objects, always with a window from which to observe the world outside (Figure 9.1). This was to cause a significant antinomy between the

9.1
Bernard Rudofsky,
Hotel room at
Arles, **1926**
(Research Library,
The Getty
Research Institute,
Los Angeles
(920004))

lack of a real place to which he belonged and the continuous search, through his travels and writings, for the construction of a sense of place and similarly, given the absence of a home, a special predilection for investigating domestic spaces, which represented the main theme running through his work.

> I shall have to say more about the serene subject of travel in the pursuit of architecture's roots because it was one of my annual trips that not only determined my outlook on domestic architecture but also made me for the rest of my life a displaced person.[2]

This condition caused a sense of restlessness which led Rudofsky in a creative quest for the unusual and the existential. Rudofsky's search for other cultures and places undoubtedly reflected his immense intellectual curiosity but at the same time his frustration with his own epoch, a critical approach to established customs and codified culture and his rejection of the partial vision offered by Western culture. His intellectual restlessness spurred his curiosity about what had been forgotten and excluded from the historiography of architecture which he found centered on a few select cultures.[3] The polemic and even aggressive style of his talks revealed his "countercultural" stance and a radical form of thought which compelled him to re-examine the issues from their earliest stages without ever taking anything for granted. Travel represented the opportunity to learn "what could not be found in books,"[4] constructing for himself an alternative to an academic vision of the world. Vernacular architecture therefore became the "point of departure for the exploration of our architectural prejudices."[5] Exhibitions were the main vehicle for expressing his polemical stance towards contemporary culture in order to demonstrate the incongruity of accepted conventions – *Are Clothes Modern?* – to show the relevance of past cultures, and the connections with oriental cultures, questioning the meaning of progress just as he did with the meanings of wild and primitive, demonstrating the presence of the modern in the past and ridiculing the contemporary world.

Travelogue

The way in which Rudofsky studied the places he visited was both analytical and sensorial. Rudofsky prepared for a journey by reading widely, taking notes – kept in the Getty Center in Los Angeles – in which, despite the fragmentary and varied nature of the themes, he defined what would become his perceptual orientation. Preliminary preparations did not prevent him from assimilating what the direct experience would enable him to discover. For Rudofsky, travel meant a readiness to observe and meet with surprises. In one of his travel notes he denounced the change in the art of traveling: "The element of surprise, the exhilaration which derived from personal discovery no longer exist: in their place remain the pure and simple act of 'recognition' . . . The tourist is perfectly satisfied if what he sees coincides with what he expected."[6]

By contrast, Rudofsky interpreted travel as a sensorial experience, favoring itineraries that enabled him to enjoy the seaside and the sunshine; here he immersed himself in lifestyles which included first of all the flavors of food and wine, which he also recorded in his notebooks. Although driven by curiosity, he did not specifically seek out adventure or the discovery of new experiences at any cost. Instead, he focused on personal experience and on the complete absorption of a place. This enabled him to record details which became essential for understanding the local culture, customs and the architecture as a whole. For instance, in his travels in Japan, featured in *Domus* in 1956–57, he described traditional inns with customary rituals of bathing, meals, clothing and sleeping; he illustrated the use of sliding paper screens, the *shoji*, the traditional house or similar wooden platforms, meeting places at sanctuaries or beaches which are described together with the solid, decorated stone structures used for storing and preserving valuables.

The study of places became multidisciplinary; apart from architecture, it also involved graphics, design, clothing and the study of materials and techniques. From the various places he encountered, Rudofsky extrapolated particular interests which became themes and forms of discussion, which were published in magazines and journals with eloquent images and concise texts.[7] He became interested in Japanese printing and maps, the paving of the tortuously narrow streets in small towns in Apulia, the covered walkways, rush matting of Naples, fabrics, baths, the human body and clothing, the art of shop window displays and of the reuse of ancient materials in architecture. From his travels in India he recounted the stone screens ("petrified veils"), the extraordinary interiors of astronomical observatories and the meaning and use of decoration ("an alternative to the curtain wall").[8] Taken together, they represented "visual portfolios,"[9] a complex of images and ideas of an architect traveller: his own personal travelogue.

In Japan, as in the south of Italy, Greece or India, architectural spaces were explained from the reality of everyday life, and filtered through direct experience. As an architect, Rudofsky sought to understand "architectural situations," in which architecture expressed specific ways of inhabiting and occupying a place. Thus, it was not the extraordinary or the monumental aspects which Rudofsky recorded, but rather the familiar, the domestic sphere, and the daily life of architecture. His comments and images trace experience back to the details of circumstance, to a specific moment in a certain light and therefore to immediacy and to details.

Watercolors, drawings, notes and, above all, photographs are what remain from these experiences of travel. This set of materials reveals Rudofsky's way of reflecting upon places, which was utterly at odds with a conventional academic approach. The material gathered during his travels, which was mixed together when used for exhibitions or publications, was a personal set of architectural records, a collage of ideas and images, from different cultures and places. The images were not organized according to specific categories, or a geographical or temporal origin. Rudofsky did not tell about the itineraries of his journeys, or the map of his movements; instead, he provided a set of images which were a mixing up of different places and times, resulting in a series of space-events. The places he visited overlap; images combine with each other, similarities emerge between distant places, as happened for Japan and Italy:

> Walking one August day along the shores of the Inland Sea, along narrow
> paths flanked by walls of living stone, amongst fig trees and medlars

(which, coincidentally, originally come from Japan), olive trees and white and pink oleanders, it is easy to imagine you are close to Sorrento. The optical illusion is reinforced by the acoustic one. Through the milk-white mist arrive the lengthy calls of the fishermen which sound exactly like those of their fellow fishermen in Mergellina. The catch includes squid, cuttlefish and clams; but I don't want to confuse things even more so I shall refrain from making further comparisons.[10]

Rudofsky's approach to traveling has many similarities with the interpretation of sites that takes place in the ancient Japanese maps Rudofsky collected, commented on in his writings, and which became the subject of one of his exhibitions at the Museum of Modern Art (Figure 9.2).[11] These maps seem to invent a new way of considering places, with multiple levels of describing territory. They lack high or low points, and are designed to be read from the margins towards the center; they must be laid out on the floor – due to the irrational scale of representation – and are at the same time both abstract and descriptive. Indeed, since they are both a plan and an elevation with information about inns and routes, they represent topographic "stories" rather than "objective" geographical maps. Rudofsky was unquestionably fascinated by and at ease with this way of interpreting reality which allowed for intuition and multiple interpretations.

In the text that stemmed from his journey to Japan,[12] Rudofsky commented similarly on a way of organizing and understanding places without classifications but instead by using the intuitive and narrative system of "banchi." This set of regulations "organizes" large cities like Tokyo into streets without names and houses without numbers. The search for an address, through a narrative of adventures and encounters, links the sense of place with a system of references, memories and traces of routes and therefore with a situational and relational dimension. The very concept of place is transformed from a static concept to one that acquires the dynamic nature of a journey.

Places

The images and reflections assembled by Rudofsky were not a travel guide[13] nor a free-ranging set of notes and curiosities; rather, both consciously and polemically, they were an investigation of architecture. Although taken from a range of cultures and countries, they hold intersecting and overlapping thoughts and observations which, rather than being heterogeneous, contain recurrent research themes. Despite their immense variety, the exhibitions and published texts are united by architectural themes which the images appear to communicate, revealing an unexpected coherence to the complexity and fragmentary nature of the work.

The themes he identified were captured through the creative act of painting or photography – a method which is neither external nor abstract, like a historical or theoretical interpretation, but rather by creative juxtapositions, associations and impressions, a means central to architecture itself. Above all, Rudofsky's work involved images, most of which had a strong evocative power, suggesting solutions and leading through a development of these ideas, allowing space for and inviting further exploration. Rudofsky's work was an invitation to appropriate these images.

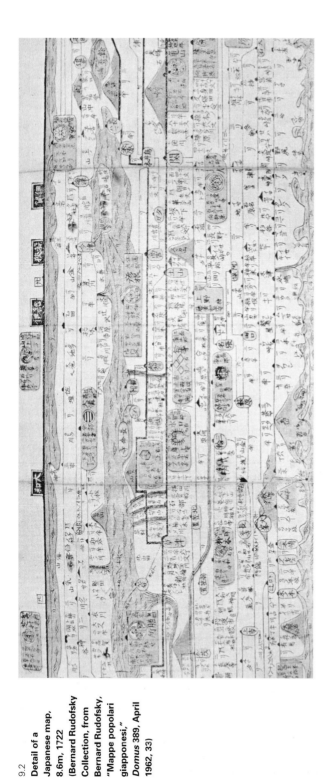

9.2
Detail of a
Japanese map.
8.6m, 1722
(Bernard Rudofsky
Collection, from
Bernard Rudofsky,
"Mappe popolari
giapponesi,"
Domus 389, April
1962, 33)

His work was essentially visual and evocative rather than theoretical or academic. The places he portrayed were not actually "studied" and he made no attempt to explain the reasons and needs which led to selecting the illustrated architecture. The images acquired an autonomy that was independent of the time and place of their origin, despite being rooted in these times and places.

This is particularly clear in *Architecture without Architects*, the most important of his exhibitions organized at the Museum of Modern Art and in the text-catalogue which accompanied the exhibition. The exhibition, in 1964, brought together many of the images gathered over the years, beginning with his travels in the 1930s and covering a diversity of places. The enormous success of the event derived from both the seductive power of the images as well as Rudofsky's skilled exhibition choreography. The installation sought to immerse the visitor in the experience of the images, arranged at various levels and reproduced in various formats. It was not an "ordered" and explanatory vision of the material, but rather a rich visual experience, fragmentary and stimulating, similar to the style of his journeys. Even the text contained no attempt to "catalogue" the material but left freedom for a scattered sequence of interpretations. Images had the most important role in the book-catalogue too; the words merely provided information about the contexts and places of origin, confirming what was strongly expressed by the images. In his introduction to *Architecture without Architects* Rudofsky clarified this creative approach by stating that the examples of architecture represent "the largest untapped source of architectural inspiration for industrial man." "This exhibition, the first of its kind, approaches architecture not with a historian's mind but with a naturalist's sense of wonder," Rudofsky explained in his lecture in Virginia.[14]

If the aim of Rudofsky's investigations was not a speculative examination, but rather a quest for inspiration for design through visual and architectural material, the significance of his work cannot be reduced merely to the study of vernacular architecture – as it is generally understood. Rudofsky did not study vernacular architecture in the sense of researching reasons for, and the development of, the forms and spaces in a specific culture. On the contrary, he explored architectural solutions linked with local culture, then exported the investigation into a broader perspective through a process of de-contextualization, mixing contrasting cultures and places, and creating a visual collection of architectural themes.

In contrast to the physical and cultural differences of his destinations, his analytical eyes discovered a continuous path, selecting similar architectural themes from various locations, cultures and times. In particular, he observed and reproduced forms of architecture that created a strong relationship with the ground. Many of the villages visited and depicted in his watercolors and photographs are localized in difficult orographic situations, to which the architectural forms respond with the clarity of volumes rooted in the ground (Figures 9.3, 9.4). Architecture is therefore interpreted as a forceful act of appropriation of the natural landscape, rather than a simple continuation of the environment.

Rudofsky developed the theme of architecture's relationship with the ground; photographs of staircases, passages, stone paving, details of steps, stones and bases, taken in various parts of the world, to reveal numerous solutions and

9.3
Bernard Rudofsky,
Watercolor of the
Corricella, Procida
(Naples, Italy),
1935 (Research
Library, The Getty
Research Institute,
Los Angeles
(920004))

physical interactions between buildings and the ground. The vast number of powerful images of quarries and caves he gathered demonstrated his fascination with this subject. Through this, Rudofsky shifted attention toward topography, recording architecture in its initial act of construction. His images are not just a study of beautiful details around the world, rather they are a recalling – without nostalgia – of the necessity of architecture as action on the earth.

Moreover, Rudofsky's investigations focused in particular on the study of settlements of towns and villages from contrasting world cultures and traditions. Compositions from different parts of the world appear as variations on the same

9.4
South Italy,
photo by Bernard
Rudofsky
Research Library,
The Getty
Research Institute,
Los Angeles
920004))

theme – the development of a communal architecture, where the individual building, reduced to a simple prismatic shape, loses its primacy, while the overall picture is a rich complex of sculptural masses and their reciprocal relationships create plays of solids and voids, light and shadow.

A large number of images show an inventory of urban settings and spaces. Arcades, roofing systems, covered streets, markets, tree-lined avenues, porticoes, pergolas, drapery, and materials from the streets of Osaka or Seville are noted. Through his series of images, rich in the play of light and shadow, he created an idea of space reaching beyond the abstract division between public and private, between architecture and city, between interiors and exteriors. His attention was drawn more to the space "in-between" and the dynamic between components rather than a single building or space. Beyond definitions and labels, he considered the built environment as a succession of spaces which in turn generated other spaces. The street, in particular, becomes a sort of corridor within the whole unique collective construction of global architecture.

Rudofsky's images do not interpret space as simply a physical and geometrical format of a mere architectural solution but where specific styles of living and occupying spaces are expressed by the architecture itself. These spaces respect the definition of Michel de Certeau: "space is like a word when it is spoken . . . In short, *space is a practiced place.*"[15] They are the spaces of popular everyday culture. The photographs of Southern Italy, for example, with children, women at windows or on terraces, people at markets, fountains, sitting outdoors or just passing by, comment on the street and its sense as relational space, rather than its role as infrastructure or a functional thoroughfare. The street is the place where patterns of daily life converge, and here architectural features express the dynamic between objects and people participating in the construction of space. All this envelops an idea of architecture being developed with a relationship to human activities.

The study of human activities itself became a topic of investigation for Rudofsky, looking into the peculiarities of various countries and cultures. This was not a social examination of local habits but an attempt to understand the real meaning behind our actions in order to question the spaces relating to life's primary activities. In other words, a re-defining of domestic space. Detailed notes, images, reflections on customs and traditions created a broad investigation on fundamental living habits – eating, cooking, dressing, sleeping and washing. Throughout his life, Rudofsky continuously investigated these primary activities, organizing the exhibitions: *Are Clothes Modern?* (1944), *Textiles USA* (1956), *Now I Lay Me Down to Eat* (1980), *Golden Eye* (1985), *Sparta / Sybaris* (1987). Then a number of texts on the subjects that further developed the research: *Are Clothes Modern?* (1947), *Behind the Picture Window* (1955), *Streets for People* (1969), *The Unfashionable Human Body* (1971), *The Prodigious Builders* (1977), *Now I Lay Me Down to Eat* (1985) and *Sparta-Sybaris* (1987).

Through these works Rudofsky showed that the Western way of living and occupying spaces was an irrational and non-functional response to our needs, that the spaces we inhabit are impoverished in meaning when compared with those in use in ancient societies and other cultures today. In the images of domestic spaces in Japan, Turkey, even ancient Rome, Rudofsky finds "tangible evidence of more humane, more intelligent ways of living."[16] His notes and images taken in various parts of the world re-construct an alternative way of considering domestic space that holds a closer relationship with the human body and pleasures of life. Those investigations could be explained using the words of Georges Perec:

> To question the habitual . . .
>
> What's needed perhaps is finally to found our own anthropology, one that will speak about us, will look in ourselves for what for so long we've been pillaging from others . . . What we need to question is bricks, concrete, glass, our table manners, our utensils, our tools, the way we spend our time, our rhythms. To question that which seems to have ceased forever to astonish us. We live, true, we breathe, true; we walk, we open doors, we go down staircases, we sit at a table in order to eat, we lie down on a bed in order to sleep. How? Where? When? Why?[17]

Rudofsky found answers to his existential questions in architecture from around the world which, besides its differences and specifics, held a quality of "permanence, in both the material and spiritual sense."[18] The so-called architecture of the vernacular became a "timeless subject"[19] and his images comprised architectural investigations on universal themes that linked architecture to its initial status: the relationship with the ground and the relationship between parts, which entailed architecture as essentially made of relational spaces.

Through his image collection, Rudofsky reconstructed a sense of place not intended as belonging to a particular site, but as an expression of an essential and universal condition of habitation. In the image which is reproduced in the photograph, Rudofsky *inhabits* the places he visited. The images he brought back from his travels were fragments and notes about inhabitation. Despite the fragmentation and differences, the images, taken as a whole, construct the sense of a place, combining space, time and human action in everyday life.

> I shall take you . . . to places where life goes on much as it did in former times; . . . it is not an escape from reality. It is, on the contrary, an attempt to rediscover the cultural ties that once united large parts of mankind.

The Place of the House

The ideas and investigations that emerged from Rudofsky's travels, exhibitions and published texts appear even clearer when reviewed with his design work. The themes of his travel images return in his designs for houses in Italy, Brazil, the United States and Spain. The similarities do not concern the aesthetic aspect, but rather, the architectural themes.

Villa Oro in Naples (Figures 9.5, 9.6), designed with Luigi Cosenza in 1935, is an investigation of the composition of architectural spaces in the Mediterranean. Overlooking the Bay of Naples, and set in impervious orographic conditions, the villa is a cluster of volumes arranged on various levels inserted within the tuff hill: modern white prisms with different forms and proportions, separated from each other and partially excavated in order to create external spaces and connections between the different parts. Some volumes are cantilevered, supported by thin iron pillars, others rooted in the tufa. The daylight and night views show the play of voids and solids: dark excavated spaces due to shadow during the day become rooms of light at night, contrasting with the solidity of the volume.

9.5
Bernard Rudofsky
and Luigi Cosenza,
Villa Oro, 1935–37
(Research Library,
The Getty
Research Institute,
Los Angeles
(920004))

9.6
Bernard Rudofsky
and Luigi Cosenza,
Villa Oro, detail
(Research Library,
The Getty
Research Institute,
Los Angeles
(920004))

The house has two levels above the ground, and a level inside the hill. The plan disposition is apparently simple: the rooms are set in succession, but the differentiated paths produce a spatial experience that instead of forming a sequence, constitutes a fragmentation that is maze-like. The spaces on split-levels recall those by Adolf Loos. But unlike Loosian architecture, the various rooms are not compacted in one solid. They remain autonomous and differentiated. The architectural whole consists of a continuous series of interiors and exteriors arranged on different levels. A labyrinthine experience within the porosity of the material and volumes become an interpretation of the spatial conception and the relation with the ground of Mediterranean villages, with specific similarities with those in Procida, the island where Rudofsky lived while working on the design (Figure 9.3).

The entrance is on a private road; a simple door opens to a small space from where one can either go to the atrium or directly reach the upper floor. From the atrium the path is split again, and then again. There is the option of climbing to the master's rooms upstairs, or to go into the living room, from which one can pass on one side to the dining room or to the library on the other side. From the library one can descend to the bar-living room cut into the hill or go to an open-air covered space, a room open toward the garden and the panoramic view. The terrace garden unifies all those spaces (Figure 9.7).

The project develops the theme of the *room*. The whole villa is a succession of rooms which keep the traditional differentiation of the various parts of the house: bedroom, dining room, library, studio, etc. All the rooms are inhabited, designed with the main pieces of furniture, chairs, tables, together with materials, paving and textiles. The project consists of the arrangement of the rooms, and in the orchestration of the path through the spaces. Photographs showing Berta and Maria Teresa, the wives of Rudofsky and Cosenza, in visual conversation from different terraces of the villa, communicate the spatial dialogue between the parts and the play of volumes and spaces one after the other.

While Villa Oro was a house designed to be a cluster of volumes, a "house-as-a-city" – similar to the watercolours of urban settlements – the hotel that Rudofsky designed at Anacapri with Gio Ponti in 1938 is a composition of individual and differentiated houses. The rooms, each with its own name, are connected by a path set amidst the countryside. In order to prepare their clients for a heightened way of experiencing the hotel, the architects even went so far as to design the clothes that they should wear on their arrival. The idea of initiating the spatial experience, which involved the clothing, was later re-experienced by Rudofsky himself when he visited Japanese inns, and he makes reference to the project of the hotel in Anacapri in his travel notes in *Domus*.[20]

9.7
Bernard Rudofsky and Luigi Cosenza, Villa Oro, plan (Research Library, The Getty Research Institute, Los Angeles (920004))

A direct relationship between spaces and ways of living was established in the design for a house along the coast of Positano, studied with Cosenza in 1937 as the response to a request from Ponti for *Domus*. The house consists of two volumes of different heights, one of which is plastered and the other in calcareous stone – a "structural continuation of the rock."[21] Slabs set between the two volumes define the house as a series of open spaces around the roof garden with a magnolia and fig tree: the living room with the fireplace, a kitchen top, a semi-cylindrical unit for the shower. The house is meant for "spontaneous living"[22] in close contact with the sea and the sun and therefore dissolves at the open air, becoming essentially the place of the relationships between the two volumes and around the main and symbolic elements. The project is demonstrative of an idea of architecture as an expression of a way of living, going beyond the first and simplistic meaning of architecture as shelter. Although only intended to be an ideal design, it was developed as though it were a real commission, published with details and calculations, together with a discussion with an imaginary client who fails to understand the radical nature of a house without rooms, closed-off spaces and entrances: "Where do you dine? Where do you receive guests? Where do you go in?" The architects reply that the house is like a medicine so that "you will be educated to live differently."[23]

The reappraisal of domestic spaces together with ways of living was also explored in the design for a house for Rudofsky himself and his wife Berta in Procida (Figures 9.8, 9.9). The design has powerful abstract tones, as a design manifesto

9.8
Bernard Rudofsky, house in Procida, 1935–37, model (Research Library, The Getty Research Institute, Los Angeles (920004))

demonstrating new kinds of lifestyle, even though it was done with the intention of being built. The house was intended for living in close contact with the ground and all the spaces have a sensorial experience. You live barefoot to "go back and feel the delight of the sole of your foot being tickled by the sand, well-mown grass, or smooth marble."[24] The bed is a room entirely occupied by mattresses. The bath is sunken into the floor. One eats lying on triclinia in the Pompeian manner. The whole design has clear references to Pompeian houses which Rudofsky was interested in due to the theme of the courtyard, which he returned to in his designs for houses in Brazil. Moreover, the use of triclinia became the central feature around which he developed studies, publications and exhibitions. The radical nature of the lifestyle suggested by this design corresponds to the simplicity of the architecture which, though seemingly rigid, reveals a complexity in the asymmetry of the whole. "What is needed is not a new way of building; what is needed is a new way of life" was the title of the article with which Rudofsky presented this project, summarizing his alternative response to the much-debated theme of the house in the modern world.[25]

The design of open air spaces for the house of the artist Constantino Nivola at Long Island, New York, in 1949 is a composition of simple features – a

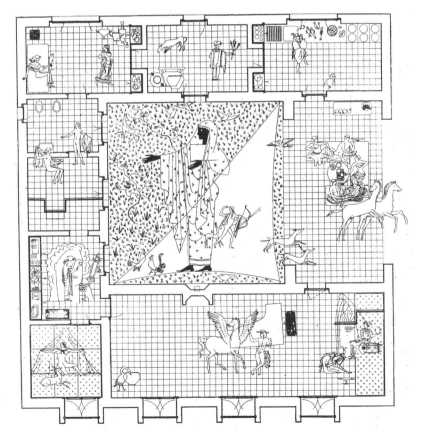

9.9
Bernard Rudofsky, house in Procida, 1935–37, plan (Research Library, The Getty Research Institute, Los Angeles (920004))

solarium, a pergola, a free-standing wall, a long bench, a table, and a system of seating (Figures 9.10, 9.11). This design represents a reflection on the spaces of habitation: the various features create the spaces of the house, even though they are in the open. The architecture is reduced to its essential vocabulary: *the* room, *the* wall, *the* frame. Simplicity is what characterizes each of the different parts; the pergola, made using thin white poles, underlines the abstract and geometric space of the emptiness that it circumscribes; the solarium is a room without a roof and doors, resting on the ground to which access is gained from above, by means of a ladder. The house becomes a simple catalogue of distinct, separate features which stand out poetically on the green of the lawn and among the trees. The branches of an apple tree pass through the free-standing wall, creating shadows which move over the white surface of the wall. From the solarium, sheltered within an intimate domestic space, it is possible to observe the clouds passing in the sky, while one can engage in nude sunbathing at any time of the year, thanks to the heat from the reflection of the sun's rays.

In all his house projects, Rudofsky continued to explore issues which he had discovered in his travels and investigated in the critical activities of exhibitions and publications. His modern domestic spaces were based on the rediscovery of the original and archetypal meaning of habitation. The house is broken into its main parts, the bedroom, dining room, the bathroom, etc. re-considering the original meaning of the spaces devoted to these activities. Architecture is then reinvented without prejudices, reviewing ways of occupying spaces. Architecture is not reduced to its forms but is inseparable from the meaning of the spaces and the human condition.

The room becomes the main constituent of the house. It is a space of intimacy and concreteness: defined among the walls, on the ground, under the sky.

9.10
Bernard Rudofsky, Nivola house today (Photo: Alessandro Como)

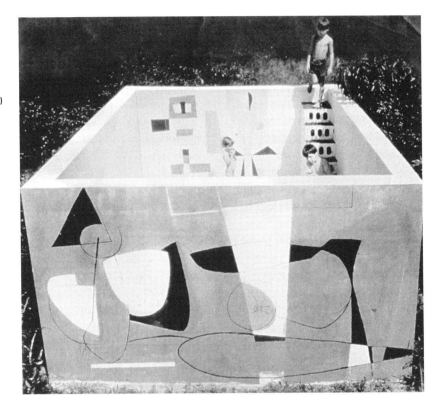

In some projects the room becomes an open-room, communicating even more the essence of architecture and the meaning of dwelling, free from the function of sheltering. Here a stronger relationship with the ground and the sky is experienced.

Other essential elements create the space of the house. Among those, the fireplace, the table, the window, and some others, according to the various design projects. The project of the house becomes simply the arrangement of a series of elements which have always been part of the domestic sphere but which find new meanings and use in the relationship between the parts.

The path through the rooms realizes a complex experience, similar to that of the Mediterranean settlements: a continuous passing through exterior and interior spaces, creating a piece of urban space. The project of the house therefore becomes a comment on urban space, proposing a re-appropriation of urban space through the experience of crossing and inhabiting the various parts.

Rudofsky revised the modern way of habitation, privileging the experiential over the functional, intimacy and solidity over visibility and transparency, separation of parts over the free plan, though his projects are clearly modern and the language of modernity is not questioned by Rudofsky. The simplicity and the essentiality of Rudofsky's architecture shifted the attention toward the meaning of the spaces and the sense of the operation in itself, rather than on forms and language. As a consequence, his designed spaces are profoundly complex, a complexity that is hidden by the apparent simplicity of the white modern volumes that characterizes his architecture.

Rudofsky's modernity represented the search for the true essence, the archetypal form, the initial element that constitutes the whole. His modernity was expressed in the freedom to rethink and reformulate what is generally evident, and in the capacity to reconsider architecture from his unprejudiced view of history and culture. Instead of being an architecture based on the unchangeable, it lies in the *relational condition*; it is a living architecture, sensitive to differences and to the time of day and the seasons.

Comparison with Rudofsky's design work enables one to understand the real sense underlying his critical investigations. It also clarifies misunderstandings and ambiguities which the exhibition *Architecture without Architects*, despite its incredible success, provoked both among his critics and his supporters in the duality between *architecture* and *non-architecture*, between *modern* and *vernacular*.[26] Rudofsky's design work shows that he did not want to propose vernacular architecture as a direct reference for contemporary architecture. On the contrary, vernacular architecture helped Rudofsky to anchor modernity to those universal themes and solutions where man finds a "primitive" relationship with the world, and in which the act of dwelling is expressed.

Rudofsky looked for the roots of architecture in the concreteness of the world of reality because he did not conceive architecture in the abstract sense of theoretical and programmatic statements but in things already written in the world. It is here that Rudofsky went to search for architecture, and to rediscover it in the images that he gathered together.

This is how Ponti introduced the exhibition *Architecture without Architects* in *Domus*:

> Neither critical exegesis nor erudition has guided Rudofsky's choice of images, but a touching love for architecture, which will be propagated amongst all of us who conceive culture not as something that is "produced" but as something that is received, by looking, listening and loving. How many things we already love, having discovered them in these pages, or we love once again, after rediscovering them here.[27]

Notes

1 Lecture at the IDCA Aspen, 1980, in Andrea Bocco Guarneri, *Bernard Rudofsky: A Humane Designer*, Vienna, New York: Springer-Verlag, 2003, p. 244.

2 Ibid.

3 Bernard Rudofsky, *Architecture without Architects: A Short Introduction to Non-Pedigree Architecture*, New York: Museum of Modern Art, 1964, p. 2.

4 See the introduction to the articles "Introduzione al Giappone," in *Domus* 319, June 1956, *Domus* 320, July 1956 and *Domus* 330, May 1957.

5 Rudofsky, *Architecture without Architects*, p. 3.

6 Rudofsky, *Domus* 330, 36.

7 Gio Ponti, "Stuoie Napoletane," *Domus* 119, November 1937, 18–20; Bernard Rudofsky, "Decadenza del Bagno," *Domus* 288, November 1953, 37–40; Bernard Rudofsky, "Japanese Vernacular Art: town maps, village maps, plans of castles and shrines, maps for pilgrims and for

emperors, hunting maps and battle maps . . ." *Domus* 389, April 1962, 29–34; Bernard Rudofsky, "Japan: Book Design Yesterday," *Design Quarterly* 55, 1962; Bernard Rudofsky, "Roads and Inroads," *Horizon*, January 1962; Bernard Rudofsky, "Architettura Senza Architetto: In Puglia," *Domus* 431, October 1965, 58–62; Bernard Rudofsky, "Uncleanliness and Ungodliness," *Interior Design* 55(6), June 1984, 212–221; Bernard Rudofsky, "Lessons from India: The Optical Distiller," *Interior Design* 56(8), August 1985, 230–235; Bernard Rudofsky, "Lessons from India: Interiors Extraordinary," *Interior Design* 56(9), September 1985, 248–253; Bernard Rudofsky, "Lessons from India: Alternatives to the Curtain Wall," *Interior Design* 56(10), October 1985, 236–241; Bernard Rudofsky, "The Art of Artless Display," *Interior Design*, March 1986; Bernard Rudofsky, "Débrism or, don't throw away your broken Limoges," *Interior Design* 57(5), May 1986, 280–285.

8 Rudofsky, "Lessons from India: Alternatives to the Curtain Wall."

9 Introduction to the series of articles in *Interior Design*, March 1986, May 1986, September 1986 and May 1987.

10 Rudofsky, *Domus* 330, 37.

11 *Japanese Vernacular Art*, Museum of Modern Art, 1961.

12 Bernard Rudofsky, *The Kimono Mind: An Informal Guide to Japan and the Japanese*, Garden City, New York: Doubleday, 1965, pp. 263–276.

13 Rudofsky, *Architecture without Architects*, p. 3.

14 Lecture in Virginia, at the Getty Research Institute, Bernard Rudofsky papers, ca. 1910–1987, Series I. Working papers, Box 5, F 4.

15 Michel de Certeau, *The Practice of Everyday Life*, trans. Steven F. Rendall, Berkeley and Los Angeles: University of California Press, 1984, p. 117.

16 Lecture in Virginia.

17 Georges Perec, "Approaches to What?" from *L'Infra-ordinaire* (1989) in *Species of Spaces and Other Pieces*, trans. John Sturrock, Harmondsworth: Penguin, 1997, p. 206.

18 Lecture in Provincetown, 1973.

19 Ibid.

20 Rudofsky, *Domus* 319, 49.

21 "Una villa per Positano e altri lidi," *Domus* 109, January 1937, 11–17.

22 Ibid.

23 G. Cosenza and F. D. Moccia (eds), *Luigi Cosenza: Opera Completa*, Napoli: C.L.E.A.N., 1987, p. 110.

24 "Non ci vuole un nuovo modo di costruire, ci vuole un nuovo modo di vivere," *Domus* 123, March 1938, 6–15.

25 Ibid.

26 Felicity Scott, "Review of *Architecture without Architects: A Short Introduction to Non-Pedigree Architecture* by Bernard Rudofsky," *Harvard Design Magazine*, Fall 1998, 69–72 and Felicity Scott, "Bernard Rudofsky: Allegories of Nomadism and Dwelling," in Sarah Williams Goldhagen and Réjean Legault (eds), *Anxious Modernisms: Experimentation in Postwar Architectural Culture*, Cambridge, MA: MIT Press, 2001, pp. 215–237.

27 Gio Ponti, "Architettura Senza Architetto," *Domus* 431, October 1965, 59.

10

Hot Springs, Geysers and Animated Matter

Sarah Treadwell

There is a certain sort of place that, above all others, is described in terms of wonder. Where ground literally bubbles, reversing its interiority, when stones of permanence become molten and are flung explosively into sulphur rich air, when gas-filled rocks float on water – then the world emits expressions of wonder. Thermal "wonder-lands," replete with reversals and anomalies, exist in volcanic regions across the globe and throughout time, attracting visitors and their commentaries:

> A vast volume of boiling water, surrounded by glittering jets of spray and curling wreaths of steam, rises in one grand bouquet to the height of 40 or 50 feet, an altitude which it retains for some seconds, and then slowly subsides into the bay whence it rose, where it dies away in a surf of seething foam, leaving huge banks of steam rolling slowly up the dark hill-side. An exceedingly grand sight![1]

Inklings of surprise, enchantment and recognition of an uncanny quality are found in nineteenth-century naval officer Herbert Meade's expressions of wonder on visiting the Maori settlement of Ohinemutu in a thermal region of New Zealand in December 1864.[2] Water, like a bouquet of flowers, dematerialized and rolled up darkened hillsides; wonder emerged in an uncanny surfacing of both the familiar and the strange. Political theorist Jane Bennett writes of "a contemporary world sprinkled with natural and cultural sites that have the power to 'enchant' "[3] and Ohinemutu, in the center of the North Island of New Zealand, is such a site.

    The idea of wonder, with its attribute of enchantment, persists as a counterpoint (but not an opposition) to notions of the diabolical in relationship to a volcanic landscape that is powerfully material; boiling mud-pools operate as caricatures of matter with their excessive smell, noise and texture. At a moment when architecture might be thought to be impossible through reasons of instability, toxicity and danger, the landscape becomes wondrous, raising questions about the possibility or impossibility (or the desirability) of a wondrous architecture. In New Zealand, the "natural" might be seen as a category that consumes the wondrous but consideration of images of the thermal landscape of Ohinemutu suggests instead that landscape and architecture meet in the wondrous through a material collaboration between diabolical instability (and the necessity for structure) and atmosphere.

Bennett's attention to wonder springs from an uneasiness caused by the prevalence of images and stories of modernity constructed as disenchanted – modernity as a place of dearth, control and alienation as seen in the Pruitt-Igoe housing whose demolition, so it has been argued, signaled the death of modernism. While tales of disenchantment account for quite a lot of the contemporary world there are events that warrant, according to Bennett, a counter-story.[4] A story that might operate as an opening to new assemblages which have the potential to emerge from the dissolution of architecture's utilitarian responses to ground. To understand the earth as a wonderland, induced in the shimmering separation between consumption and occupation of the earth, is also to recognize the extension of architecture in its atmospheric condition.

The volcanic region in New Zealand was complexly occupied when Europeans arrived in the nineteenth century and the newcomers, traveling across the thermal landscapes, recorded their responses in terms of both anxiety and wonder. Not only did the terrain operate as a metaphor for fiery, ambivalent relationships with local Maori but also the hot springs and warm waters suggested amniotic beginnings, wonder and possibilities of transformation. Meade reported on a landscape that was architecture and which shaped the space of communal occupancy; he described the use of the steam and heat from hot pools in cooking and a social deployment of volcanic warmth:

> In an open space in the middle of the settlement, stone flags have been laid down, which receive and retain the heat of the ground in which they are sunk. This is the favorite lounge; and here at any hour of the day, but especially when the shades of evening are closing round, all the rank and fashion of Ohinemutu may be seen wrapped in their blankets, luxuriously reclining on the warm stones.[5]

By focusing on existing moments of enchantment, which do not seek a return, Bennett finds openness and imagines an ethics of generosity. Entertaining and analyzing wonder she experiments with "a fable of everyday marvels in order to uncover and to assess the ethical potential of the mood of enchantment."[6] The image that Meade projects into the future (wrapped bodies conversing on heated ground on a cold night), is an everyday image of enchantment that suggests an architecture that is not confined to building nor premised on separation. The earth is not a means to permanence or stability but rather it participates wonderfully in the everyday events of occupation.

Following nineteenth-century travelers through thermal "wonderlands" of Aotearoa New Zealand (the name wonderland persists into the present tourist literature[7]), such moments of enchantment appear – small events and images that complicate the usual tale of progress and redemption that infected colonial relationships. A narrative of wonder emerges, fraught with longing and closeness (between matter, bodies, classifications and landscapes), and formally played out in darkness with water and high temperatures. Meade, on an exploratory trip around New Zealand at a time of incipient conflict between Maori and Pakeha and between tribes, stopped at Ohinemutu on the 27th December 1864 and wrote:

> Ohinemutu, a settlement on the southern shore of the lake [Lake Rotorua], built in the very midst of the hot springs, which surround what is considered by one who has seen also those of Iceland, the largest geysers in the world, and an infinite number of hot springs; so that, except during a strong southerly breeze, the inhabitants live in a perpetual cloud of steam.[8]

Characteristic of the thermal regions is the presence of visible atmosphere; Epicurean primordia, tiny, alert and mobile particles of water and gas that combine and recombine with each other, animating matter. Steam, mist, shifty surfaces – secretions that operate as a kind of mesh net that sways, emanating from the thermal region, pervasive, light and inescapable. A mesh that repeats the molecular structure of matter at a visible scale, clinging to surface/skin, dissolves boundaries and distinctions between objects that become shifty and patchy dependent on a clearing puff of wind:

> Within a world of animate primordia continually entering into particle-ular proximity with each other, within a world where objects are macrolevel assemblages of billions of invisible primordia, within a world where the mind is a form of body, but a form made up of particles so fine and fragile that their survival requires the larger composite body as a protective shell – in *this* world, thinking, like sensing, is a matter of perception.[9]

An understanding of the material world as a continuum of active assemblages that shape both body and mind allows the possibilities of material thinking – a fluid conjunction of intelligent senses. As the steam fogs vision it clings, damply, to warming skin and, seeping through the feet, the thermal activity of the earth can be momentarily understood. Animate matter constructs both the thermal landscape and the affective responses of wonder that it induces.

Visual Clouding

Describing Te Tarata, a geyser with basined terraces that was near Rotorua, Meade stated that "To convey an idea of its beauty on paper is impossible; Hochstetter, the historian of the Austrian exploring expedition, got out of the difficulty simply by saying that it baffles description – and he is right."[10] Geologist and explorer Dr Ferdinand Ritter von Hochstetter (1829–84) nevertheless spent many words describing the terraces and basins of Te Tarata as a scene in which color, with its synaesthetic effects, slides easily from the optical to the bodily. Having activated Te Tarata visually Hochstetter reserved his gentlest words for the "scientific collector" and the physical gathering of stalactites.

> Such is the famous Tetarata [sic]. The pure white of the silicious deposit in contrast with the blue of the water, with the green of the surrounding

vegetation, and with the intensive red of the bare earth-walls of the water-crater, the whirling clouds of steam, – all together presents a scene unequalled in its kind. The scientific collector, on the other hand, has ample opportunity of filling whole baskets with the most beautiful specimens of the tenderest stalactites, of incrustated branches, leaves etc.; for whatever lies upon the terraces, becomes incrustated in a very short time.[11]

Vision, as a medium of wonder, is both critical and difficult; it will not work alone. Inseparable from affective bodily responses, it is "intensive" and "whirling." The very tender regard of the collectors is absorbed into the fresh, untouched stalactites about which the language exhibits both a passionate and scientific interest. Epicurean thinkers would sense the particle emanations that swerved off Hochstetter's assemblage; in his image not only objects left in the volcanic atmosphere become encrusted but also its image of beauty adheres to the collector – a film of pleasure etching into the mind and imagination of the visitor. Sensitive surfaces were needed for the reception of tender stalactites.

Surface Warmth

Skin slipping into warm water on the evening of 28th December 1864, Meade and companions immersed themselves in Lake Rotorua:

Young and old of both sexes meet in the lake every evening, almost the whole population taking to the water, which is of an agreeable temperature, like that of an ordinary warm bath, all over the bay, except where the water boils. The whole lake seemed alive, for the rising steam prevented any more than a portion containing the bathers being visible, and the scene was a curious one.[12]

Physically awash, his skin and the warm water merging, Meade wrote of the evening and described his shifting and partial vision and the enjoyment, singing and strangeness of the night; "Joyous peals of laughter came ringing along the surface of the water from behind those misty veils."[13] The water rendered bodies partial – he could see only the heads of the old men and more of the young women:

the prettiest young girls in the settlement were seated in a circle in very shallow water, looking like mermaids, with the moonlight streaming over the well-shaped busts and raven locks. They sang us a wild song, and beat their breasts to the changing time with varied and graceful gestures.[14]

The surface of the water was a sounding board – a surface of reflection changing the young women into mythical creatures – mermaids, associated with allure, captivity and pain. Bennett asks what it is about such crossings, or mythical conjunctions, that have the power to enchant? She suggests that it lies in "their mobility, that is in their capacity to travel, fly or transform themselves; in their morphing transits . . . [that] enact the very possibility of change; their presence carries with it the trace of dangerous but also exciting and exhilarating migrations."[15]

Geyser

The enchantment of the night when Meade lay in the warmth of Lake Rotorua listening to laughter and song across the water was heightened by the periodic eruption of a large geyser. He wrote:

> But ever and again even these voices [of the young women] were hushed and stilled, while, with a weird and rushing sound, the great geyser burst from the still waters, rising white and silvery in the moonbeams which shone from the dark outlines of the distant hills, and dashing its feathery sprays high against the starry sky. The scene was the very incarnation of poetry of living and inanimate matter.[16]

Surrounded by water Meade was molecularly inundated in the event his words constructed. The darkness of the night heightened the effects of a luxurious warmth (that might become extremely hot) and the sound of the geyser, springing from within the waters in which he basked, silenced other voices that traveled across the water. The water that bore his weight and warmed his muscles and bones was not a passive receiver. In his description of the geyser playing on the lake, matter had become animated; he wrote, "The whole lake seemed alive."[17]

Meade made an image of the night bathing in Lake Rotorua that was published as a chromolithograph in the volume of his travels that his brother prepared for circulation after Meade's death. The first edition locates the image alongside the text that tells of the evening's pleasures and alarms. In landscape format the chromolithograph (Figure 10.1) stretches to encompass darkness, water, femininity and Mokoia Island which Meade had visited the day before. The island is the site of a local legend that Meade recounted:

> Hinemoa, the ancestress of the present inhabitants of the island, and of the town of Ohinemutu on the mainland – a chief's daughter of the

10.1
"Ohinemutu Geyser, Mokoia Island, and Lake Rotorua," chromolithograph (In Lieut. The Hon. Herbert Meade, *A Ride through the Disturbed Districts of New Zealand*, London: John Murray, 1870, 1st edn, to face p. 39)

greatest beauty and the bluest blood in all New Zealand, who, finding her family (the powers that were, on the mainland) opposed to the marriage she longed for, answered the midnight trumpet of her island lover by swimming across the lake, supporting herself when tired by a string of gourds round her neck, and concealed herself in the warm bath, till her lover found her hiding beneath the rocks, and throwing her garments on her as she "rose from the waters beautiful as the wild white hawk, and stepped on the ledge of the bath graceful as the shy white crane", took her home as his wife, and lived happily ever after, &c., &c., &c., &c.[18]

As Meade lay in the water on the enchanting night, with the terraced Mokoia Island in the distance, he might have recalled the story of Hinemoa and her swim across the lake. The illustration that Meade made of his night bathing, published as a chromolithograph, has something of the fluidity and pleasurable darkness of the legend. Constructed with horizontal layers the image situates Meade's mermaids across the bottom edge; they are at play, modesty constructed with concealing water, inclined heads and flowing hair. Hybrid, like Hinemoa, who in Meade's recounted version of the legend was both white hawk and white crane, the young women are creatures at ease in the elements – falling into the water, trailing through its surface.

Chromolithograph

Above the young women hovers Ohinemutu, a collection of structures, buildings and vegetation stretched along a peninsular. *Whare* (houses) can be discerned and raised houses and platforms – an assemblage of architecture that includes some substantial buildings. Buoyed up by its own reflection, the settlement, now aquatic, seems to float. Above Ohinemutu is the lake which reflects the island Mokoia and the opposite shore. Floating over the hills of the opposite shore (which parallel the settlement) some clouds drift and, in their similarity to the hills, they set the layered landscape into a floating relationship with the dark starry night. A world is made in strata that suggest equivalences through similarity of contour; the heights of the raised *whare* and structures are echoed by the mountainous shapes of both landscape and cloud.

The repeated horizontality in the image has an affinity with the surface of the water that floats the settlement as well as the island. The lake as a body of water mirroring the night sky shapes a silvery darkness that seems, in Meade's image, to sustain the pleasures of immersion. If the horizontal traditionally has had associations with base matter and has been set against the vertical transcendent products of upright human figures, then this image complicates the opposition. The figures suggest a relationship to gravity that is playful – in this watery world gravity does not cause downfall nor can it punish physical lapses; horizontality is pliable and the vertical droops.

Disrupting the layered floating world, flaring at the corner of the image, the geyser destroys the rectilinear framing of the page. Its spurting fire and water works induce a migraine effect of intermittent visual clarity. Streaming upward to fall in glittering arcs, dropping gilded rain into the water of the lake, the glow of the geyser colours the skin of the young women. The image resists the scenic through its blurring-at-the-corner-of-the-eye; an unfinished aspect in which the edge of the image disappears in the flare of the geyser exploding over peninsular and water. Barely present as an object the geyser registers as an effect that disturbs the containment that the frame of an image conventionally offers. On the edge of picturesque, a celebratory and slightly threatening whiteout effect occurs which skews the plane of the image pushing forward and disappearing as glare at the same time.

The uncontrollable and yet temporally regular force of the geyser explodes over the roofs of the *whare* and obliterates distant mountains. But the geyser is a power that comes from *within* the settlement of Ohinemutu and it is not pictured in the chromolithograph as a malevolent event. The young women seem to revel in its glow; bodies are warmed and a carefree quality is induced. Having the power to cancel clarity and distinction, the geyser colors the scene as explosive and festive. Its reflected brightness spreads across the now molten and luminous lake. Pleasure is evident; the young women seem to be coated wondrously in the gold of the exploding light.

The chromolithograph was published in the first edition of Meade's book[19] and each of the colored images[20] was right-angled to the text to be viewed with a physical turn away from the written word; with rich and muted colors the images might have seemed wondrous in a world in which color printing was novel. In the second edition of Meade's journeys they were replaced with grey scale engravings and the view of Meade's magical night in Lake Rotorua was altered and shifted, becoming an engraved frontispiece to the edition (Figure 10.2). The layered stretched-out space of the chromolithograph was compressed and reshaped as a vertical image that, despite similarities, created quite a different account of Meade's wondrous night.

Engraving

Moving from a horizontal format to the vertical the engraved image registers the traditional plane, which occupies the viewing subject, as a transparent window transecting the cone of vision. The vertical image becomes pictorial and didactic losing the sensuous qualities of the earlier image and intimating both transcendent awe and falls from grace. The liquidity of the lake that pools and spreads, flooding the chromolithograph, setting peninsular, island and distant shore afloat, has been contained by the upright structure of the engraving. Wonder, it seems, was no longer to be found in the pleasurable conjunction of warm water, darkness and explosive femininity, but rather the geyser as object dominates.

The geyser shapes the engraving occupying a large proportion of the image; spectral and unnerving it shoots rills of thin light into the air; unearthly, it turns the playful young women into abject pale creatures. A woman at the corner of the engraving is transformed from an androgynous figure to a fearful femininity; she cowers as she faces the geyser. Reduced from seven to five, the figures are Europeanized and sexualized. The viewer, with the shift in orientation, stands over them no longer sharing their immersion. The water level has dropped leaving the women, who no longer seem childlike, exposed.

Beneath the engraving as frontispiece is the title: "Ohinemutu Geyser, Mokaia [sic] Island and Lake Rotorua."[21] The women are incidental to the landscape

OHINEMUTU GEYSER, MOKAIA ISLAND AND LAKE ROTORUA.

items that the title collects. The engraving has, however, deleted Mokoia Island from the landscape. Whereas in the chromolithograph Mokoia Island with its *pa* or fortified, terraced village, was situated as a counterpoint force to the geyser; in the engraving it has been cropped. The architecture of the *pa* (that had resisted British forces at the battle of Gate Pah near Tauranga[22]) was removed from the image. Mokoia Island, named but not present, is translated to either the unfortified Ohinemutu or the distant hills.

Mokoia Island was an important place for Te Arawa, the local people, and around 1822 it was the site of an incursion into Te Arawa territory by northern Nga Puhi.[23] From this encounter the island became associated with an act of bravery and cunning by an important woman Aokapurangi. The journal *Te Ao Hou* recounts the story of how Aokapurangi, wife of Te Wera, a Nga Puhi chief, in an act of intercession for her people, a sub-tribe of Te Arawa, positioned herself over the doorway of a great carved house on Mokoia Island. A woman was always the first person to cross the threshold of a new and *tapu* (sacred) house in an act that would destroy its sanctity.

By passing under her (an act which also generally is said to destroy the sacred or *tapu* nature of the head) into the house, besieged Te Arawa were able to be saved (through an agreement with leader Hongi of the invading Nga Puhi). In this case, the journal *Te Ao Hou* pointed out, the action of Aokapurangi was one that would ceremonially allow new life. The story describes an architectural act that was specific to women and acknowledged their generative capacity. The site of the story of courage and regeneration, Mokoia Island, is erased from the engraving in the second edition of Meade's book and the women in the foreground of the image seem to be set apart from the protection that its depiction in the chromolithograph offered.

Hinemoa and Tutanekai[24]

While the story of Aokapurangi is not generally well known, Mokoia Island is the site of a story that is immensely popular, the legend of Hinemoa and Tutanekai. Meade's account is a truncated version of the love story based on Governor Grey's version of the legend.[25] But the story is also, like the retelling of the exploit of Aokapurangi, an account that involves the generative aspects of women operating at landscape and architectural levels. The enchantment of the story of Hinemoa and Tutanekai lies in its lack of grounding, its wateriness; in Hinemoa floating through dark water, with submerged dangers half seen and named, drawn by sound. Swimming in the dark, buoyed up with dried fruits, with gravity's grip loosened, her skin would no longer have seemed an impermeable barrier and, waterlogged, she would become continuous with the lake.

The legend of Hinemoa and Tutanekai is an image/story in which water is connective and expansive, and where, as in Meade's chromolithograph, land is interleaved between water and sky. A Pacific story, as described by Epeli Hau'ofa, that acknowledges the mobility of people of Oceania in opposition to Western accounts of the fixity and boundary.[26] Hau'ofa, writing against the idea of island confinement, describes a vast surface of water to be traversed, layered below with a "fire-controlling and earth-shaking" underworld and above with a dark sky bright with stars and constellations as signs of the possibility of movement. Lake Rotorua as a surface and body of water was not confined by land but could be seen as a continuation of the condition of the sea interrupted by surrounding earth. The earth, however, particularly in its volcanic conditions, was also acknowledged to be liquid.

Governor George Grey (1812–98), an important figure in New Zealand's colonial history, recorded the story of Hinemoa and Tutanekai. He noted the prevalence of legends and stories in the speeches and language of Maori and saw in them allusions, explanations and intentions that he did not necessarily understand. Grey's desire for secure regard and for confidence in British interests led to his project of collecting legends; a project that was complicated by repetition, language difference and by a destructive fire.

The Story of Hine-Moa; the Maiden of Rotorua[27]

Sir George Grey claimed that he was telling the story of Hinemoa and Tutanekai as it was recounted to him on a visit to Rotorua and this seems to be confirmed by George Sisson Cooper (1825–98) who was also on the expedition:

> As . . . we should not be able to leave Mokoia for some time, the Governor availed himself of the opportunity of obtaining on the spot . . . the legend of Hine-Moa and Tutanekai, and which is here subjoined verbatim, as taken down from the dictation of an inhabitant of the island by his Excellency, as he sat upon a rock by the margin of the very Waiariki which was, many years ago, the scene of the story.[28]

Grey's version starts with an account of the illegitimate birth of Tutanekai and his location on Mokoia Island which separated him from Hinemoa – a maiden of rare beauty and high rank – who lived on the mainland. After the genealogies of the two protagonists the next line describes an architectural act: "About this time Tutanekai built an elevated balcony, on the slope of the hill just above you there, which he called Kaiweka."[29]

Nineteenth-century images of Maori architecture frequently depict platforms, as do Meade's images of Ohinemutu, and they have been identified as storehouses, lookouts and burial platforms. The balcony of Tutanekai may have been such an elevated platform – of the land but removed from the land – skimming over ground and, in its resurfacing, constructing a performative space. Homi Bhabha described such a space when he writes about places of otherness and difference – he imagines the contour of difference as occupying "a space lying on the borderline between outside and inside, a surface of protection, reception and projection."[30] The balcony of Tutanekai shaped the space of his association with Hinemoa.

Grey's description of the platform as an elevated balcony connects it to English balconies, which operate as ambiguous extensions to the house, or building being partially external yet still of the house and spatially oriented elsewhere. Associated with longing, in its construction of removal with a distant prospect, the balcony is the site of both desire and frustration. On the balcony/platform Tutanekai and his friend Tiki played musical instruments projecting the sounds over the lake.

Hinemoa and Tutanekai had already met at assemblies of local people and had conceived a secret passion for each other. Eventually, through an intermediate, they acknowledged their mutual feelings. Tutanekai, in a "large warm house of general assembly," spoke to his family of the love between them and told of how Hinemoa would come to him when he played. One night she heard Tutanekai and Tiki playing on the balcony and desired to paddle across to Mokoia, but found the canoes had been pulled too far up onto the land and were too heavy for her to shift. Grey described or transcribed the "soft measures [that] reached her from the trumpet of Tutanekai, and the young and beautiful chieftainess felt as if an earthquake shook her to make her go to the beloved of her heart;"[31] the land itself was instrumental in provoking her desire.

The passage of Hinemoa to Tutanekai is described in a landscape in which things are named. A contemporary account repeats the names given in Grey's record of the story:

> Hinemoa decided the only way to join her sweetheart was to swim across to Mokoia Island. Taking six large, dry, empty gourds she lashed them together with flax. Strapping them to her back she went to the rock Iriiri-kapua. From there she went to the pot Wai-rere-wai and, discarding her clothes, plunged into the water. At the stump of a massive tree called Hinewhate she rested a while, then she swam on out into the darkness of the lake.[32]

Rocks, geological formations, hot pools and sunken tree are named in a comprehensive system of relating to the natural world. Naming is an act that both acknowledges agency in a nature that then becomes acculturated and also a name is conferred as a mark of singularity and an acknowledgement of a relationship of reciprocity. As Bennett suggests, "human agency is essentially bound up with non-human manifestations of it."[33] Landmarks in the legend of Hinemoa and Tutanekai are meetings of matter – points of touch – distinguished and remembered in a night that stripped vision away. In a 1928 film, *Land of Hinemoa*[34] she was shown leaving the shore in remnants of daylight, her naked body visible as she cast aside her cloak to plunge into the water; the written legend cloaks Hinemoa in darkness and her modesty was preserved.

In the darkness Hinemoa could not see her destination and she followed the sound from Tutanekai until she reached the island of Mokoia. Hinemoa swam supported by gourds that she had assembled into flotation devices. No visible points of direction were available and she was guided by the refrain from the putorino (flute) of Tutanekai in a flow of active longing. The refrain becomes part of the territorial assemblage of tree, rock, spring and lake in which Hinemoa navigated:

> At the place where she landed on the island, there is a hot spring separated from the lake only by a narrow ledge of rocks; that is it – it is called, as I just said, Waikimihia. Hine-moa got into this to warm herself, for she was trembling all over, partly from the cold, after swimming in the night across the wide lake of Rotorua, and partly also, perhaps, from modesty, at the thoughts of meeting Tutanekai.[35]

In A.W. Reed's version of the legend, with an active sense of touch and smell, "Hinemoa felt her way carefully until she touched rocks which were strangely warm. There was a smell of sulphur laden steam and a few moments later she lowered her body cautiously into the luxurious warmth of a hot pool."[36] The warmth of the rocks may have been strange to Reed rather than to Hinemoa but his language suggests the wonder of a place that was disturbing, diabolical (sulphuric) and pleasurable in its luxurious warmth.

Bennett describes a state of wonder as "a temporary suspension of chronological time and bodily movement."[37] She wrote that "To be enchanted . . . is to participate in a momentarily immobilizing encounter" – with an absence of association the body and its thoughts are stilled while senses are sharpened.[38] Once Hinemoa reached the warm pool, she stopped. The servant of Tutanekai came to the lake nearby the hot spring to fetch water for his master and Hinemoa three times impersonated a male and broke the calabash intended for Tutanekai. Tutanekai eventually came down to the hot pool and discovered Hinemoa; they departed from there to his *whare* and the act of marriage.

In the story of Hinemoa and Tutanekai it is Tiki – sometimes named as the companion of Tutanekai or in other accounts a servant – who is a figure of ambivalence. In Queenie Rikihana Hyland's contemporary account of the legend, Tiki is the figure who moves between the balcony and the hot spring – as an unknowing intermediary between Hinemoa and Tutanekai. Tiki was the water bearer whose calabashes were broken by Hinemoa and through his agency Tutanekai discovers naked Hinemoa immersed in the hot water.

While the protagonists, the lovers that affirm genealogies and alliances, remain stable in versions of the stories – Tiki alters becoming either servant or good friend or disappears entirely. In the story that was told to Governor Grey, and which he published, Tiki was the figure at the start of the dalliance and, after Hinemoa and Tutanekai consummate their relationship, he ends the story: Tutanekai, despite his marriage to Hinemoa, grieves for Tiki who departed from Mokoia Island for his home village heartbroken by the loss of his bachelor companion. The temporary metamorphosis of Hinemoa into a male in the hot pool is paralleled by the close friendship between Tiki and Tutanekai who, after his marriage, persuaded his father to let Tiki, his companion of the balcony, marry his sister so that their friendship could continue.

Warm volcanic water is the generative heart of the legend. It restores Hinemoa in a transformative amelioration that would be taken up in following decades with the creation of medicinal and therapeutic spas throughout New Zealand. Lake Rotorua became the center of the Government of New Zealand's tourist-centered exploitation of hot springs. Both the healing capacity and the tourist potential of thermal waters occupied the Government Balneologist as he trod between science and pleasure.[39]

More particularly, the *ngawha* was a site for enchantment in its crossings and attachments. In the amniotic warmth of the hot pool an enchantment takes place in the transformation of Hinemoa into a male who attracts investigation by Tutanekai. In the discovery of Hinemoa as female the illegitimate Tutanekai is transformed by his alliance with the high status young woman. The hot pool named Waikimihia with its steam that concealed the form of Hinemoa was one element of an active landscape architecture operating at the limits of body and matter; the wonder of a warm and liquid world is both a return and an anticipation of change.

In the legend an architectural space was shaped in the landscape stretching from the balcony of Tutanekai that projected sound across the reflecting surface of the lake. Within the surface of the lake Hinemoa floated, navigating a liquid world marked by known and named material moments. A partial dispersed architecture, an assemblage that swerved together, emerging in conjunction with the animated matter of the thermal landscape. The final stage of the design occurred in the transformative immersion of Hinemoa in the enchantment of the *ngawha* or hot spring.

In Oceania, water predominates and landscape, a concept structured by pictorial fixity, dissolves as the proportions of land and water differ from Western measures. Land becomes particular – small gritty particles washing into the reaches of the Pacific Ocean colors the turquoise and indigo water momentarily ochre, an earthy liquid. Water, not landscape, shapes the architectural space of occupation. Over its various surface conditions the eye travels restlessly acknowledging that water is understood through more than just the visual sense; bodies submerged and floating maintain their condition through breath and muscle. Water in its mobility and mutability cannot become an equivalent to landscape, even as it unsettles the category dear to the Western imagination. The steam and warmth of the waters of Ohinemutu in Oceanic New Zealand refuse location as prospect and actively permeate viewing bodies, leaving a lingering trace of sulphur on their skin.

In New Zealand in 2005, a prison was designed and built at Ngawha, a settlement in the North Island of New Zealand. Much controversy surrounded the location of the project with local people arguing that it was inappropriate for such a purpose because of cultural sensitivities. Architect Rewi Thompson, however, acting as a consultant for the project, in a country that has a high rate of imprisonment, felt that Ngawha with its hot springs might elicit metamorphoses and its healing and transformative qualities were drawn into the design.[40] That the hot springs were deployed as an architectural effect was signaled by the repetition of the colors of the hot pools in the colors and materials of the prison. The amniotic waters of the hot springs colored both the skin and surface of bodies and building in what was hoped to be a transformative architecture.

Notes

1 Lieut. The Hon. Herbert Meade, RN, *A Ride through the Disturbed Districts of New Zealand; Together with some account of the South Sea Islands Being Selections from the Journals and Letters of Lieut. The Hon. Herbert Meade, RN, Edited by his Brother*, 2nd edn, London: John Murray, 1871, p. 38.

2 According to the Preface of *A Ride through the Disturbed Districts of New Zealand*, Meade was sent on an expedition into the interior of the North Island by Governor George Grey as a mark of good will to the tribes that supported the Government, p. iv.

3 Jane Bennett, *The Enchantment of Modern Life: Attachments, Crossings, and Ethics*, Princeton, NJ: Princeton University Press, 2001, p. 1.

4 She finds effects of enchantment in things such as "the discovery of sophisticated communication among nonhumans, the strange agency of physical systems at far-from-equilibrium states, and the animation of objects by video technologies" (Bennett, *The Enchantment of Modern Life*, p. 4).

5 Meade, *A Ride through the Disturbed Districts of New Zealand*, 1871, p. 36.

6 Bennett, *The Enchantment of Modern Life*, p. 4.

7 For example, a recent publication on the national airline of New Zealand aimed at both locals and tourists starts with an article on Rotorua: "Rotorua's thermal and cultural wonderland is undergoing a face lift." "Full Steam Ahead," in *Air New Zealand Magazine*, March 2006, 51.

8 Meade, *A Ride through the Disturbed Districts of New Zealand*, 1871, p. 34.

9   Bennett, *The Enchantment of Modern Life*, p. 82.

10 Meade, *A Ride through the Disturbed Districts of New Zealand*, 1871, p. 45.

11 Ferdinand von Hochstetter, *New Zealand: Its Physical Geography, Geology, and Natural History: With Special Reference to the Results of Government Expeditions in the Provinces of Auckland and Nelson*, translated from the German original, published in 1863 by Edward Sauter, with additions up to 1866 by the author, online ed. prepared by John Laurie, Auckland: University of Auckland, 2005, p. 413.

12 Meade, *A Ride through the Disturbed Districts of New Zealand*, 1871, pp. 38–39.

13 Ibid.

14 Ibid.

15 Bennett, *The Enchantment of Modern Life*, p. 17.

16 Meade, *A Ride through the Disturbed Districts of New Zealand*, 1871, p. 40.

17 Ibid., p. 39.

18 Ibid., p. 33.

19 Lieut. The Hon. Herbert Meade, RN, *A Ride through the Disturbed Districts of New Zealand*, 1st edn, London: John Murray, 1870. The image (with no title) is opposite page 39.

20 Of the 24 illustrations in the first edition four are chromolithographs. In the second edition the chromolithographs disappear with the exception of the view of "Ohinemutu Geyser . . ." which becomes an engraving and a frontispiece.

21 Meade, *A Ride through the Disturbed Districts of New Zealand*, 1871, frontispiece.

22 The second chromolithograph, "Gate Pah Redoubt, Tauranga," is another such instance. Gate Pah, which had been the site of a battle between Maori and British forces at which large numbers of British infantry were defeated by both a much smaller number of Maori and the technology of the *pa*, is pictured in the chromolithograph as "The Gate pah has been built up into a small sand-bag redoubt, mounting an Armstrong field-piece." Meade, *A Ride through the Disturbed Districts of New Zealand*, 1870, p. 8.

23 "How Aokapurangi Saved her People," *Te Ao Hou The New World* 41, December 1962, 13–14.

24 Leonard Bell has discussed the many retellings, poetry and paintings that have been made of the story. He points out that the images of Hinemoa are related to a common nude type depicted by European and British painters in which the reclining females "often equipped with literary, historical and biblical titles, posed for the display of breasts and limbs, eyes averted, with slightly open mouths, seemingly passive and submissive in demeanour." Leonard Bell, *Colonial Constructs: European Images of Maori, 1840–1914*, Auckland: Auckland University Press, 1992.

25 Sir George Grey, *Polynesian Mythology and Ancient Traditional History of the New Zealand Race, as furnished by their Priests and Chiefs*, London: John Murray, 1855.

26 Epeli Hau'ofa, "Our Sea of Islands," in *A New Oceania: Rediscovering our Sea of Islands*, Suva: University of the South Pacific, 1993.

27 Sir George Grey, *Polynesian Mythology and Ancient Traditional History of the New Zealand Race, as furnished by their Priests and Chiefs*, 2nd edn, Auckland: Printed by H. Brett, Evening Star Office, 1885.

28 George Sisson Cooper, *Journal of an Expedition Overland from Auckland to Taranaki, by way of Rotorua, Taupo, and the West Coast: Undertaken in the Summer of 1849–50 by his Excellency the Governor-in-Chief of New Zealand*. Facsim. ed. Christchurch: Kiwi Publishers, 1999, p. 190.

29 Grey, *Polynesian Mythology*, p. 147.

30 Homi Bhabha, "Signs Taken for Wonders," in *The Location of Culture*, London and New York: Routledge, 1994, p. 110.

31 Grey, *Polynesian Mythology*, p. 148.

32 Queenie Rikihana Hyland, *Paki Waitara: Myths and Legends of the Maori*, Auckland: Reed Publishing, 1997, p. 81.

33 Bennett, *The Enchantment of Modern Life*, p. 163.

34 *Land of Hinemoa*, Television Films, New Zealand Ltd., Sydney, Film editor – Watty Batty, Producer and photographer – Lee Hill. The New Zealand Film Archive/Nga Kaitiaki O Nga Whitiahua, Ref. No. 23659.

35 Grey, *Polynesian Mythology*, p. 149.

36 A. W. Reed, *Legends of Rotorua*, Auckland: Reed Books, 1958, p. 62.

37 Bennett, *The Enchantment of Modern Life*, p. 5.

38 Ibid.

39 Ralph H. Johnson, "Arthur Stanley Wohlmann: The First Government Balneologist in New Zealand," in Roy Porter (ed.), *The Medical History of Waters and Spas*, London: Wellcome Institute for the History of Medicine, 1990.

40 Pers. comm.

11

Not Another Waikiki?

Mobilizing Topophilia and Topophobia in Coastal Resort Areas

Daniel O'Hare

This chapter explores international discourses of love and aversion relating to the development of coastal tourism areas throughout the twentieth century. Particular attention is paid to the way that urban planning, design and development decisions relate to the broader discourse. Examples from Australia, Thailand, Spain and the United States are used to support an argument that topophilic and topophobic attitudes, in relation to some of the world's best-known coastal mass tourism resorts, are used to inform development decisions in less developed coastal settlements.

In this chapter, a discourse is understood as "any discussion or exchange of ideas, expressed through conversation and dialogue . . . and/or writings that treat a subject systematically and at some length."[1] The formal and informal narratives of coastal resorts reveal patterns that arguably constitute systematic discourses. In the discourse of place, a process that employs national and international narratives of comparison and contrast, "meanings are produced, connected into networks and legitimized."[2]

"Topophilia" is defined here simply as "love of place," a definition consistent with Tuan's stress on "the affective bond between people and place or setting."[3] "Topophobia," as used, encompasses both "fear of place" and "aversion to place." A landscape of love for some may be a landscape of fear or aversion for others,[4] and such is the case with the coastal mass tourism resorts of the twentieth century. One of the strongest strands of topophilia, identified in this study, appears to be a desire for coastal villages set in natural landscapes, and this is accompanied by an apparent phobic reaction against the built form and intensity of cities and urbanized coastlines. This chapter provides examples that confirm Tuan's contention that urbanized societies attribute a heightened value to nature.[5] The discourse presented here reveals tensions between attitudes to nature and attitudes to urban places.

Coastal resort areas have become major areas of urban growth, not just for tourism but also for second homes[6] and in-migration of "permanent tourists" (those who move to such areas permanently, for retirement or lifestyle enhancement).[7] Tourists, second home-makers, retirement migrants and lifestyle migrants seek what they perceive to be an ideal environment. Unlike the majority of the earth's human population, these people are able to choose from a variety of potentially ideal environments, increasingly in a number of countries. They are major participants in, and consumers of, myth-making narratives of place. The affective bonds that they form with places are, therefore, bonds of choice rather than habit.

Coastal urban expansion has been accompanied by widespread concern that tourism – and lifestyle migration – "spoils unspoilt places." Tourists and in-migrants are "looking for differences."[8] Yet the discourses by which these differences and "unique" qualities are defined are frequently couched in disparaging reference to well-known coastal resort areas dominated by mass tourism. In the popular discourse, the emphasis is frequently placed on how a "special" or "unspoiled" resort area is *not* like Waikiki or another well-known beach resort area such as Benidorm (on Spain's Costa Blanca), Pattaya (Thailand), or Australia's Gold Coast.

This chapter examines the use of topophilic comparison and topophobic contrast as twin means of defining what is special about coastal resort areas. A relationship is established between the "popular" discourse of travel writing, tourist guidebooks, and ephemeral tourist brochures, and a more formal professional discourse in planning and urban design practice. International and local literature reviews are supplemented with key informant interviews and urban morphological observations made during fieldwork in Australia, Thailand, Spain and Hawaii.

Mobilizing Myths of Topophilia and Topophobia

In this chapter, the term "myth" is used in the sense of "an intellectual construction which embodies beliefs, values and information, and which can influence events, behavior and perception."[9] The focus here is, then, on what people believe and value about the places they love – or fear or detest – rather than on the degree of "truth" underpinning those beliefs and values. The myths of coastal places – whether "true" or "false" – influence decisions relating to holidays, second homes, retirement, investment, planning, design and development.

The myths of beach resorts are constructed by a range of mythmakers, formal and informal, intentional and unintentional, inside and outside of a particular place. Beliefs about particular places are shaped by a range of unofficial and quasi-official tastemakers in ephemeral sources such as weekend newspapers, glossy magazines, television travel shows, tourist brochures and published guidebooks. At a more formal level, place myths are created by novelists, travel writers, and the writers of place. In this chapter, Paul Theroux, a prolific travel writer, is seen to articulate myths of topophobia in relation to coastal mass tourism resorts. James A. Michener's 1971 novel, *The Drifters*,[10] set predominantly in Torremolinos on Spain's Costa del Sol, is drawn on for examples of how novelists may contribute to the construction of myths of topophobia. Writers of place have often amplified the topophilia associated with valued smaller coastal resorts such as Noosa,[11] on Australia's east coast, and Carmel in California.[12] These writers, and others such as journalists, may thereby inadvertently contribute to a little known coastal village becoming a sought-after resort.

Travel guide books, often ostensibly aimed at a more discerning group – "travelers" rather than "tourists" – are particularly effective at putting previously unknown places "on the map." A backpacker character in Alex Garland's 1997 book, *The Beach*, set on Thailand's Ko Phi Phi Leh, notes, "There's no way you can keep it out of Lonely Planet, and once that happens it's countdown to doomsday."[13]

Many beach resorts have assumed greater popularity via the endorsement bestowed by celebrities, creative people and powerful people choosing to holiday there. Hua Hin in Thailand achieves prestige as the chosen summer home of the Thai royal family since 1922,[14] in a similar way to Brighton's early popularity due to key members of the British royal family having holiday homes there in the eighteenth century.[15] State Governors enhanced the prestige – and stimulated the growth – of Southern Queensland resort areas by building their private holiday homes there in the 1880s and 1930s.[16] Association with well-known or controversial artists has led to certain places achieving cache as tourist resorts and second homes – for example Salvador Dali settled at Cadaques on the Costa Brava, giving it some of the bohemian mystique of the Surrealist movement.

Other beach places have assumed popularity through films being made there, or through film stars residing or holidaying there. St Tropez attracted attention, and gained in prestige, when Brigitte Bardot starred in a popular 1956 movie that attracted papal disapproval. Carmel in California is well known partly because the actor Clint Eastwood was the local mayor in the 1980s. A previously undeveloped beach on tiny Phi Phi Island, in Thailand, continues to develop – despite almost total devastation in the 2004 tsunami – as a significant resort following the 1999 filming there of *The Beach*, starring Leonardo DiCaprio.

The myths of coastal tourism places are further interpreted, articulated, refined and redefined through the work of professionals and marketing people in the planning, urban design and development fields.

Borrowed Topophilia: The Early Coastal Mass Tourism Resorts as Exemplars

The earliest coastal mass tourism resorts established a new kind of cultural landscape, offering a built form and experience not previously known. In the eighteenth and nineteenth centuries in Britain, several of these new beach resorts became very well known, including, for example, Brighton, Southport and Blackpool. By the twentieth century, newer resorts on the European Mediterranean shores and in the warmer parts of the United States were added to the list of famous beach resorts. By the middle of the twentieth century, cheaper travel and better working conditions meant that places such as St Tropez, Miami and Honolulu were becoming more accessible to a mass tourist market.

It seems that, for most of the history of beach tourism, well-known coastal resorts have been evoked in the naming and aspirations of emerging coastal resort areas. Development of newer beach resorts, from the late nineteenth century until the mid-twentieth century, was accompanied by a topophilic borrowing of these "tried and proven brandnames," which were looked to as models. The borrowed topophilia of the established resorts included both the literal adoption of the same place names and the use of such place names as descriptors of the newer resorts. In Australia, as elsewhere, there are many examples of the adoption of an existing resort name: for example, in the nineteenth century the name Brighton was given to new beach resort suburbs in Melbourne, Sydney, Adelaide, Perth and Brisbane, and the earliest resort town on Queensland's Gold Coast was called Southport in 1875.[17] By the twentieth century, American resorts were perceived as the model of beach sophistication and desirable development, and we see the name Miami applied to a popular Australian Gold Coast resort area developed early in the century.

Up to the third quarter of the twentieth century, the major beach resort areas retained their status of exemplar. While formal adoption of famous resort names was extensive, the metaphorical use of such names in promotional boosterism was even more widespread. British Railways advertised Cornish resort towns as "the Cornish Riviera."[18] In 1889, Noosa (Queensland, Australia) was promoted in the nearest prosperous town – and source of tourists – as "the Brighton of Gympie."[19] Around the same time, operators of beachside cabins in Waikiki were also likening the emerging resort to Brighton.[20] During the twentieth century, Honolulu itself became the exemplar. Byron Bay, at Australia's most easterly point, with its contemporary reputation of being "not another Gold Coast," was promoted in 1925 as "the Honolulu of New South Wales"[21] (see Figure 11.1). Paul Theroux, in his grand tour of the Mediterranean, notes "the Riviera of Israel," "the St Tropez of Tunis" and a resort in Crete named Waikiki.[22] These few examples from the many available indicate that the major coastal mass tourist resorts have been the focus of a topophilic discourse in which they were regarded as exemplars to be emulated.

11.1 Byron Bay, the Honolulu of New South Wales, c. 1925 (QGITB, no date, c. 1925 – courtesy of State Library of Queensland)

In the 1980s and 1990s, Pattaya was still being promoted by the Thai government[23] and independent tourist guide books as "Thailand's Riviera."[24] The power of the Mediterranean resort myth is of interest, as by 1990 Pattaya was not only recognized as Asia's most well-known mass coastal tourism resort, it was also experiencing post-resort-maturity problems including falling tourist numbers due to sewage pollution and a tawdry reputation for sex tourism. Perhaps Pattaya was trying to connect with "the Mediterranean dream":

> The dream of the Mediterranean . . . is the dream of the Riviera as a brilliant lotophagous land – the corner of the Mediterranean from the outskirts of Toulon eastward to Monte Carlo, a hundred-odd miles of Frenchness – food, wine, style, heat, rich old farts, gamblers and bare-breasted bimbos. All that and art too.[25]

The references to "Thailand's Riviera" are, however, neither topophilic nor topophobic: they simply recognize that Pattaya is the major center in the expanding coastal urbanization on Thailand's eastern Gulf coast.

Coming to Terms with a New Form of Urbanization

Derogatory observations on the coastal mass tourism resorts, in the academic literature, can be tracked back to Turner and Ash's polemic, *The Golden Hordes*.[26] Such topophobic attitudes have reached a broader audience through popular novels such as Michener's *The Drifters*.[27] More recently, David Lodge reinforces the topophobic stream of Hawaii discourse through his novels *Paradise News*.[28] The topophobic narrative of the mass coastal resort is perhaps at its most comprehensive in travel writer Paul Theroux's grand tour of the Mediterranean.[29]

One of Michener's characters presciently observes that the Torremolinos coastal high-rise sprawl is a new form of urbanism: "It's not a city. It's not a village. It's nothing seen on earth before."[30] In the academic sphere, Mullins, using Australia's Gold Coast as his example, describes the new form of coastal urbanization as the formation of "landscapes of consumption" and "cities for pleasure."[31] In Australia, population movement from the capital cities to coastal areas has been so significant at the turn of the twenty-first century that it has been called the "Sea Change" phenomenon.[32] Jones dismisses taste-based criticisms of the Gold Coast on the basis that Australians and the urban design and planning professions are yet to recognize that it represents a new type of city.[33] MRVDV, in the book *Costa Iberica*, are among the few to go beyond acceptance, to celebration of this new form of urbanism.[34]

Michener and his characters were early critics of the new urban landscape of vast sections of the Spanish Mediterranean coast. A Michener character describes "a vision of the new tourism when cities of more than twelve thousand could be constructed from scratch for the pampering of [international] travelers."[35] The 1971 observation is prophetic; indeed the population estimates have been greatly exceeded in Spain and elsewhere. Nevertheless, progress toward recognition of this new coastal urban form has been slow, no doubt due to its newness. Twenty years before Theroux's scathing critique, a Michener character observes:

From Torremolinos to Fuengirola a concrete forest had grown up, a plethora of high-rise apartments crowding the waterfront, a jungle of shacks and hot-dog stands inland where the money was being made. What little open land he did see was being converted into golf courses.

And it was ugly, ugly beyond the operation of chance. It looked as if Spain had invited to its southeast corner a convocation of the world's worst architects.[36]

"See it Before it's Spoilt": The Rise of Topophobia

By the 1990s, media reports of tourism spoiling previously "unspoilt" places became commonplace. An article headed "Tourism the Destroyer," in the consumer magazine *Choice Travel* is typical of the anti-tourism tone of the time.[37] Using a common language, such reports depict the transformation of "famous places" into "tourist meccas," whereby "hordes of tourists" turn "picturesque honeypot towns" of "rustic tranquility" into crowded "theme parks" (to conflate the messages of two separate articles in just one issue of *The Times*).[38]

Many tourist brochures carry the message "see it before it is spoilt."[39] Some reports suggest that the global expansion of the tourism industry consists of a process of discovering "unspoilt" places, exploiting them until they are "spoilt," and then moving on to develop a seemingly endless supply of "unspoilt" and "pristine" places. This process was noted by Christaller as early as 1963.[40] The frontiers of tourism are constantly pushing outward to include the "undiscovered." Turner and Ash refer to this process as the expansion of the "pleasure periphery" by pioneer tourists seeking to keep ahead of the wave of mass tourism – yet paradoxically hastening the arrival of mass tourists.[41] By the 1970s, pioneer tourists were moving on from crowded Hawaii to Tahiti and Fiji, from Majorca to Greece, North Africa and the Indian Ocean.[42] Regular updates on which formerly "trendy" destinations have become "passé" appear in the press. For example, Cuba, "the only place in the Western hemisphere where US tourists are notable by their absence," is now among the "most fashionable" and "trendy" destinations for "trend-setters," while Tuscany has faded from the itinerary of "the style-conscious traveler."[43] Such reports privilege the "explorer traveler" over the tourist masses who follow: "serious travelers regard Thailand, Malaysia and Indonesia as hopelessly Eighties."[44] These reports provide evidence that not only do tourism landscapes change over time, but tourist tastes also change.

A David Lodge character observes the novelty factor associated with the continuous outward expansion of Turner and Ash's pleasure periphery: "I mean, Majorca, who'd go to Majorca anymore? It's dead common, Blackpool by the Med. Same with Florida, even the Caribbean. You got to keep going further and further to get away from the Joneses."[45]

Aldous Huxley complained in 1925 that "[f]orty miles of Mediterranean coast have been turned into . . . one vast shuffling suburb."[46] There are claims that the Riviera became too crowded and built up by the end of the 1920s and especially after the introduction of paid annual holidays for French workers from 1936.[47] Such resorts quickly filtered down from the social elites to the newly mobile masses. Turner and Ash describe the 1920s summer Riviera as the "direct ancestor" of the 1970s Spanish costas "with their pre-packed, simplistic formula of sun, sea, sand and sex."[48] The Spanish Mediterranean had reportedly been a "snob destination" in the 1950s, but popular resorts like Torremolinos were already showing signs of becoming a "Blackpool of southern Spain" by the 1970s.[49] The reference to Blackpool suggests an elitist disdain for the mass tourism of the working class.[50]

The 1970s saw a spate of tourism publications addressing the question of whether tourism destruction of the cultural landscape was inevitable.[51] Relph's pessimistic view, of tourism as "an homogenizing influence [involving] the destruction of the local and regional landscape that very often initiated the tourism"[52] voices a criticism that continues to be raised afresh thirty years later. Whether or not Reelph's claim is true, tourism continues to grow, resorts are transformed, and although declining popularity is sometimes reported, there are few reports of coastal resorts closing down because of destruction by tourism.

"Tropical paradises" seem to have fared particularly badly in the transformation of coastal landscapes by tourism. Hudson claims that some former tourists to Jamaica and Barbados, hearing that these places are "spoiled by tourism, . . . now go elsewhere to seek places which retain their unspoiled tropical beauty."[53] In the case of Kingston, Jamaica, the replacement of the former "charm and uniqueness" of the waterfront by "bland international style architecture" has obliterated the urban tourism resource.[54] "Homogenization of the tourist landscape"[55] is exacerbated by the involvement of large international companies in airlines, travel agencies, shops, hotels, restaurants and other facilities. The result is that "a tourist resort [is recognizably] a tourist resort whether in the Balearic Islands, Bali or Barbados."[56]

A reluctant tourist in Lodge's *Paradise News* notes the sameness of the Mediterranean resorts depicted in travel brochures: "They seemed extraordinarily repetitive: page after page of bays, beaches, couples, windsurfers, high-rise hotels and swimming-pools. Majorca looked the same as Corfu and Crete looked the same as Tunisia."[57]

Sack writes of a process of place homogenization and loss of authenticity through consumerism, in which "the vastly different historical geographies of Hawaii, Florida, and Majorca have become obscured by an industry providing low-cost access to mixtures of sand, sun, and surf."[58] Figure 11.2 illustrates superficially similar coastal built environments that have evolved in the United States, Spain and Australia over the past fifty years. Hudson builds a persuasive argument that prolific unplanned tourism development will destroy both the tourism resource and the sustained economic success of the local and regional tourist industry.[59] Nevertheless, a search of the internet under "tropical paradise" brings up over three million entries. This suggests that the demand for, and supply of, such tourist destinations are both very much alive. The question of whether new "unspoilt" destinations are created to replace "spoiled" ones, remains unresolved.

Turner and Ash detail how Florida's tourist resources were "ruined by slack planning."[60] The "rape of a state" involved serious degradation of the beaches, the Everglades and Florida Keys through unchecked property speculation. Australia's

(a)

11.2
The superficially
similar urban
forms of
(a) Waikiki;
(b) Benidorm, and
(c) the Gold Coast
(Photos: Daniel
O'Hare)

(b)

(c)

Gold Coast, with references to Florida in the naming of beaches such as Miami, has faced many of the same environmental problems, including the erosion of the coastline through the construction of roads and buildings on the frontal dune systems.

The rise of topophobic myths, whereby the mass coastal resorts have come to be disliked by some influential commentators since the 1970s, is not necessarily based on the critics' direct experience of the subject resorts. Bill Bryson, the sardonic travel writer, observes that some Australians deride the Gold Coast despite never having been there.[61] Frequent derogatory comments regarding the mass tourist resorts referred to in this chapter, offered spontaneously to the author by both casual commentators and key informants, indicate that myths of topophobia are widely held.

Pre-emptive Topophilia: Resisting Mass Tourism in Valued Coastal Places

Two of Spain's mass tourism resorts of the 1950s and 1960s, Sitges and Tossa de Mar, later resisted large-scale mass tourism, and have since come to be regarded as among the Spanish Mediterranean's most prestigious seaside towns.

Sitges is located on the Catalan Coast 38 kilometers south-west of Barcelona (Figure 11.3). With easy rail access from Barcelona, by the turn of the twentieth century Sitges had developed as a fashionable summer beach resort. Sitges established and maintained a high-class aura by attracting wealthy Barcelona residents and internationally renowned artists and writers.[62] These characteristics of Sitges were reinforced with the 1919 low-density subdivision of seafront land adjoining the historic village center, and the subsequent building of mansions, many of which were designed by avant-garde Catalan architects including Antoni Gaudi.

In 1960, Sitges, along with Benidorm and Lloret de Mar, was one of the three principal international tourist destinations on Spain's eastern Mediterranean coast.[63] Nevertheless, Sitges residents, with the support of influential Barcelona

1.3
Sitges, on Spain's
Catalan coast
Photo: Daniel
O'Hare)

parties, have continuously rejected the development of large-scale mass tourism infrastructure such as major hotels and large marinas. This has allowed Sitges to maintain its status as an elite resort for Barcelona.[64] During Sitges' peak period as an international resort, from 1956 to 1967, local political pressure and high beachfront property values resulted in tourists being mainly accommodated in small hotels and converted mansions within the town center. When the international tourism industry adjusted to the oil crisis of 1973, major tour operators concentrated their business in resorts with large hotels (such as Benidorm and Lloret de Mar) and Sitges reverted to its historical – and prosperous – role as an upmarket second home resort.[65]

According to Priestley, the main development pressures causing urban coastal sprawl in the Spanish Mediterranean now are associated with second home development rather than with mass tourism.[66] In Sitges, at the end of the twentieth century, these pressures were compounded by the expansion of Barcelona associated with the 1992 Olympic Games. In particular, the 1992 opening of a toll motorway reduced the driving time from Barcelona from 45 to 25 minutes, effectively bringing Sitges within the urban dynamics of metropolitan Barcelona.[67] Sitges is thus becoming home for new permanent residents who commute to jobs in Barcelona. These new residents – who could perhaps be called "permanent tourists" – are attracted by the same qualities that attracted holiday-makers to Sitges throughout the twentieth century.

The development of Tossa de Mar, approximately 70 kilometers northeast of Barcelona, differs from Sitges (Figure 11.4). Tossa was one of the first places on the Costa Brava to attract international tourists. A "small colony of artists and writers" favored Tossa in the 1930s.[68] The French painter, Marc Chagall's residency in 1934 established Tossa's reputation as "the Blue Paradise."[69] Tossa, in 1954, was the first of the Costa Brava fishing villages to commence international tourism development, following Ava Gardner – and the town – starring in the film, *Pandora*.[70] As tourist numbers grew and pressures for development increased, local residents

11.4
**Tossa de Mar,
Costa Brava,
Spain (Photo:
Daniel O'Hare)**

successfully exerted political pressure to restrict the scale and extent of tourism. A young entrepreneur in neighboring Lloret de Mar saw the opportunity to fill the gap, and mass tourism subsequently developed there rather than at Tossa.[71] Tourism development at Tossa has been significant, nevertheless, though its impacts have been mitigated by a very vocal local community that stresses the historic character, low-key atmosphere and the natural setting of the town.

Defining Topophilia Through an International Topophobic Discourse

A detailed study of the Australian east coast resort of Noosa (Figure 11.5) highlights the use of constructive place comparison and contrast in the way that local residents, tourists, investors, developers and government bodies negotiate the values and desired urban form of a tourist resort area.[72] Interpretation of in-depth interviews and documentary, published and ephemeral literature reveals that this small coastal settlement employs an active informal process of "constructive comparison" to determine the desired characteristics of the place.[73] This continuing narrative of an evolving coastal town contains both topophilic and topophobic strains, comparing Noosa with well-known international resort areas. For example, the data sources compare Noosa's relaxed informality and valued natural setting with the "natural" ambience of New Zealand beach towns, the low-rise village atmosphere of some of the smaller Mediterranean resorts, and the environmental ethos evident in Carmel, California. Such topophilic streams of the discourse are offset by more vociferous topophobic contrasts with mass tourism resorts. Noosa is seen as being more "natural" and "low-key" than Waikiki, the Spanish Mediterranean resorts and Australia's Gold Coast, largely because high-rise development has been prevented in Noosa.

11.5
**Noosa Heads,
Australia (Photo:
Daniel O'Hare)**

Negotiation of the low-rise built form has been conducted in a forty-year process of topophobic contrast to mass tourism resorts, particularly the Gold Coast, but also to Waikiki in Hawaii.

The Noosa myth that "no buildings may be higher than the trees" is a local manifestation of a catchphrase that is familiar in many of the world's beach resorts, including Bali and Tahiti. Noosa's anti-high-rise movement began in the late 1960s as a reaction to the Council's approval of an eight-storey building on the beachfront. Local objections to high-rise development were based on knowledge and experience of well-known resorts with high-rise development on the beachfront, including on the Queensland Gold Coast. Articulate and well-traveled permanent residents of Noosa were aware of the fierce debates over high-rise tourism development in Hawaii around that time.[74]

Resolution of the building height issue in Noosa was slow. The approved eight-storey building was never built, due to a fortuitous combination of severe cyclonic storm seasons, public pressure and the economic fall-out of the 1973 global oil crisis.[75] The "no higher than the trees" wording gradually moved from the informal to the formal narrative in a succession of Council policies. High-rise buildings in Noosa were only ruled out legally in 1991, with the introduction of a planning scheme prohibiting the erection of buildings higher than four storeys. The prohibition on high-rise development was a formalization of a strong informal sanction that had been in place since the great anti-high-rise battle of 1969–70. During this twenty-year period, a topophilic Noosa narrative based on low-rise built form grew to eventually eclipse the topophobic "not another Gold Coast" discourse that initiated it.

In Hua Hin (Figure 11.6), on Thailand's western Gulf coast approximately three hours south of Bangkok, the topophobic discourse appears to have been less effective in restraining trends towards conventional mass tourism development. The royal Thai resort town of Hua Hin is frequently contrasted – and increasing compared, negatively – with Pattaya and the southern Thai resort of Phuket. In 1980s travel literature, Hua Hin was contrasted with these mass tourism resorts, as the village lacked

11.6
**Hua Hin, Thailand
(Photo: Daniel
O'Hare)**

their high-rise development, water pollution, crowds, bars, street prostitution and commercialism. By the 1990s, although still highly regarded, Hua Hin began to be likened to these places.

Although the travel literature reveals fears that Hua Hin is showing signs of becoming "another Pattaya," the "not another Pattaya" myth does not seem to have been overtly used in official planning and urban design for the smaller resort, other than in a planning study commissioned by the Tourism Authority of Thailand (TAT). After establishing that visitor numbers to Hua Hin and adjacent Cha Am were second only to Pattaya, that study expressed fears that "uncontrolled development could easily result in deterioration of the natural and social environment of the [Hua Hin] Study Area impairing its attractiveness both for tourists and residents."[76] The study went on to recommend a 20m building height limit, aesthetic controls and landscaping guidelines to retain and enhance the image of "royal resort."[77] A visit to Hua Hin immediately shows that the height limit has not been enforced. Hua Hin retains its distinctiveness from the mass tourism resorts, however, due to the influence of the Royal family.[78]

In various international tourist guidebooks, Patong, the main resort town on Phuket, is described as "a second Pattaya," "a mini-Pattaya" and "another Pattaya." Critics have even been known to liken Pattaya (unfavorably) to Torremolinos, as one British tourist guidebook illustrates:

> With its murky sea, streets packed with high-rise hotels and touts on every corner, Pattaya is the epitome of exploitative tourism gone mad. But most of Pattaya's visitors don't mind that the place looks like Torremolinos or that the new water treatment plant has only recently stopped businesses from dumping their sewage straight into the bay – what they are here for is sex.[79]

Because of the strength of the "not another Pattaya" myth in Thailand, there is scope for further research into the extent to which this myth is influencing tourism planning and development in the more recently developing coastal resorts.[80]

Resuscitating Topophilia in the Mass Coastal Resorts

One of the ironies of the long-running debate on the tourism transformation of coastal places is that, while residents of many resorts have feared loss of local identity through "Waikikianization"[81] – or "Waikikification" – Waikiki itself has commenced a campaign of "restoring Hawaiianness."[82] Waikiki's own form of tourism development is regarded by influential Hawaiians as having destroyed its Hawaiian character and sense of place because promoters reduced its rich identity to a mere "sandpit."[83] Recent Hawaiian planning documents directly adopt the principle of restoring Hawaiianness, partly because of evidence that tourists now demand more variety in a beach holiday than the staples of sun, sand and surf.[84] Some critics, however, question the cultural authenticity of recent planning and development processes for recapturing Waikiki's sense of place.[85]

Waikiki was not the only iconic coastal mass tourism resort area to reassess its character in the 1980s and 1990s. In Spain, major Mediterranean resorts were experiencing a decline in tourist numbers by the late 1980s, due to problems including water pollution, overcrowding, poor quality urban development, poor waterfront access, inadequate infrastructure, cultural impacts, and competition from newer destinations.[86] Similar problems were reported in Pattaya, Thailand's major mass tourism resort.[87] Australia's Gold Coast was hit hard by a national economic recession in the early 1990s, with tourism numbers declining for the first time and with prominent properties sitting vacant due to stalled developments. In each place, strategies were developed to reinvigorate these flagship tourist cities. In both Spain and Thailand, the scale of the problems attracted a national response; in Hawaii, there was a state government response to match that of the City and County Council, while on the Gold Coast, the City Council (Australia's second largest local government) led the response with little or no state or national assistance. It appears that major problems have been addressed and that each of these coastal resort cities has emerged more robust than before; however, further comparative international research is needed before conclusions can be drawn.

Conclusion

The narratives of newly emerging coastal urban environments employ topophilic comparison and topophobic contrast to articulate both desired and undesirable future urban forms. The coastal mass tourism resorts of the twentieth century are used as reference points in these topophilic and topophobic discourses. The familiar slogan, "not another Waikiki/Benidorm/Torremolinos/Pattaya/Gold Coast" conveys a simplistic vision of these places as high-rise coastal urban strips where the features and sense of a natural landscape have been obliterated. These mass resorts are used as benchmarks by which to evaluate the degree of transformation from the (desirable-topophilic) natural state to the (spoiled-topophobic) city resort state. Some coastal resort areas, such as Noosa on Australia's east coast, have skillfully embodied positive elements of topophobic discourses into their planning instruments, resulting in a strong topophilic narrative of local distinctiveness despite significant transformation by coastal urban development. Comparison of Noosa with Hua Hin also reveals, however, that the strength of the narrative is arguably more important than legislative controls.

Meanwhile, the mass coastal tourism resorts are themselves undergoing "narrative surgery" to ensure that topophilic elements outweigh the increasingly topophobic discourses they are attracting. The move to "ReHawaiianize" Waikiki is a vivid example of the way that planning and design processes engage in the discourses of topophilia and topophobia. If such approaches to tourism regeneration are motivated by elitism, as claimed by critics,[88] reinvention of the mass resorts may conflict with their roles as both popular holiday destination and home for local people.

The international case studies reviewed in this chapter provide support for mobilizing the myths of place through a process of constructive comparison by which the topophilic qualities of distinctive coastal places are articulated and celebrated as a place is transformed by tourism and urban development. These examples suggest the potential for a more positive approach to tourism transformations, beyond the disempowering assumption that tourism "spoils unspoilt places."

Notes

1 Michael Jones, "The Concept of Cultural Landscape: Discourses and Narratives," in Hannes Palang and Gary Fry (eds), *Landscape Interfaces: Cultural Heritage in Changing Landscapes*, Dordrecht: Kluwer Academic Publishers, 2003, p. 25.

2 Derek Gregory, "Discourse," in Ronald Johnstone, Derek Gregory, Geraldine Pratt and Michael Watts (eds), *The Dictionary of Human Geography*, 4th edn. Oxford: Blackwell, 2000, pp. 180–181, cited in Jones, ibid.

3 Yi-Fu Tuan, *Topophilia: A Study of Environmental Perception, Attitudes, and Values*, New York: Columbia University Press, 1974, p. 4.

4 John Bale, "Space, Place and Body Culture: Yi-Fu Tuan and a Geography of Sport," *Geografiska Annaler* 78B(3), 1996, 168.

5 Tuan, *Topophilia*, p. 92, pp. 102–112.

6 Xavier Campillo-Besses, Gerda Priestley and Francesc Romagose, "Using EMAS and Local Agenda 21 as Tools Towards Sustainability: The Case of a Catalan Coastal Resort," in Bill Bramwell (ed.), *Coastal Mass Tourism: Diversification and Sustainable Development in Southern Europe*, Clevedon: Channel View Publications, 2004, pp. 220–248.

7 Daniel J. O'Hare, "Tourism and Small Coastal Settlements: A Cultural Landscape Approach for Urban Design," unpublished PhD thesis, Joint Centre for Urban Design, Oxford Brookes University, 1997; Bernard Salt, *The Big Shift: Welcome to the Third Australian Culture*, South Yarra: Hardie Grant, 2001; Ian Burnley and Peter Murphy, *Sea Change: Movement from Metropolitan to Arcadian Australia*, Sydney: UNSW Press, 2004.

8 Michael Hough, *Out of Place: Restoring Identity to the Regional Landscape*, New Haven, CT: Yale University Press, 1990.

9 John Rennie Short, *Imagined Country: Environment, Society and Culture*, London: Routledge and Kegan Paul, 1991, p. xvi.

10 James A. Michener, *The Drifters*, London: Mandarin, 1971.

11 Nancy Cato, *The Noosa Story: A Study in Unplanned Development*, Brisbane: Jacaranda Press, 1979; Michael Gloster, *The Shaping of Noosa*, Noosa Heads: Noosa Blue Publishing, 1997.

12 Harold Gilliam and Ann Gilliam, *Creating Carmel: The Enduring Vision*, Salt Lake City: Peregrine Smith Books, 1992.

13 Cited in Steven Martin and Joe Cummings, *Thailand's Islands and Beaches*, Melbourne: Lonely Planet Publications, 2002, p. 296.

14 Ibid., p. 253.

15 John K. Walton, *The English Seaside Resort: A Social History, 1750–1914*, Leicester: Leicester University Press, 1983.

16 Robert Longhurst, *Gold Coast: Our Heritage in Focus*, South Brisbane: State Library of Queensland Foundation, 1995; Robert Longhurst, *Sunshine Coast: Our Heritage in Focus*. South Brisbane: State Library of Queensland Foundation, 1995.

17 Longhurst, *Gold Coast*.

18 John Towner, *An Historical Geography of Recreation and Tourism in the Western World, 1540–1940*, Chichester: Wiley, 1996.

19 Aleck. J. Ivimey, *All About Queensland*, Maryborough: Garvie, Alston and Anr, 1889, p. 60.

20 Mary McDonald, "Who Owns Waikiki?" in Deborah W. Woodcock (ed.), *Hawaii: New Geographies*, Honolulu: Department of Geography, University of Hawaii-Manoa, 1999, p. 187.

21 Queensland Government Intelligence and Tourism Board, *From Noosa to the Tweed: Mountain and Seaside Resorts of Southern Queensland*, Brisbane: QGITB, no date (c.1925).

22 Paul Theroux, *The Pillars of Hercules: A Grand Tour of the Mediterranean*, London: Hamish Hamilton, 1995.

23 Government Public Relations Department, *Thailand in Brief*, Bangkok: Thai Government, 1990.

24 Hans Hoefer, *Insight Guide: Thailand*, Singapore: APA Productions and Prentice Hall, 1985, pp. 239, 250.

Daniel O'Hare

25   Theroux, *The Pillars of Hercules*, p. 101.

26   Louis Turner and John Ash, *The Golden Hordes: International Tourism and the Pleasure Periphery*, London: Constable, 1975.

27   Michener, *The Drifters*.

28   David Lodge, *Paradise News*, London: Penguin, 1991.

29   Theroux, *The Pillars of Hercules*.

30   Michener, *The Drifters*, p. 42.

31   Patrick Mullins, "Cities for Pleasure: The Emergence of Tourism Urbanization in Australia," *Built Environment* 18(3), 1992, 187–198.

32   Salt, *The Big Shift*; Burnley and Murphy, *Sea Change*.

33   Victoria Jones, "Invisible Landscapes: Cultural Landscapes of the Gold Coast 1959–1999," unpublished MBltEnv (Urban Design) dissertation, Queensland University of Technology, 2001.

34   MRVDV, *Costa Iberica: Upbeat to the Leisure City*, Barcelona: A.C.T.A.R., 2000.

35   Michener, *The Drifters*, p. 326.

36   Ibid., p. 411.

37   Consumer Association, "Tourism the Destroyer," *Choice Travel*, May 1990, 100.

38   Ben Macintyre, "Tourist Hordes Threaten Provencal Idyll," *The Times*, 30 July, 1996, 13; Libby Purves, "Once Britten, Twice Shy," *The Times*, 30 July, 1996, 16.

39   John Urry, "The Tourist Gaze and the 'Environment'," *Theory, Culture & Society* 9(3), 1992, 24; Tom Selwyn (ed.), *The Tourist Image: Myths and Myth-Making in Tourism*, Chichester: Wiley, 1996.

40   Cited in Richard W. Butler, "The Concept of a Tourist Area Cycle of Evolution: Implications for Management of Resources," *Canadian Geographer* 24(1), 1980, 5.

41   Turner and Ash, *The Golden Hordes*, p. 12.

42   Ibid.

43   S. Calder, "Holidays Made in Heaven – and Hell," *The Independent*, 20 July, 1996, 3.

44   G. Cooper, "How to Travel Places and Impress Your Friends," *The Independent*, 20 July, 1996, 3.

45   Lodge, *Paradise News*, p. 5.

46   Cited in Turner and Ash, *The Golden Hordes*, p. 86.

47   Ibid., p. 85.

48   Ibid., p. 88.

49   Ibid., p. 99.

50   Compare Dean MacCannell, *The Tourist: A New Theory of the Leisure Class*, London: Macmillan, 1976.

51   For example, Turner and Ash, *The Golden Hordes*; and MacCannell, *The Tourist*.

52   Edward Relph, *Place and Placelessness*, London: Pion, 1976, p. 93.

53   Brian Hudson, "Landscape as a Resource for National Development: A Caribbean View," *Geography* 71(2), 1986, 119.

54   Ibid., 8–9.

55   Brian Hudson, "Technology, Tourism and Heritage: Waterfront Redevelopment in the Caribbean," unpublished manuscript supplied by the author, p. 14.

56   Ibid.

57   Lodge, *Paradise News*, p. 32.

58   Robert D. Sack, "The Consumer's World: Place as Context," *Annals of the Association of American Geographers* 78(4), 1988, 642.

59   Brian Hudson, "Tourism in Jamaica and Grenada," in Stephen Britton and William C. Clarke, *Ambiguous Alternative: Tourism in Small Developing Countries*, Suva: University of the South Pacific, 1987, p. 55.

60   Turner and Ash, *The Golden Hordes*, p. 111.

61   Bill Bryson, *Down Under*, New York: Doubleday, 2000, p. 206.

62 Campillo-Besses *et al.*, "Using EMAS and Local Agenda 21 as Tools Towards Sustainability," p. 230.

63 A. Miguelsanz-Arnalot and G. Higueras-Miro, *El Tourisme a Sitges*, 1964, cited in ibid.

64 Priestley, 2004, pers. comm.

65 Campillo-Besses *et al.*, "Using EMAS and Local Agenda 21 as Tools Towards Sustainability," p. 230.

66 Priestley, 2004, pers. comm.

67 Campillo-Besses *et al.*, "Using EMAS and Local Agenda 21 as Tools Towards Sustainability," p. 230.

68 Damien Simonis, *Catalunya and the Costa Brava*, London: Lonely Planet Publications, 2003, p. 150.

69 Ibid.

70 Priestley, 2004, pers. comm.

71 Ibid.

72 O'Hare, "Tourism and Small Coastal Settlements."

73 Ibid.

74 Cato, "The Noosa Story."

75 O'Hare, "Tourism and Small Coastal Settlements."

76 Japan International Cooperation Agency, *Hua Hin and Cha-Am: Tourism Development Study*, Bangkok: JICA, for Tourism Authority of Thailand, 1992, p. 6.

77 Ibid., p. 16.

78 Interview with Mr Khun Niti Kongrut, Director TAT Pattaya Region, 28 June 2004. Kongrut noted that the Royal family has considerable control over development through their own extensive land holdings, and that the local government and private landowners respect their wish that Hua Hin not develop an extensive red light district.

79 Paul Gray and Lucy Ridout, *The Rough Guide to Thailand's Beaches and Islands*, 1st edn, London: Rough Guides, 2001, p. 177.

80 The Hua Hin research provides some indication of such a relationship, but that research was limited to English language sources.

81 This issue is raised in 1979 by Cato, *The Noosa Story*, although the term was apparently coined later. "Waikikianization" is mentioned in David Zurick, *Errant Journeys: Adventure Travel in a Modern Age*, Austin, TX: University of Texas Press, 1995. An earlier, equivalent derogatory term, "Waikikification," was cited by Turner and Ash in *The Golden Hordes*.

82 George S. Kanahele, *Restoring Hawaiianness to Waikiki*, Honolulu: Queen Emma Foundation, 1994.

83 Ibid., p. ii.

84 For example, see City and County of Honolulu, *Waikiki Planning and Program Guide*, Honolulu: CCH Planning Department, 1996.

85 Jon D. Goss and Serge A. Marek, "Clearing the Jungle: The Politics of Redevelopment in Waikiki," undated draft paper located at http://jongoss.info/papers/waikiki.htm, accessed 4 April 2007.

86 Michael Barke and John Towner, "Learning from Experience? Progress Towards a Sustainable Future for Tourism in the Central and Eastern Andalusian Littoral," in Bramwell (ed.), *Coastal Mass Tourism*, pp. 157–175.

87 Khun Niti Kungrat, 2004, pers. comm.

88 McDonald, "Who Owns Waikiki?"; Goss and Marek, "Clearing the Jungle."

12

Economy and Affect

People–Place Relationships and the Metropolis

Peter Murphy

Yi-Fu Tuan, in his renowned geographical work, focused the attention of scholars on the myriad ways in which human beings form and express subjective relationships to their surroundings.[1] These *affective relationships* result from the qualitative assessments that people make of the places that they interact with on a day-to-day basis, either through direct experience or second-hand through the people they know and through reportage. Such assessments influence not just their states of mind but also the decisions that people make about where to live, where to work and where to play.

The metropolis, or large urbanized region, is too large, too complex and too little related in its parts to be the locus of those close-quarter engagements that produce affective relationships, either positive or negative, with places. When people say that they love a city they do not mean that they love the metropolitan totality. Rather, they mean that they love (or hate, or are ambiguous about) parts of the whole, typically small parts: districts, neighborhoods, precincts, parks, beaches, waterways, buildings, assemblages of buildings, and so forth. Of course, it is not just the physical fabric of the city to which people relate but also the types of people who inhabit the city and the experiences that they accumulate during their lives in it. So the notion that there can be affective relationships with a city, construed as a metropolitan region, is unconvincing. If such relationships do exist, they can only be at the most abstract, attenuated level and in reality derive from the intense experiences that we have of the parts.

But far from being irrelevant to an understanding of the strength and forms of the affective relationships that people have with the places they inhabit, or might inhabit, the metropolis as an aggregate establishes, in quite critical ways, the economic, social, cultural and political circumstances that shape its components. In the absence of the metropolitan frame (a circumstance that is admittedly hard to imagine), those places around which people make meaning would either not exist at all, or else would lack the resonance that vivifies or darkens them. The strength and structure of the metropolitan economy drive a myriad of micro-scale processes that produce the physical and social forms to which people relate in their daily lives. This "big picture" perspective informs our understanding of changes in the city. In a period in which cities compete strongly for geographically mobile investment flows and consumption spending, the physical and social states of the metropolis are critical variables influencing economic growth. As well as being the engine rooms of national economic growth, cities are also assemblages of sub-systems based on decisions made by firms and households. Collectively those systems define the conditions of localities that make cities more or less livable, more or less good places in which to do business. And, of course, places that are good for business are often places that are good to live in. Reciprocally, places that are good to live in are places that are often good for business.

In thinking about the relationships people have with the places that they inhabit it is useful to distinguish between residents and visitors. It is further useful to distinguish between the physical and non-physical environments of cities. The physical dimension includes elements of both built and natural environments. The non-physical includes social and cultural characteristics of the population and the economic bases of urban life. It may be conjectured that in their non-physical characteristics Western cities are very similar (although the details vary) because they are shaped by the same external circumstances and consumer preferences. The physical dimensions may be unique although, in the case of the built environment, much of what is seen is held in common because the urban fabric itself is a response to similar economic and social conditions. Only the natural environment of cities is unambiguously unique. Bringing environment and people together it may be conjectured that residents relate primarily (although not exclusively) to the non-physical environment whereas tourists respond primarily to the physical dimensions. These categories of people and place suggest that disentangling the ways in which people relate affectively to place is complex although in all configurations the framing power of economy is present.

To develop this argument the chapter is in two parts. The first considers how the metropolitan economy works to produce sub-metropolitan conditions for capital accumulation and collective consumption. How these macro-economic processes produce spatial forms that generate affective relationships over time is illustrated against the backdrop of economic history. The second part of the chapter considers the scope for public policy to influence the qualities of places to which people relate. It deals, in particular, with the ways in which micro-economic forces (decisions by firms and households), playing out over space and time, intersect with the broader economy to produce more or less livable cities, and parts of cities, and how a knowledge of these forces leads to policy instruments to shape change.

Metropolitan Sydney is used to ground the discussion. This is appropriate for three reasons. First, it is the city that the author knows best and is thus a source of authentically portrayable cases. Second, Sydney is a city that is well known internationally and has all of the universal characteristics of large Western cities as well as distinctive physical attributes that are significant factors in its competitive advantage. Third, the metropolis is large enough to contain the full spectrum of spatial forms, built forms and social configurations that characterize the contemporary Western city. Sydney is unique but largely in terms of its physical and built environment and even then the built environment is a variant or simulacrum of what is observable elsewhere.

Sydney is the capital city of the Australian state of New South Wales (NSW) and its population – at 4.2 million – represents 21 per cent of the Australian total; approximately half a million more people than the next largest Australian city, Melbourne. Sydney is by general acclaim a beautiful city with high levels of physical beauty and a high quality built environment, especially in its central public domain and its more affluent residential areas. Its environmental amenity is based on an equable climate (warm summers and mild winters), a large and beautiful harbor, and renowned ocean beaches. By any measure Sydney is Australia's most globalized city and scores highly on all the standard indicators.[2] To quote from the NSW Government's place-marketing material:

> Sydney provides international investors with unparalleled access to Australia's high-growth economy and an ideal platform for expansion into Asia Pacific markets. Sydney is a global city servicing the needs of hundreds of multinationals. It is also the headquarters of Australia's finance, information communications technology (ICT) and biotechnology industries.
>
> The city is Australia's major business and financial centre, being the location of 65 per cent of finance industry business such as banking, insurance and funds management. Close to half of the finance industry's gross product and more than 45 per cent of Australia's 263,600 finance sector employees are concentrated in Sydney and NSW.
>
> The world's largest international accounting and consultancy firms have offices or regional operations centers in Sydney, with an equally high concentration of law, management and marketing firms.[3]

Tourism is Australia's most important service export and Sydney, as is typical of global cities, attracts a disproportionately large share. Some 30 per cent of international visitor nights are spent in Sydney, compared with 15 per cent in Melbourne and less than 10 per cent in each of Perth and Brisbane. Sydney's dominance is accounted for by its airport's gateway function to Australia, together with the city's disproportionate share of internationally orientated businesses and immigrants, both of which generate tourism.[4] Important, too, is the fact that Sydney is the one Australian city that is widely known in Asia.[5] Again typical of global cities, over 30 per cent of Sydney's residents were born overseas, making the city home to 45 per cent of Australia's Asian language speakers and 29 per cent of European language speakers. This diversity is unmatched by many other cities in the world and provides international companies with a pool of Asian, European and Middle Eastern language skills.

Metropolitan Implications of Economic Globalization

At the metropolitan scale Sydney's globalization since the early 1980s (and on-going at the time of writing) has been paralleled by an unprecedented period of economic growth.[6] The volume of business investment and consumer spending has driven Sydney property prices to stratospheric levels and vastly expanded demand for restaurants, coffee shops and all the other accoutrements required by a large and affluent population. Globalization has also accentuated the cosmopolitan character of the metropolis, a feature that, in itself, makes it attractive to members of the so-called "creative class" who Richard Florida argues now drive urban economic growth (see below).[7]

Globalization, as everywhere, has had its dark side. Welfare contrasts between those who have fared best in the new economic regime, and those who have lagged or missed out altogether, have increased over the past quarter century. High levels of immigration from non-Anglo/European sources have generated considerable anxiety over the dilution of "traditional" Australian cultural habits and values and competition for jobs among the lower paid.[8] The sheer size of metropolitan Sydney, combined with the strength of spending power in its population, has driven housing prices to new highs, with attendant worsening of affordability for lower-income earners and those otherwise wishing to enter the market.

These patterns of wealth, relative deprivation and general social change have imbued the metropolis, as an amorphous collectivity, with positive and negative resonances in the minds of its citizens. For some, the metropolis has become a thriving, exciting place to live. For others, an unaffordable and rather frightening prospect from which escape to other places is the best option. Within this over-arching frame is the infinite variety of spatial scales, social and physical forms variably influenced or produced by general economic change and its accompaniments.

In this first part of the chapter the traces of economic change on Sydney's places and spaces are identified and conjectures are made as to how these shifts both reflect and drive changes to the ways in which people relate to them. The material is organized into three spheres: the domestic, the public and the economic.

The Domestic Sphere

The Inner City

The inner areas of Sydney have changed enormously over the 200 and more years of white settlement. Typical of Western cities, the areas around the central business district were initially populated by factories, warehouses and workers' housing. In line with early spatial models of the city the middle and upper classes lived in more capacious housing either beyond the inner city, or within the inner city but in parts distant from the industrial districts. This familiar story has more affluent citizens relocating to detached housing in suburban settings serviced by railway and tramlines from the late nineteenth century onwards.[9]

After World War II, the long economic boom of the 1950s and 1960s saw the acceleration of low-density, suburban development that was fuelled by the affordability of private motor vehicles and the desire on the part of many citizens to live in what they regarded as ideal residential settings away from the grime and poverty of the inner city. In this period the areas of inner city workers housing were so little thought of that anyone who could do so escaped from them as soon as possible. These interconnected processes of valorizing the suburbs and de-valorizing the inner city were further fuelled by the de-camping of factories to the suburbs in pursuit of proximity to workers and cheaper land. By 1950, when Sydney's first metropolitan plan, the County of Cumberland Scheme, was promulgated, large areas of inner city housing were slated for demolition because of their presumed slum status and the need for more inner city industrial land to accommodate the booming manufacturing sector. While conditions were nowhere as depauperate as the de-industrialized ghettoes of American inner cities, in the 1950s and 1960s inner Sydney was not the place to be if you were Anglo-Irish and upwardly mobile.

Yet just as the bulldozers were moving in, the great post-WWII immigration boom was kicking in.[10] Many immigrants sought work in the factories, and in low-end service economy jobs in the downtown. Inner city workers housing suited them well because it was accessible and cheap. They used these areas as sites on which to establish themselves in Australia prior to the growing affluence that permitted many to realize the suburban dream (which many did as soon as they could afford to). In effect, immigrants, despite typically very different residential experiences to those of the native-born population, rapidly adjusted their preferences to local norms. Despite this propensity to move up and out of areas of initial settlement migrants and their Australian-born children retain strong affective relationships with these places. A notable example is the Sydney suburb of Leichhardt that was colonized by Italian migrants in the 1950s and 1960s. Since then Italian migration has diminished to a trickle but Norton Street, the main drag, is still entirely Italian in flavor (Figure 12.1). Not only are the shops and restaurants patronized by immigrants and their progeny, the street is also the focus of significant Italian-themed events such as the 2006 World Cup Soccer. Obviously enough, these "ethnic places" have also become part of the rich mix of cosmopolitan eating and shopping opportunities used by Sydney-siders of all ethnic backgrounds. Sydney's first Chinatown, in the Haymarket on the southern edge of the CBD, serves a similar function but, unlike suburban Leichhardt, has been revalorized by the influx of Chinese migrants into the many high-rise apartment blocks that have emerged in the inner city. Whereas Leichhardt might be seen as a simulacrum – history in aspic – Chinatown is both tourist haunt and a lively domestic hub for the latest wave of migrants (Figure 12.2).

Back-tracking to the late 1960s, post-WWII migration played a significant role in preserving much of the inner city from demolition. Around this time the ground was laid for the next round of transformation as young, university-educated Australians began to colonize the inner city, much to the chagrin of their parents for whom the suburban idle was the norm and the inner city was a slum. The history of gentrification has been exhaustively studied so the drivers are clear: access to the cultural delights of downtown, proximity to downtown jobs and a nostalgic attachment to older housing forms and the folkways thought to be attached to them. There is nothing in the Australian experience that readers familiar with the history of gentrification around the Western world would be unfamiliar with but the significance of

2.1
Jorton Street
afés, Leichhardt,
ydney
Photo: Asim
Aly-Khan)

12.1
Norton Street
Cafés, Leichhardt,
Sydney
(Photo: Asim
Aly-Khan)

the trend is undoubted and its connection with romantic ideas of heritage, community and the working class are uncontested.

What might have been seen as an exhausted pre-occupation for urbanists gained new momentum in the late 1980s and 1990s when new forms of economic globalization imprinted themselves on the metropolis. Gentrification accelerated and, as well as consuming older housing, was manifested in rising demand for new medium density and high-rise housing. This shift was driven not merely by a continuation of the gentrification impetus established in the 1960s. As well it was driven by growth in the globally focused service economy of downtown Sydney. The new knowledge workers wanted to live near their downtown jobs, the quality of remaining older housing was poor, and poorly located, and such folk, many of them widely traveled, were favorably disposed to living in newer housing at densities not heretofore regarded as being acceptable to low-density oriented Aussie culture (Figure 12.3). This shift towards high-density living is quite remarkable in the Australian context. While to some degree it is driven by government policy designed to promote a higher density city, it also reflects, as did the initial phase of gentrification, a quite fundamental re-evaluation of what constitutes a quality living environment. A further layer in understanding the connection between the metropolitan economy and the recent round of investment in inner city housing is the relationship between land prices and metropolitan population size. Elementary land economics tells us that the larger a city's population, the higher the value of land in areas favored by businesses and people. As population grows so central land prices grow. The only way people can continue to live in highly priced areas (unless they are inordinately rich) is by living at higher densities; i.e. using less land per dwelling unit. Because strong economies attract population, the relationship between population numbers, land prices and

densities is driven by economic globalization and facilitated by the preferences of cosmopolitan workers.

A curious feature of Sydney's gentrification is that its beachheads of gentrification were the suburbs of Paddington, Balmain and Surry Hills, all away (but not far) from the sea coast and harbor; curious because an elemental feature of

Australian self-mythologizing is a preoccupation with the beach. In the past decade or so, however, the beachside suburbs have been strongly incorporated into the gentrification process, with younger generations re-discovering the beach mythology and sharing the beachside suburbs with the multitude of tourists for whom Bondi beach, in particular, is an Australian icon.

Another interesting sidelight to Sydney's gentrification story has been its displacement to the outer edge of the metropolis into areas of high natural amenity on the coast and in the mountains well served by commuter rail. Such areas require long-distance commutes (at heavily subsidized prices – a matter to be addressed below) but allow many of those who in the past would have preferred the inner city to access better, cheaper housing in settings conducive to the reproduction of the social and cultural values associated with earlier cohorts of gentrifiers.

Ideology of Suburbia and the Suburban-Urban Debate

This business of gentrification has highlighted a rather fundamental contrast in the living preferences of Australians, a contrast that has engendered a politics around elite perceptions of the urban and a more democratic preference for the suburbs. The gentrifiers not only prefer the grungier settings of the inner city, they actively decry the "desert of suburbia." This cultural elitism plays itself out in interesting ways. At one end of the spectrum are the followers of Jane Jacobs who, not universally perhaps, tend to laud not just the benefits of mixed use, high-density inner city living but actively denigrate what they regard as the cultural and aesthetic poverty of the suburban desert. At the other end of the spectrum are those who applaud the democratic ideal of suburbia and decry the urban cultural elites who presume to declare the program for what constitutes a proper urban citizenry.[11] While essentially a sideshow in the politics of academia and among some writers in the quality press, the debate has some political significance in the contentious domain of densification.

At issue is the extent to which government – by forcing citizens to live at higher densities – is materially affecting their welfare; the reality is that by far the larger part of the Australian body politic prefers the detached house on a suburban allotment, not a flat or a town house in the inner city (or elsewhere) and the suburban lifestyle of backyard barbecues, weekend sporting events, shopping malls and football clubs.

Gay Spaces

The public emergence of gay culture in Australia reached its apotheosis in Sydney – of all the possible Australian cities – and is symbolized by the annual "Gay and Lesbian Mardi Gras" festival.[12] While there is an interesting geography of gay places (with the commercial and to some degree residential focus being in Sydney's inner city suburbs of Darlinghurst, Newtown and Leichhardt), this more or less parallels mappings in cities worldwide; mappings explored by many cultural historians and urbanists of assorted shades. Of more direct interest for the present chapter is the association of gay culture with ideas of cosmopolitanism and social tolerance, qualities that Florida argues are essential elements of a city's competitive advantage.[13] Cities strong in those qualities are argued by Florida to be conducive to attracting/retaining members of what he terms the "creative class." Writing much earlier than Florida, Robert Reich coined the term "symbolic analysts" ("knowledge workers" are much the same thing).[14] Such people are assumed to be instrumental in driving economic development because they innovate in business as owners or employees. Sydney's enmeshment in the processes of economic globalization since the 1970s has arguably created conditions favorable to the public positioning of gay culture, although its emergence predates and presages globalization. Although not emphasized in city marketing texts, Sydney's gay scene is certainly part of any sophisticated understanding of the city's competitive advantage.

Spaces of Disadvantage

As was noted above, social polarization is a universal feature of global cities. This is no less the case in Sydney, although Australian circumstances arguably lessen the material significance of differentials in incomes (as opposed to the opportunities for political grandstanding that such differentials permit).[15] Nevertheless, the presence of the poor in any affluent city will influence the attitudes that the better-off have towards those parts of the city inhabited by the poor. This may be illustrated in a number of ways.

In Australia, social housing exists in two settings. High-rise apartment blocks were constructed in the inner cities in the 1950s and 1960s. This was possible because pre-gentrification land prices were low. While this housing stock-still exists – and lower rise extensions of more recent vintage have occurred in suburbs like Waterloo and Glebe in Sydney – it is increasingly isolated in a sea of affluence (Figure 12.4). This naturally generates local social climates that worry the gentrifiers (undesirable, apparently threatening neighbors) although it would be inaccurate to inflate the material, as opposed to the affective significance of these juxtapositions. Certainly the presence of social housing has not inhibited gentrification. Social housing also exists in low-density settings in the outer city. Decanted to the periphery to take

advantage of lower housing prices, these enclaves of poverty and social disfunc-
tionality, and the anti-social behavior of many of their younger residents, have come
to symbolize the welfare gap between the haves and the have-nots in contemporary
Sydney. As is the case elsewhere in the world, the middle class has responded by
patronizing the gated communities that are sprouting up in the suburban and inner
city landscapes accompanied by hand-wringing by critics who – with not much in the
way of evidence – conjure up frightening images of a dystrophic divided city.[16]

It is important, for international readers, to know that levels of socio-spatial
polarization in Sydney, and other Australian cities, are probably less than in other parts
of the Western world and certainly less significant in welfare terms. In a pioneering
article on this subject, Murphy and Watson proposed a number of explanations for
the lesser significance of location in determining levels of welfare: while the welfare
gap between rich and poor has widened, the poor have not got poorer because of
the (still) generous Australian welfare system; moreover local government is a relatively insignificant supplier of services so where you live matters relatively little as
health, education and police services are provided by State Governments.[17]

Immigration has always been contentious around the world and this
appears to have sharpened in recent times. In the urban context the focus of anxiety
within "host" populations has been the putative formation of ghettoes.[18] This propo-
sition came to the fore in the 1980s in Australia in response to the shift of migration
to predominantly Asian sources – especially refugees from Indochina. The association
of high ethnic concentrations, in outer Sydney suburbs such as Cabramatta, with high
unemployment (especially among young people) and the drug trade raised alarm bells
in an Anglo-Celtic and European population already uneasy about Asian migration.
Careful analysis of the ghetto hypothesis conclusively discounted it but this did not
prevent the opponents of immigration continuing to deploy it in their rhetoric.

211

In recent years the social panic has shifted to a focus on migrants from Islamic countries. Needless to say, the era of global terrorism makes the settlement of people from such source countries more problematic than it would have been heretofore. More material is the reality that youth unemployment is typically high and social norms are very different in some respects from those of the pre-existing populations. Areas of high Islamic settlement, such as Sydney's Lakemba, are therefore conceived of as problematic in large sections of the public imaginary. In reality, however, places like Cabramatta and Lakemba are also sought after for the ethnic eateries that abound there – most likely by members of the creative class rather than the wider metropolitan populace.[19]

The Public Domain

Contesting the Public Domain: the Cronulla Riots

In early 2006, major riots broke out in the beachside suburb of Cronulla, south of central Sydney. The riots were sparked by violent reactions on the part of local youth to incursions by Lebanese Muslims into the locality. The latter were threatening the locals and, in particular, women who, in the Australian idiom, dress scantily for the beach. This is a complex story that no doubt will be the subject of numerous research theses and scholarly publications but, in essence, the cause is simple (Figure 12.5). The riots reflect a high level of disquiet on the part of many Anglo-Celtic Australians at the high level of immigration from Islamic countries and the values Muslims bring with them that are regarded by many as incompatible with the Australian way of life. Immigration is of course a marker of economic globalization and the place of cities in the international economic system. But not all immigrants come with the language and job skills that enable them to fit quickly into their new settings. This was certainly a factor in the Cronulla riots since many of the Lebanese youth were unemployed and had come from rural areas where metropolitan value sets were absent. The upshot of the riots was that Cronulla, and other Sydney beaches south of the Harbour were, for a short period no-go zones, heavily policed sites of fear. The areas of the metropolis in which the Lebanese Muslims had settled were similarly demonized, unfairly, no doubt, but certainly on the basis of objective indicators such as high rates of violent crime.

The site of the riots, on and near one of Sydney's major surfing beaches, was particularly significant. Beach culture, with its bronzed lifesavers and sybaritic sun worshipping, is a powerful element of the Australian imaginary – up there with "the outback" in our sense of national identity. So to be challenged in this domain, by "outsiders," in a period of great change and challenge to traditional ideas of Australian-ness, was flashpoint of, in retrospect, major proportions. Had the riots occurred at Bondi, the symbolism would have been perfect.

Re-valorizing the Public Domain

Another way in which economic globalization has impacted on central Sydney has been through the growth of international tourism and business travel. Again, this is widely recognized and well documented in other so-called global cities. An area

2.5
Newspaper
coverage of the
Cronulla riots,
Sydney

known as Darling Harbour, on the western edge of the downtown, exemplifies this trend.[20] A railways goods yard and port area until the 1960s, changes to freight handling had made the area redundant for industrial and other port-related activities. In the late 1970s, the NSW Government, which owned the land, decided to transform it into a tourism/recreation precinct, along the lines of the famous Baltimore inner harbor precinct that was the forerunner of many similar schemes for urban revitalization around the world. In its initial decade the re-development attracted tourists but relatively few Sydney-siders. While close to the CBD, its connectivity was poor so city workers did not develop a taste for the bars and eateries that were part of the scene. Over time, however, major new high rise housing developments on the eastern and western flanks of Darling Harbour brought a ready-made population of consumers into the area with a resulting strengthening of the area's economy, thus connecting two separate manifestations of globalization (Figure 12.6).

The other salient example of a place that has been transformed in response to the changing structure of Sydney's economy is the "The Rocks."[21] This

12.6
**King Street
Wharf, Darling
Harbour, Sydney
(Photo: Asim
Aly-Khan)**

historic precinct at the northern edge of Sydney's central business district – consisting of nineteenth-century workers' housing and port buildings – has been refurbished and is now a major tourist attraction with many restaurants and hotels (Figure 12.7). Readers can identify the simulacra for the cities of their own experience. The Rocks is also reasonably attractive to locals, in part because of its adjacency to the Museum of Contemporary Art and the Sydney Opera House. Unlike Darling Harbour, there is little adjacent new housing (although there is some high-end high rise at Circular

12.7
**The Rocks,
Sydney
(Photo: Asim
Aly-Khan)**

Quay) to leaven the artificial quality that characterizes historic districts "frozen in aspic" and de-natured of the lifeways that created them.

The Economic Domain

Morphed Spaces

These major changes in land use, driven by shifts in the drivers of metropolitan economic growth, themselves driven by Australia's changing position in the global economy, were paralleled, in an area south of the CBD, known as the Central Industrial Area (CIA).[22] Until the late 1960s, the major site of Sydney's factory employment, the CIA, for a combination of reasons, has been massively transformed over the past 30 years. The factories have largely gone, to be replaced by warehouses and freight handling facilities (with much lower employment numbers and largely unskilled jobs) and increasing numbers of high-rise apartment blocks. Currently islands in a wasteland of warehouses, residual factories and pockets of poor quality workers housing, their revalorization has yet to be converted into locality shifts around which the new residents can form affective relationships, although no doubt this will happen in time.

The CIA itself has in part been revitalized by two major infrastructure developments, themselves directly necessitated by both technological change and Sydney's insertion in the global economy. Port Botany was commissioned in the late 1970s and has created demand for industrial land in its vicinity. Relocation of shipping and related land-based activities from Sydney Harbour simultaneously released waterfront industrial land at the very time that demand for inner city high density housing was emerging and governments were keen to encourage it. Sydney's international airport is on the southern edge of the CIA and massive growth in air traffic, including freight traffic, has impacted on demand for industrial land for storage and freight handling activities. In combination, the port and airport have, however, generated nowhere near the demand for industrial land being vacated due to de-industrialization and the relocation of factories to the suburbs. But the clean, quiet activities they generate have accentuated the improvement in amenity that has enabled the flowering of new housing in this former industrial heartland.

Managing the Metropolis

The collective capacity to influence the trajectory of places through public interventions, or at least those aspects around which people form affective relationships, is quite limited; certainly much more so than city boosters, and academics worrying about the public interest implications of their studies might want to argue (or at least hope for). Places evolve primarily through market forces – the myriad decisions made by firms and households – and public interventions can at best steer change at the margin. This steering capacity, while generally modest, is not, however, to be underestimated. The matching of appropriate tools to circumstances, together with political backing, can make a difference. Good architecture, landscape architecture and urban design can have a major impact on the quality of urban life. Good community planning can alleviate the stresses of living in all sorts of ways. However, from a metropolitan economic perspective, the position from which this chapter is based, the questions revolve around the extent to which an understanding of the metropolis, as a set of complex micro-economic systems, can yield policy prescriptions that will make it more livable.

The general question of livability is quite vital in the governance of post-industrial cities and has been acknowledged as such since at least the early 1980s.[23] The best-known contemporary proponent of this view is Florida who proposes a simple and seductive hypothesis, namely that urban economic development depends on a city's capacity to attract creative people.[24] This stands in contrast to traditional development models that emphasize the attraction of businesses. The corollary of Florida's thesis is that cities must work on the quality of their built and natural environments and their social and cultural facilities and ambience. Whatever the validity of Florida's views, and their utility as a basis for public policy, there is little doubt that in post-industrial cities environmental quality is an important driver of firm and household location decisions.

Traffic congestion, poor air and water quality and the destruction of natural and agricultural lands are generally regarded as being things that make living in cities less desirable for people and businesses. The larger cities become, the more concern is expressed about these environmental problems. However, are they inevitably the consequences of urban size or can they be managed at acceptable levels that put no limits on how large cities can become? The question is important because if such problems are not actually, or at least not inevitably, the outcomes of urban size, then cities can become as large as their economic potential allows without dystopic consequences. Again, since cities are the engine rooms of national economic growth, enabling them to develop to their fullest potential is highly desirable.

There is a well-developed theoretical and empirical literature on the economics of urban size.[25] Key concepts in this literature are agglomeration economies and diseconomies. Agglomeration economies refer to the un-priced advantages that firms and households obtain by living in larger rather than smaller places. Larger cities provide, for example, markets of sufficient size to enable the financially viable offering of goods and services that smaller places cannot. The availability of these things encourages businesses to set up and expand and also influences decisions by individuals and households about where to live. Examples germane to the case of twenty-first-century global cities include access to higher-order financial and cultural services. As noted earlier, the defining feature of global cities is their capacity to attract "command and control" functions of transnational corporations. Such global coordinating activities require the support of "producer services" such as banking, advertising, law and IT and such services are only available in large cities. On the cultural side, the availability of high order cultural services – theatres, opera houses, high-end fashion stores, etc. – is essential if the global cultural elite that services and drives the global economy is to be enticed to settle. Of these attractors, nothing can be done to alter the provision of higher-end commercial and personal services (they are simply the products of market size). Something can, however, be done to improve collective provision of quality of life things, such as high-end cultural facilities, urban design and architecture, although the ambiance of places that have arisen through market forces, and which are therefore attractive to the creative class, cannot in reality be recapitulated.

One set of urban quality indicators, which also impact on business directly, can, however, be manipulated if governments are prepared to grasp the nettles of externality pricing and cost-recovery pricing. At the risk of offending those who may already be entirely familiar with the basics of pricing, or those who may not be and do not care to be, here is a brief explanation.[26]

In the real world, everyone makes consumption decisions based on prices. While price is not the only factor taken into account, it is highly influential in determining what and how much is purchased. The primary determinant of the price that sellers ask for their goods and services is the costs they incur in production. At a minimum those costs need to be recovered. Resource economists distinguish between private costs and *social costs*; the latter are also known as *negative externalities*. Producers should make production decisions based on full costs (i.e. both private and social) otherwise production decisions are distorted. Private costs, unlike social costs, cannot be avoided; producers have to pay for privately owned goods and services.

This way of thinking can be readily applied to urban environmental problems such as air and water pollution. Air pollution, in post-industrial cities like Sydney, results predominantly from private automobile use. When people use their cars, they are conscious of petrol and other running costs but do not factor in the generation of pollutants. While many motorists are ethical and would not choose to pollute the atmosphere, they are unaware that the additive effect of many small decisions causes the problem. In order to change behavior, governments have to use measures, such as petrol taxes, to make motoring more expensive and thus suppress demand. There are well-known complications, of course, both political and behavioral. On the latter point, it is well known that when prices increase motorists hardly change their behavior at all. They will take money away from other parts of their household budgets rather than reduce reliance on cars. A major reason for this is that car dependency is built into urban structure so it is difficult for people to adapt (more on this below). Governments, of course, are always conscious of the political backlash in taking unpopular decisions. The same story can be told about water pollution and also about levels of water consumption that cause environmental damage when dams have to be built or extended in surface area. Table 12.1 shows recent dollar estimates of externalities associated with three forms of transportation in Sydney. If multiplied by the numbers of kilometers traveled in the city over any given period of time, very large numbers result.

In addition to social costs, which encourage over-consumption because market prices are lower than they should be, most urban services (water and sewerage, roads, public transport etc) are under-priced. That is, the prices charged by suppliers, historically governments in Australian cities, are less than the costs of producing the services. The effects are over-consumption with resulting environmental effects. The over-consumption associated with under-pricing is in turn embedded in urban structures. This embeddedness makes it especially difficult to engender change. Public transport is a special problem since it is held out as an environmentally

Table 12.1 Rail and road externalities, NSW (cents per kilometer)

Externalities	Rail	Car	Bus
Air pollution	0.86	1.77	4.52
Greenhouse gas emission	1.08	4.56	10.77
Noise pollution	3.44	0.34	9.04
Accidents	0.04	8.38	5.17
Road damage	0.00	0.22	3.88
Total	5.43	15.26	33.37

Source: NSW Railcorp (2006)

and socially friendly alternative to private cars. Yet in Sydney only a fraction of the costs of providing public transport, especially commuter rail, is covered by fares (Figure 12.8). The balance is funded from general taxation. Many taxpayers do not use the systems so there are equity and political issues here.[27]

The two aspects of metropolitan form that are influential on quality of life are densities and accessibility. Both are a function of pricing so, to the extent that low densities and poor accessibility are judged to be negative features of big cities,

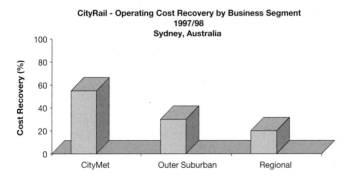

12.8
State (Sydney) Government contribution to State Transit Authority (STA) and CityRail operating costs (Source: CityRail and STA)

they can be addressed by the measures just reviewed. It is probably with respect to these macro-forms and environmental conditions that the notion of affective relationships with the metropolis as an entity makes some sense (although even there is much differentiation within the aggregate).

Conclusion

Human beings inhabit places that provide for their material, social and aesthetic needs. The many types of urban places generate affective relationships based on experience and second-hand information. Some experiences and observations generate positive relationships while others produce ambiguous or negative responses. This chapter has argued that to varying degrees the physical material of cities, both human-constructed and natural, as well as the social and cultural formations of city life, represent the outcome of economic forces. The economic history of cities is sharply etched in both their physical and non-physical forms and those forms are the basis on which, as well as the reflection of, the behavior and attitudes of residents and visitors. The day-to-day decisions of business operators and households are conditioned by the wealth of the urban economy and directly reflect the values of decision makers. Because people experience the city at sub-metropolitan scales – although there may be rather inchoate and abstract attachments to the aggregate – it is at this scale that affective relationships are formed. To the extent, however, that the small places reflect formative economic conditions, affective relationships can be read as formed by, if not always understood, as fundamentally economically conditioned. The argument is not intended to be reductionist. Rather, the intent is to highlight the power of economy in a context in which cultural theory and architectural history and critique are the primary explanatory frameworks. Perhaps there is an analogy with sociobiology that, counter to the predilections of those committed to social explanations of the human condition, argues the underlying biological and evolutionary basis for all aspects of human behavior. Convenient illusions and second-order explanations of people–place relationships are valid, or at least comforting, within their own frames of reference. Scratch the surface, however, and the substructure is revealed. Sometimes nakedly, sometimes subtly, but ever present.

Notes

1   Yi-Fu Tuan, *Topophilia: A Study of Environmental Perception, Attitudes, and Values*, New Jersey: Prentice-Hall, 1974. This book was path-breaking at the time when human geography was in the thrall of the so-called quantitative revolution. The discipline was evolving in two quite separate directions: spatial political economy and a new cultural geography.

2   Peter A. Murphy, "Sydney Now: Going Global in the Space of Flows," in Kevin O'Connor (ed.), *Houses and Jobs in Cities and Regions: Research in Honour of Chris Maher*, Brisbane: University of Queensland Press, 1999, pp. 167–178.

3   NSW Department of State and Regional Development, *Facts and Statistics* 2006 www.business. nsw.gov.au

4   Peter Forsyth, Ian Burnley, Larry Dwyer and Peter A. Murphy, *Economic Impacts of Migration Induced Inbound Tourism*, Les Cahiers du Tourisme, Series C, No. 194, 1995, p. 39.

5   Peter A. Murphy and Sophie Watson, *Surface City: Sydney at the Millennium*, Sydney: Pluto Press, 1997, pp. 37–61.

6   Murphy, "Sydney Now."

7   Richard Florida, *Cities and the Creative Class*, London: Routledge, 2005.

8   Peter A. Murphy, Bette O'Brien and Sophie Watson, "Selling Australia, Selling Sydney: The Ambivalent Politics of Entrepreneurial Multiculturalism," *Journal of International Migration and Integration* 4(4), 2003, 471–498.

9   Peter Spearritt, *Sydney Since the Twenties*, Sydney: Hale and Iremonger, 1978.

10 Ian H. Burnley, *The Impact of Immigration on Australia: A Demographic Approach*, South Melbourne: Oxford University Press, 2001, pp. 31–34.

11 Patrick N. Troy, *The Perils of Urban Consolidation*, Sydney: The Federation Press, 1996; Hugh Stretton, *Ideas for Australian Cities*, Melbourne: Georgian House, 1970; Brendan Gleeson, *Australian Heartlands: Making Space for Hope in the Suburbs*, Sydney: Allen & Unwin, 2006.

12 Murphy and Watson, *Surface City*, pp. 62–73.

13 Florida, *Cities and the Creative Class*.

14 Robert B. Reich, *The Work of Nations: Preparing Ourselves for 21st Century Capitalism*, New York: A.A. Knopf, 1991, pp. 177–178.

15 Peter A. Murphy and Sophie Watson, "Social Polarization and Australian Cities," *International Journal of Urban and Regional Research* 18, 1994, 573–590.

16 Mike Davis, *City of Quartz: Excavating the Future in Los Angeles*, London, New York: Verso, 1990.

17 Murphy and Watson, "Social Polarization and Australian Cities," 573–590.

18 Ian H. Burnley, Peter A. Murphy and Robert H. Fagan, *Immigration and Australian Cities*, Sydney: The Federation Press, 1997.

19 Murphy, O'Brien and Watson, "Selling Australia, Selling Sydney," pp. 471–498.

20 Murphy and Watson, *Surface City*, p. 46.

21 Spearritt, *Sydney Since the Twenties*.

22 Peter A. Murphy and Sophie Watson, "Restructuring of Sydney's Central Industrial Area: Process and Local Impacts," *Australian Geographical Studies* 28(2), 1990, 187–203.

23 Peter A. Murphy and Chung-Tong Wu, "Globalization and the Sustainability of Cities in the Asia-Pacific Region: The Case of Sydney," in Fu-Chen Lo and Peter J. Marcotullio (eds), *Globalization and the Sustainability of Cities in the Asia-Pacific Region*, Tokyo: United Nations University Press, 2001.

24 Florida, *Cities and the Creative Class*.

25 Harry W. Richardson, *The Economics of Urban Size*, London: Macmillan, 1973; George Tolley and John Crihfield, "City Size and Place as Policy Issues," in Edwin S. Mills (ed.), *Handbook of Regional and Urban Economics*, vol. 2, Amsterdam: North-Holland, 1987, pp. 1285–1311.

26 Peter A. Murphy, "Pricing the Metropolis: Economic Instruments for Urban Management," paper delivered at IMFRD 06 Conference, Shanghai Jiaotong University, 2006.

27 Ibid.

Epilogue

The Architectural Project as Dialogue

Vittorio Gregotti

It is quite reasonable, but also insufficient, to link the topophilia-topophobia alternative to the broad debate internal to the relationship between global-local and communitarianism-globalism. A great deal has been written (often in a fatalistic manner) about the cultural and political reasons for the excessive technical and economic power of global market ideologies over the weakened awareness of the histories of different identities and of their capacity for favorable interpretation of external forces. When such forces are imposed or endured, they are transformed into anonymous and homogeneous developments measured only by quantity, or else into buildings that are exceptional only in a forced way. In such cases, the marketing concept replaces the concept of the monument, and the city becomes a string of colossal objects erected in aesthetic and economic competition with each other. And this is happening more and more often these days.

But if we were to carry out a dialectical dialogue between topophilia and topophobia instead of a radical dispute, this would bring to the fore the main material for the construction of architecture as an artistic practice. Architectural history abounds with innumerable examples of interweavings of external influences and local traditions, which are always constitutive of any renewal.

Convinced as I am that empirical and cultural conditions make up the essential material of our discipline's artistic practice, I believe that a debate, *a critical debate*, on the nature and meaning of context is of great importance for the architectural project.

For this reason, the other indispensable dimension of *topos* is the specific nature of the site as a perceptibly close, physical context, as well as a vast landscape, whether transformed by man or by nature. There are those (myself among them) who consider *topos*, its history and justifications, as the very material with which the foundations of architecture are laid by its own constitution. But what happens when this context is destroyed by the growth of architecture itself? I do not have an answer in the face of the growth of urban sprawl, which is the main problem facing us throughout the world today. I think the first and oldest act of architecture is not to take shelter in a cave or to build a hut but to lay a stone on the ground, name it and mark it, and then live in it. In other words, to open up a dialogue with the specific context.

In any event, the planning and building of architecture always mean designing and building somewhere else, whether far away or near. The project must somehow be drawn out of itself in order to bring about a critical dialogue between specific conditions, new problems and the state of the discipline. This assumes as a truth the necessity of recognizing the existence of a center, essential to the art of architecture, so that the inconstant boundary of its territory can profitably open itself up to a conversation with the other sciences, as well as with other places and their histories. Essential to setting up the dialogue is an agreement that it be based, on the one hand, on the diversity of topics, and, on the other hand, on the common element, that is, the specificity of the diverse architectural traditions, and their comparison.

Architectural changes prior to the twentieth century occurred without making a choice between topophilia and topophobia in building something new, and often by favorably interpreting the external influences on the traditions of the specific community. Even the violent Jesuit colonization of South America, in the end, produced a colonial architecture quite recognizable in its identity. Even the internationalism of Gothic architecture in Europe is expressed in France, England and Spain according to interpretations based on their diverse characteristics. English culture of the first half of the eighteenth century rejected the Baroque but then embraced Palladianism, endowing it with its own specific identity.

It is worth pointing out in this regard that the literature on architectural history is generally concerned with comparisons with the past rather than with the future. But history as a value in itself appears today to be damaged. The new, however, was once free of this fixation on the future, which has been viewed as an absolute value since the beginning of the twentieth century. Today the future is a representation of the absolute positiveness of progress seen as technological progress and of the global unification of opinions understood as economic opinions. It cannot be denied, at any rate, that the current widespread topophobia (in other words, the current tendency towards homogenization) is closely connected to the political decisions that guide development, and that development corresponds, according to the dominant opinion, to market ideology. The more recent or politically weak the development, or the more it considers its own cultural identity in a weak way, the more it is prone to homogenization – often in its lowest and most superficial forms of aesthetic appearance – indifferent to diversity or, worse, such differences are used only as folklore material.

Now and then, the impetus of economic and political development, and its acceleration, do not allow the fulfillment even of the best intentions, which are overwhelmed, except for urgent needs, by indifference with respect to the quality of its own cultural plan and of its critical dialogue with the dominant cultures.

Is it possible that architecture will become the most effective portrayal (without sublimation) of the least lovable aspects of social cohabitation? Turning to Shanghai, but even more to Beijing, this question seems to prove founded in all its ambiguous dramatic force with respect to architecture's vindictive capacity just when it is foundering as an artistic practice. Therefore, together with an irresistible attraction to the forewarning of the future void, there is the temptation to fill it with the uncontrollable yearning for the known, familiar and trusted, as an irrepressible reaction of fear at the inability of the mind to confront the new metropolitan event.

It is the idea itself of a city that is no longer a whole, interconnected and recognizable as a representation of relationships, but instead, only as the daily oppression of the realized megalopolis. Every constituent element shouts at its neighbor without the event ever reaching the greatness of battle but only the coarseness of an advertising campaign. At the same time, it is amazing how architecture is able to convey boundless hostility and self-importance in such an accomplished manner. Even the ancient planimetric orthogonal system is entirely without equivalence in three dimensions. Only its unrecognizable echo remains imprinted in the ground by an angry confusion of blind construction violence that prattles about itself vociferously.

Each architectural work can no longer in any way be isolated and judged in itself. On the one hand, the context devours it without regard for quality. It no longer presents a point of view of the world but, instead, presents the world itself. Thus, one can say that it portrays the world beyond any subjectivity whatsoever. In this "new picturesque" (a picturesque not deriving from "picture" but from other forms of representation), the role of the project is to become a cell of a totalitarian organization of values and current objectives.

There is no longer a trace of the sense of necessity but only of accumulation, in the boundless expansion of the desire for awe without marvel: the marvel is the unity of this absence of a unique specificity.

Everything is big, enormous, out of proportion to itself, an exception within the exception, a redoubling of a hypertext that quashes any possibility of difference. There is no building form that has not been made use of, distorted, enlarged, adorned, crowned or varied in any number of ways.

The expansion and exceptional and ancient care of parks and gardens, and of street furniture in general, are assimilating to the wasteland of never-ending construction, and the derelict fragments of the noble and poor past. Everything is immersed in a grey haze – the dust of demolitions and polluting dampness.

It is obvious that discussion of the issue is needed for Chinese cities in the twenty-first century: the great expansion of cities; the speed of their expansion, and of the internal renewal and social changes; the violent introduction of foreign economic forces; the manifest aim of institutions and of the people to regain an important position in the world by their own ability; the overwhelming necessities of trade, of provision of energy and other supplies. These are all issues, by the way, that Chinese cities have confronted sensibly. Nevertheless, it is astonishing how everything can function with a high level of efficiency. (The airports that serve 15–20 million people in any city are much more efficient than those of Milan or Rome.) The built-up area of a city like Beijing covers about 17,000 sq km, which is almost the size of the whole of Belgium.

In the light of such impetuous development (which, moreover, restores to China a supremacy that lasted for thousands of years and was only interrupted for 150 years by a crisis that today we can read as temporary), what can the reaction of the European city be, built as it is according to a more layered temporality, with an architecture and urban design that is undoubtedly more solid and articulated, if not to look for diverse forms of thoughtful modernization, of a better balance between the new and the existing, of the return of meaning to a readable differentiation? All this certainly goes far beyond the independent capabilities of our artistic practice, but not of its duty to suggest possibilities.

The metropolitan scale of Asian cities (as well as some in the Third World) eludes our concrete comprehension, and this makes us see for ourselves how we belong to the last century, from our position as a transitional generation. We can still have the experience of remembering a different concept of the city and can therefore measure what has been lost.

It is important, however, to point out the shift of the organizational human mind in the light of the boundless expansion, from the form of things to their management, with the associated consequences to architecture.

So, for example, the envelope of a building becomes a huge advertising space that points to its temporary function and connects it to others of the same kind arranged throughout its territory. It does not matter where. The connection between place and thing is broken. It resumes only through use. All this clearly distinguishes the metropolises in China from those of the Third World and obviously from European ones, and yet, we cannot help thinking about the dimensional boundary of urban concentration and about how it is not possible, with the help of communications and transportation (and of the new technologies in general), to encourage or plan a more balanced territorial redistribution of urban business. At the same time, one wonders why it is not possible to foster an organic relationship between the city matrices, their installation principles, their geographies and architectural issues. If it is not possible, in other words, to agree to a shared civil, less competitive principle, to an ideal of architectural work that is less agitated, capable of coping with the slow pace that produces long duration, and to reduce the spectacular displays in favour of reuniting with the most ancient fundamentals of the task of building poetically. But perhaps all this is an impossible dream of someone who does not want to give up loving the artistic practice of architecture.

There is the undeniable dimension in the creation of architecture that concerns the physical place, both natural and man-made, and that returns, above all, to the installation principles that control the traditions of architecture's different forms on this earth. Here, concrete foundations and figurative foundations coincide.

For some civilizations such as ancient Rome, the China of builder kings and classical Greece, it is the institutional face that directly takes architectural form. For others, it is nomadism. For yet other civilizations, it is theocratic might. For others it is eventually the earth itself that chooses the places and the modes through its relationship to the universe and the seasons. The foundation also includes the geography of the terrain to be divided, an ideal city to imagine, and a prophecy to realize. Marking out the boundaries, the enclosure and the walls. Opening up to the social imagination with the precision of architecture.

The difficulties of European cities are quite renowned: besides the clearly visible problems of transportation, services, environmental ecology and the unresolved modernization in general, there are the (certainly not independent) problems of urban sprawl: unchecked external expansion and the excessive concentration of head offices, to cite two of them. To this must be added a conscious but absurd rejection of the overall hypotheses of regulation of development and even urban design. Today the aesthetic competition between brands often reduces city architecture to a collection of objects of exaggerated design.

There is no doubt that there has been a change in conditions of development and the very nature of the users, which no longer coincides with the citizens: *civis* and *urbs* seem to want to become two separate entities – indeed, to no longer love each other.

Yet the plurality of city users has a very ancient tradition, even if the tools of mobility have accelerated the frequency of visits by non-residents. The guest must still contend with the resident, who in his turn is endowed with a new mobility of his own. This makes him no less the principal urban actor, to whom the city must give reliable answers of no less quality and diversity than those given to the "city-user."

Functional and social blend; efficiency of services; environmental quality; orderly, calm and environmentally easy places in which to live, in physical proximity to the parts of reciprocal measure; with an architecture that is simple, organic and clear in its constituent relationships of urban design – these are in any case essential ingredients for the future city as well. Only thus do they become available to the social imagination, not by aesthetically imitating homogeneous peculiarities but by building spaces that can hold – along with new functions – emotions, memories and ancient passions as well. Architecture is not urban set designing or a passing event. City architecture is costly and enduring, even when it is superfluous clutter, as it has been throughout time and passing aesthetic tastes in fashion.

Productive efficiency and quality of social life, however, can often enter into conflict with each other if the former is conceived for its own sake and not as a function of the latter. Architecture can only take material from their conflict or agreement to critically transform it into a form as a foundation for the new to compare with the monuments of the past – even before comparing with the future, a future that is today often understood as a "forecast" rather than as a utopia of the real world.

It is necessary for the city to maintain a balanced quantity of differentiated and dialoguing operations. No, therefore, to specialization, and yes to specific character. The moment European cities become "entertainment machines" they simply stop being cities. This does not mean shutting off our cities to other cultures. Internationalism is a foundational characteristic of European culture.

The multicultural issue, when established as a dialogue between different cultural identities, has always been a crucial element of Euro-Mediterranean culture. Our problems today involve being able to compare cultures that are not paralyzed and rendered homogeneous by market ideologies. Even mass tourism can take on a new significance only when we succeed in increasing the assets of the weakest countries and examine the differences in a positive manner, thereby re-establishing a balance shaped by the reciprocal expression of possible choices.

But there are issues concerning this mistaken opposition between topophilia and topophobia that it would do well to recall which are connected more closely to the general, difficult state of our artistic practices. First and foremost, the fixation with subjective diversity (probably as opposition to our homogeneous condition) that seems to have stopped any critical relationship in works of art when compared with the contradictions of the real world. Architecture seems to be moving towards the representation of the state of things just as they are, as if this were the best of all possible worlds. In other words, it represents only the dominant opinions. But "an architecture worthy of man," wrote the philosopher Theodor Wiesengrund Adorno in 1965, "must have a better opinion of men and society than of that which corresponds to their real state." Contrary to critical tradition of the better culture of the modern project, today's clear approaches of forced diversity are acceptable to the majority of television viewers because they are only aesthetic and transitory. Perhaps it is the state of the subject of modern man and his estrangement from himself that makes it difficult to have a concrete image of the other. He seems only capable of obtaining an image of himself.

Every architectural act seems to be justified by the term creativity, which has now been expanded to define any aesthetic act (the widespread aesthetics has inundated us) with which designers, advertisers, fashion designers, architects and many other sectors justify their own artistry as an original innovation. But originality should not be thought of as the artist's greatest objective. There are many superfluous and even very harmful original ideas in the world.

And what type of architectural project has been conceived to respond to the mass attitude of the hypermodernists and conservatives?

It is a fairly complex and heterogeneous arrangement, formulated through the collaboration of the same architects: a bit of context, but more quantitative and stylistic in its interpretation, modernity but only in technology and communication, and perhaps a little sharp tenor here and there to lend a touch of "artistry," in particular, in the form of superfluous originality that gives a shade of ineffability to the arrangement – an ineffability necessary to demonstrate the existence of creative freedom – and, above all, a considerable amount of flexibility, which often translates into a strong adherence to profit advancement, a generous quantity of that plastic democracy known as animation, a dash of negligible involvement. No definite form. On the contrary, total plasticity and interchangeable arrangements. In other words, no architecture.

What I think should be pointed out right away are the results of these arrangements: the enormous quantity of architectures that are ambitiously obtuse and lacking any meaningful installation principle that devastate the physical environment of our cities, transforming them into a kind of compacted and inessential void, filled with objects. Often added to this is the foundering of architecture into the consensus interested in success, or into unconventional expression. And expression today is often understood as a mistaken subjectivation of artistic practice. Mistaken because such subjectivation is still obvious, as it moves inside the foreshadowed and conformist boundaries, obedient to the current state of powers. Instead of making use of the idea of freedom as a project, it is interpreted as an escape from the contradictions of the real.

All this seems aimed at shifting the very concept of artistic practice, re-establishing it on the terrain of total accord with transitoriness, completely assimilating it with the idea of meaningless newness. Thus the aim is the definitive abandonment of that metaphorical quota of truth, in other words, of eternity, which has, until now, accompanied the aspirations of artistic practice. And it is here that topophilia and topophobia definitively part company – causing severe damage to architecture and civic society.

(Translated from Italian by Ellen McRae.)

Index

Page numbers in italics indicate illustrations

Index

eBooks – at www.eBookstore.tandf.co.uk

A library at your fingertips!

eBooks are electronic versions of printed books. You can store them on your PC/laptop or browse them online.

They have advantages for anyone needing rapid access to a wide variety of published, copyright information.

eBooks can help your research by enabling you to bookmark chapters, annotate text and use instant searches to find specific words or phrases. Several eBook files would fit on even a small laptop or PDA.

NEW: Save money by eSubscribing: cheap, online access to any eBook for as long as you need it.

Annual subscription packages

We now offer special low-cost bulk subscriptions to packages of eBooks in certain subject areas. These are available to libraries or to individuals.

For more information please contact webmaster.ebooks@tandf.co.uk

We're continually developing the eBook concept, so keep up to date by visiting the website.

www.eBookstore.tandf.co.uk